The Mensheviks In The Revolution of 1917

The Mensheviks
In The Revolution
of 1917

John D. Basil

Slavica Publishers, Inc.
Columbus, Ohio

Slavica publishes a wide variety of books and journals dealing with the peoples, languages, literatures, history, folklore, and culture of the peoples of Eastern Europe and the USSR. For a complete catalog with prices and ordering information, please write to:

Slavica Publishers, Inc.
P.O. Box 14388
Columbus, Ohio 43214
USA

ISBN: 0-89357-109-1.

This book was published in 1984.

Text set by Kathleen McDermott at the East European Composition Center, supported by the Department of Slavic Languages and Literatures and the Center for Russian and East European Studies at UCLA.

Printed in the United States of America.

Table of Contents

Anybody who has written a book realizes the great extent to which it is a collective effort, and I wish to mention the names of some of the institutions and people who contributed to *The Mensheviks in the Revolution of 1917.* Firstly, the librarians at the University of Washington, the Library of Congress, the University of Helsinki and the Hoover Institution on War Revolution and Peace were helpful in locating the primary source material that rests at the base of historical scholarship. Secondly, I am grateful for the financial aid received from the Hoover Institution, the Louisiana State University Research Fund, the University of South Carolina Committee on Research and Productive Scholarship, the Daniel W. Hollis Fund and the National Endowment for the Humanities. I also wish to thank those scholars who read all or parts of the manuscript at its various stages of development and made encouraging criticisms, particularly Donald W. Treadgold, J. L. H. Keep, and Robert D. Warth. Finally, I thank the members of my family and especially my wife. They all put up with far too much for the sake of another person.

This book is dedicated to my father.

A year shall come, our blackest year of all,
in which the crown of Russia's tsars shall fall.

Lermontov — 1831

Introduction

Historians of the Russian revolution have paid little attention to the part played by the Mensheviks in the democracy that governed in Russia from the abdication of the Romanov family in February of 1917 to Lenin's *coup d'etat* in October. Speculation has been widespread about how a spontaneous agrarian upheaval and the carnage of World War I brought chaos to Russia, and how the cunning and determination of Lenin undermined the authority of the Provisional Government, but much has been left to our imagination about those revolutionary Marxists who opposed Lenin's plans to establish a proletarian dictatorship. Even in the year 1967, the fiftieth anniversary of the revolution, when more publications on 1917 saw the light of day than had surfaced to that date, mention of the Mensheviks was made only in passing and analyses of their role in the events were thin; when the Mensheviks did appear it was only long enough for the reader to learn of their conviction that 1917 brought the bourgeois revolution to Russia or that the Mensheviks would have enjoyed political success if they had thought and acted like Lenin. At the present time there is only one monograph devoted to the Mensheviks in 1917, a polemic published in Moscow the focus of which is actually Lenin.[1] In languages other than Russian, there are no descriptions of the Menshevik party organizations in 1917, only sketchy analyses of the complicated relationship between the Mensheviks and the Provisional Government and no thorough discussions about the Mensheviks and the April Crisis, the July Days, or the October *coup d'etat*.

The Mensheviks themselves have been partly responsible for their isolation from the pages of history. Their memoirs make only sparse comments on the events of 1917, despite the significance of the period and despite the active part they played throughout the year. Only Iraklii G. Tsereteli, the Georgian Menshevik leader in the Petrograd Soviet, and Nikolai Sukhanov (Himmer), the Menshevik journalist from Petrograd, made serious efforts to record their impressions of 1917, and of the two men only the maverick Sukhanov was ready to analyze events that took place after the end of July.[2] Even the most popular among the Menshevik emigre journals, *Sotsialisticheskii vestnik*, had surprisingly little to say about the year of Great October.[3] This unwillingness to discuss the revolution may be easily explained away as a defensive posture (after all, they failed to achieve their objectives in 1917), but it has obviously discouraged research efforts.[4]

Current Soviet interpretations of 1917 have also played a role in drawing attention away from the Mensheviks. The Soviet view of 1917 is shaped partly by ideology and partly by a desire to embellish the role played by Lenin, but either way it gives short shrift to the Mensheviks. Current Soviet historians, and Bolshevik party members whose memoirs have been made public, survey the events of 1917 as a great struggle between the proletariat and the bourgeoisie in which the proletariat, under the indispensable leadership of Lenin, emerges victorious. In this interpretation, the Mensheviks are either ignored or presented as the petty bourgeoisie, an ineffectual and vacillating force that quickly expires once the great antagonists settle the issue between themselves. In Soviet historiography the Mensheviks often appear as sincere fools, easily used by Russia's liberals to retard the forward march of the proletariat. In 1923 Anatol Lunacharsky wrote an obituary on the deceased Menshevik leader Julius Martov (Iu. O. Tsederbaum) which gave a typical example of the Soviet view. Martov and the Mensheviks were caught between two irreconcilable classes, according to Lunacharsky, drawn first toward the proletariat and then in the opposite direction toward the bourgeoisie; indecisive, vacillating and timid, they drifted about during the great moments of the revolution never finding the strength to become a heroic influence in their own right. Like Lunacharsky, other Soviet writers arrange the "vacillating" Mensheviks within an intellectual scheme that discourages criticism of Lenin's class interpretation of the events of 1917.[5]

In some respects, the Soviet view of 1917 is part of an anti-Menshevik polemic that began in 1903 when the Russian Social Democratic Workers' Party divided between Bolsheviks and Mensheviks. Lenin engineered the split at that time, captured the title Bolshevik (majority) for his own faction, and denounced his socialist comrades; it was also at this time that Lenin began to stress the class approach to understanding Russian history to the exclusion of institutional and cultural interpretations. The polemical spirit that characterized relations between the two Russian socialist factions intensified in the years leading up to the revolution and reached a peak of intensity just prior to Lenin's seizure of power. His political victory in October of 1917 assured a place in oblivion for the Mensheviks, at least in the USSR.

Histories written in the west have also had their serious limitations, which serve the same end as the Menshevik reluctance to speak frankly and the deliberate effort of Soviet historians to keep the anti-

Leninist socialists confined to the dustbin of history. Very little analysis has appeared in the west that concentrates on the Mensheviks in 1917, and many statements that have been made in print leave the distinct impression that their failure rested with their inability to take the correct cue from Lenin. Some excellent studies on Russian Social Democracy have appeared, of course, but they touch on 1917 only briefly or in a superficial manner. They are biographies, by and large, that focus on personalities whose significant contributions were felt in the years prior to 1917 and whose ideas represented only a small number of the many notions that inspired the Mensheviks in 1917.[6] The most important period in party history has remained hidden or has been sketchily reconstructed. One lamentable result of this neglect can be seen in popular histories written on 1917 where the word Menshevik appears infrequently, if it appears at all.

Unfortunately, the interpretations that cast the Mensheviks into passive or even into unimportant roles leave unresolved some disturbing issues about the events that culminated in Lenin's October victory. For example, the historical literature is still inconclusive about the curious and fatal attitudes held by the moderate Russian Social Democrats toward government power. After the revolution broke out in February, the newly formed Executive Committee of the Petrograd Soviet was under strong Menshevik influence, if not firmly held in Menshevik hands; current Soviet historians willingly admit that it served as a base for the Menshevik leadership until well into the summer months. If the Mensheviks enjoyed a period of strength in 1917, why did they not try to seize power as the Bolsheviks did when their opportunity arose later in the year? Why did the Mensheviks hold back in February, in April, again in July, and why did they urge Lenin to hold back in October? In other words, what made the moderates moderate, and what effect did their moderation have on the direction of the revolution? Were they frightened and unsure of themselves, or was the path away from state power followed for sound political reasons? What truth rests in the hypothesis that the Mensheviks took quite seriously the argument that a purely socialist government would be incapable of altering the conservative character of old Russia because the presence of an asiatic strain rendered the former empire immune to attempts at rapid change? This theory of the so-called oriental tradition found in some Russian institutions was analyzed by Georgii Plekhanov, and traces of its influence are to be found in the work of P. Maslov, Paul Axelrod, A. S. Martynov, A. N. Potresov and others.

These revolutionary Marxists were anything but timid and their writings contributed heavily to the Menshevik strategy that called for restraint in the areas of government reform.

Whatever the solution, the problem is important. The Menshevik reticence in matters of government power may have made Lenin and his radicals the only viable socialist candidates for the leadership of the revolution long before the chaos of September and October created what is usually considered to be the favorable circumstances that opened the doors to power for the Bolsheviks.

Another question, closely related to the first, deals with the hostility and the obstructionist tactics evident in the Menshevik relations with the liberal political parties in Russia, particularly against the Kadets. The Mensheviks turned away from positions of state power, but at the same time they prevented the Kadets, who did occupy the most important government positions, from implementing a non-socialist program. The results were catastrophic. The liberals holding government power and the moderate socialists in the Petrograd Soviet (voluntarily removed from state power) expended most of their energies between March and October fighting among themselves; even after the formation of a coalition government in May, bickering between the Kadets and the Mensheviks prevented action from being taken by the Provisional Government in the areas of land reform, industrial relations and foreign policy. There is a strong tendency in current history writing to blame the Kadet party leaders for these long and debilitating quarrels, but were the Kadets alone responsible for the anti-liberal stance of the Menshevik Internationalists? Did a dogmatic Marxist cast of mind prevent Martov, as well as Tsereteli, Dan and also Chkheidze from cooperating with precisely those non-socialists, for whom they stepped aside in late February? Did the lessons of Russian institutional history teach the Mensheviks to use restraint in government politics, but did ideology then tip the balance forward in favor of radicalism and against moderation and cooperation? One prominant feature of the revolution that stands out was Lenin's ability to remain in power in the face of the same threatening economic and social conditions that had sapped the strength of his opposition. Why did he succeed where the moderate socialists and the liberals failed? Did the Mensheviks play a part in helping to create a division between socialists and non-socialists, thereby encouraging the growth of a political dilemma that could not be resolved by peaceful means?

A number of unsettling issues also emerge from a study of the revolution's international diplomacy. At first glance, the Mensheviks and their socialist allies seem to have been helpless in the face of the bloody battle that had been raging in Europe since 1914. As a result, there is a strong temptation to view them as idealists who tried but were unable to conclude peace because they were swept aside by forces greater than any they could muster in behalf of their own cause. During April and May, however, the Mensheviks held the attention of European diplomats when they unfolded a coherent plan that promised to bring an end to the military stalemate. And despite the fact that the Petrograd Soviet leaders were the spokesmen of an extra-governmental body in Russia, representatives of the governments of England, France and Belgium undertook serious discussions with them about how to improve the international picture. Why did the Allied socialists eventually reject the Soviet peace plan? Were they too deeply committed to the cause of peace through a military victory, so refused to consider the Stockholm project when it was advanced by Tsereteli? Did the non-socialist politicians in Western Europe obstruct the progress toward a socialist peace because of fear of revolution, or did the Menshevik refusal to compromise with the Allied socialists play an equally important part in bringing the negotiations to a sterile conclusion? And when the Allies proved reluctant to accept the Menshevik plan, did "the moderates" then hope to force it onto the political stage behind a successful Russian military offensive? Both the shelving of the general peace plan and the disastrous military assault of June of 1917 have been criticized as fatal blunders made by the Allied politicians and the Russian Provisional Government, but were they alone responsible for these acts and the consequences that followed?

Still other unanswered questions come up when the events of 1917 are studied from the Menshevik point of view. Who or what, for example, was responsible for the breakup of the Menshevik party after the Kornilov revolt, and how did its dissolution change the political balance of power among the revolutionary groups? Why did a strong body of Menshevik opinion begin to drift toward a position of sympathy for Lenin in mid-July just two weeks after the moderate socialist leaders had denounced the Bolsheviks for having embarrassed the government? Why were many Mensheviks quietly allowing Kerensky to move the Provisional Government toward dictatorship in August?

None of these questions have been posed arbitrarily just to create issues out of thin air and to make a case for the study of Menshevism in 1917. The newspapers published in Petrograd during the revolution showed clearly that these same questions were raised by Lenin, Keren-sky and Miliukov, and understood by these men as being part of the problems that had to be resolved by the revolutionary leadership. Yet none of these areas of conflicting opinion has been examined from the Menshevik point of view and examined with an eye on the possibility that the Menshevik contributions had a powerful influence in setting the stage for the October *coup d'etat*.

Chapter I
Preparation for Revolution

a) The Early Plans

During its formative years, three factors developed within the character of Menshevism that were to guide its fate first toward victory but
then to defeat in the revolution of 1917. The first was a strategic plan
designed to bring about a new political and social order in Russia, the
second, a hostile ideology directed against European liberals, and, the
third, a lack of organizational structure. Other considerations certainly
did shape the movement and influence its strongest thinkers, making
the Mensheviks an important part of the history of the Russian intelligentsia, but in 1917 it was their plans to destroy the old Russian order,
distrust of liberals, and lack of party unity that proved to be the decisive points of strength and weakness. And of these three factors, the
formulation of a political strategy for reshaping Russia was the most
complicated.

It was ideas about the origins of imperial authority and how the
Romanov dynasty had survived into the twentieth century that rested
at the base of much of the Menshevik plan to change the face of old
Russia. The scant scholarly research devoted to examining these ideas
was sound and can be located mostly in the works of Georgii Plekhanov and A. S. Martynov (Pikker).[1] According to these writers, the
seeds of the old order were planted in Russian soil after the invasions
from the east in the thirteenth century. It was after these conquests
that the Muscovite grand duke emerged at the head of the only governing institution in Russia. He was not, however, a figure with
sovereign power. He was merely a collector of taxes for the Mongol
Khan ruling at Sarai. In that privileged yet servile station, according to
Martynov, the grand duke succeeded in reducing the Russians in his
assigned districts to the low level of clumsy servants, and the seeds of
despotism were sown. The power of the grand duke over his subject
peoples further increased after the defeat of the Mongols. Once freed
from the restraints imposed by his masters on the lower Volga, the
grand duke used his administration to limit the scope of legal life and
economic growth that might have given rise to internal political

competition.[2] He reserved for himself a political and economic monopoly that did not change when his title changed from grand duke to tsar, and by the time Peter the Great ascended the throne no group or institution could hope to compete against the tsar (soon to be called emperor) and his bureaucratic administration.

At no time after the Mongol conquest was the Russian landed aristocracy a threat to this monopoly. It was no more than a group of lackeys retained at the pleasure of the tsar, permitted to use land only as long as its selected members faithfully served their royal master. Its leaders never played the independent and troublesome role assumed by the great landed barons in the feudal societies of western Europe.[3] The awesome power that Peter the Great wielded over all his subjects, according to Plekhanov and Martynov, was far greater than the authority exercised by the so-called absolute monarchs of the west; the tsar could dispose of the property of all his subjects at will; the tsar was strong enough to prevent the growth of a class that drew its sources of independent power from land ownership; the tsar was strong enough to control the trade routes and manufacturing enterprises in Russia, which remained free of royal control in the west and gave opportunities to a bourgeois class that eventually destroyed the monarchies of France and England; the tsar was strong enough to prevent Russians from rising above the level of cultural bleakness.

The Mensheviks did not consider the old system to be a feudal order of the kind that Karl Marx presumed to have existed in pre-capitalist Europe before the so-called bourgeois revolutions, but a system that contained the essential features that Marx himself, as well as Adam Smith, Montesquieu, Bishop Bossuet and Jean Bodin, observed in the cultures of the orient.[4] As the Menshevik thinker Paul Axelrod concluded, the Russians were dominated by a bureaucratic system in which the governing power of one institution played a greater historical role than the class struggle.[5] This historical situation had never developed in the west, and the Mensheviks stressed the incongruence by emphasizing the importance of the imperial administration in all walks of Russian life and the total absence of rival centers of political sovereignty. Their descriptions of the power and ubiquity of the imperial bureaucracy and its uncanny ability to use the technical achievements acquired by economic progress in the west in order to prevent change in Russia indicate that the Mensheviks found few comparisons between old Russia and medieval western Europe. Some changes of the modern era had weakened the old order, the emancipation of serfs in 1861, for example, but these had not broken its stifling grip on society.[6] In the early twentieth century, it still solidified Russia and prevented its people from taking advantage of the progressive currents that had brought so many benefits to west Europeans. Paul Axelrod tried to summarize his argument on the subject in a few words: "The old order of our pre-capitalist era, it is like the Wall of China, standing in the road blocking our way to industrial development and ascent from an agricultural economy."[7]

Almost all the Russian socialists, Populists as well as Marxists, shared this view of the old Russian order, and Lenin was not an exception. They used the term bondage system, *krepostnichestvo*, or semi-bondage system, *polukrepostnichestvo*, to describe the entire social and political order where, in their opinion, economic and cultural growth had been stunted by an apparatus of bureaucratic controls.[8] Occasionally the Mensheviks used the term asiatic order, *aziatchina*, to describe the old system, but more often they relied on the term bondage system, *krepostnichestvo*, or simply despotism, *despotizm*. Very few Mensheviks used the term feudalism to describe tsarist Russia. This incorrect English translation of *krepostnichestvo* was first introduced into the literature in 1931 by Stalin for quite unscientific reasons.[9]

The means adopted by the Mensheviks to replace the bondage system with a democratic order called for some form of political cooperation between Russian socialists and Russian liberals.[10] A united effort among these enemies of the tsar was essential first to assure proper direction in the coming uprising against the Romanovs and then to fashion a strong revolutionary regime that could sweep away the remnants left behind by the old order. Centuries of bondage had successfully pulverized Russian society, so no one modern force oculd expect to meet with success in an isolated attempt to bring Russia toward democracy. The old system kept its enemies weak, according to the Mensheviks, so they would need to work together in one common cause. A deep split within the camp of anti-tsarist forces would bring doom to the revolutionary movement,[11] so political success depended heavily on the all too shaky assumption that liberals and socialists were willing to work together toward a common end.

Mensheviks should not seize power alone or encourage any other socialist group to seize state power during the revolutionary period, because a *coup d'etat* by socialists was sure to result in an unqualified disaster. A socialist seizure of power would break apart the revolutionary alliance, drive the liberals out of the revolutionary movement and leave the socialists isolated in their attempts to transform Russia into a democracy. Standing alone against the shabby mass of peasant humanity that had been molded by the bondage system, the socialists could not hope to survive, let alone introduce a democratic order. The Mensheviks were disdainful and frightened of the Russian peasants and convinced that an undiluted dose of socialism administered to these "uncultured" people would quickly draw them away as willing recruits into the ranks of a restoration movement. The inevitable result of a socialist seizure of power in the revolutionary period would be political isolation and then, as Martynov once wrote, the restoration of the old order.[12] Plekhanov also defended this important point. In fact, his constant and articulate comments on precisely this issue makes separating him entirely from the Menshevik movement a serious mistake.[13]

By calling on all socialists and liberals to agree on plans to destroy the bondage system, the Mensheviks refused to walk the path followed by the Bolsheviks. Lenin concluded that only a dictatorship of the proletariat and the poor peasantry was capable of "eradicating all the oppressive features of Asiatic bondage," and he was determined to operate either without the Russian liberals or against them.[14] The Mensheviks considered this scheme to be too risky. The urban proletariat, the main source of socialist strength, was weak, even in twentieth-century Russia, and while peasants did live in poverty, a large and politicized poor element was nonexistent. According to the Mensheviks, Lenin's scheme relied for its success on support from phantoms and a few faithful Bolshevik followers, while at the same time it rejected the services of organized liberal groups that had much to gain by the destruction of old Russia. The Mensheviks rejected Lenin's plan as early as 1905 and continued to speak out against it even after the Bolshevik seizure of power in 1917. In fact, it was Plekhanov who attributed the failure of the revolution of 1905 to the Bolsheviks whose extremist slogans drove the mobs into a frenzy and frightened the liberals into supporting the imperial government.[15]

The tactical approach of the Russian Social Revolutionaries, the agrarian reformers, was one the Mensheviks considered to be neither wise nor rigorous.[16] Despite the readiness of some Social Revolutionaries to work with the liberals, which helped bring them into a close association with the Mensheviks in 1917, they placed too heavy an emphasis on the need for peasant participation in the revolution. The agricultural population of Russia was enormous in size, but it had not attained the degree of historical enlightenment needed to recognize the evil of the bondage system. Peasant revolts against the government might be useful in sparking a general insurrection, but the Mensheviks believed that the peasants could not understand and would not follow the sophisticated political maneuver leading to the establishment of political democracy in Russia. Anti-government attitudes among the peasants were not based on political and historical savvy. Peasant outbreaks were a temporary phenomenon and might even create a danger by dispersing the energy unleashed by the revolution.[17] The peasants would revolt against the government, according to the Mensheviks, but only the liberals and the socialists working together could use this energy to destroy the bondage system and bring democracy to Russia. Moreover, the Mensheviks were not convinced that the Social Revolutionary party enjoyed a strong following among the peasantry. They considered the Peasant Union to be a tool of the Social Revolutionary intellectuals who may have correctly understood various peasant anxieties and demands but were unable to harness peasant power.

In 1917 the Mensheviks resolutely refused to seize state power and demanded that only liberals hold portfolios in the Provisional Government. When it became clear in May that the government needed socialist participation in the cabinet in order to prevent a total collapse, the Mensheviks reluctantly obliged and the Georgian Menshevik Iraklii Tsereteli took the post of Minister of Posts and Telegraphs. Both these actions were defended on the ground that liberals and socialists must work together against the old order, and after May Tsereteli and the Mensheviks made it emphatic that their presence in the cabinet did not make the government a socialist one. Socialists in power alone would bring ruin to the democratic movement in Russia. This conviction derived from an abstract notion the Mensheviks held about the non-European character of Russian institutions and how modern forces needed to cooperate for the cause of progress.

b) Contradictions with Liberals

Unfortunately, the plans to dismantle the bondage system through a socialist-liberal alliance (with the liberals running up front) ran into grave difficulty in 1917 because the Menshevik commitment to Marxism introduced a strong anti-liberal strain into the party character.

Liberals were natural enemies in the eyes of Mensheviks. They were the representatives of capitalism, a system of life that Marx had doomed in his writings and the Mensheviks were determined to help destroy. In the long run, the Mensheviks expected the force of history to remove the liberals and the capitalist order, just as they predicted it would bring an end to the Romanovs and the bondage order. In fact the Mensheviks considered some aspects of the Russian revolutionary movement to be a protest against their liberal allies as well as a revolt against the tsar.[18] And they freely admitted that their own desire to cooperate with the liberals was based less on an urge to form an alliance between comrades-in-arms and more on a calculated move to form a temporary association between enemies against a common enemy. The revolution against the bondage system became known among the Mensheviks as the bourgeois revolution, and it was to serve only as the first stage in a two stage revolution that would ultimately fulfill the prophecy of Marx by sweeping away the liberals and capitalism. As Julius Martov wrote in 1905: "Our aim is to use this bourgeois revolution in the interest of the future socialist revolution, the proletarian revolution."[19] Capitalism and its liberals had generated an essential force in the Russian revolutionary epoch. The old oriental world of dispersed villages controlled by imperial bureaucrats would break apart only under the hammer blows delivered by demanding railroad builders, bankers and industrialists; furthermore, it was this kind of action that would lead inevitably to the creation of a strong proletariat in Russia.[20] The Mensheviks welcomed capitalism and liberalism to Russia, but looked upon them both as being hostile to the final victory in the cause of freedom. They quoted Marx, on many occasions with greater precision than did Lenin, revealing a hatred of capitalism and a deep suspicion of liberals, their so-called collaborators in the business of destroying the imperial government and the bondage system.

During and soon after the Russian revolution of 1905 the strongest differences between the Mensheviks and the liberals were brought to the surface. The Russian liberals took a bold step in 1905 and organized two important political parties, the Kadets (Constitutional Democrats and later renamed the Party of Peoples' Freedom) and the Octobrists (The Union of October Seventeenth). But the Mensheviks were critical throughout the revolutionary crisis. They charged many Kadets and Octobrists with openly supporting the tsar against the masses of the people and giving more emphasis to the restoration of order in the streets than to the struggle for democracy. According to the Mensheviks, the representatives of capitalism began to share common ground with the bureaucrats of the old regime when the political crisis brought angry factory workers into the action. Russian liberals had not been as revolutionary as the Mensheviks wished. They even speculated that Russian liberalism was too feeble to attain the high degree of revolutionary fervor needed to overthrow the bondage system.[21] The Mensheviks did not abandon their conviction that cooperation between socialists and liberals was to be an essential part of a successful revolution against bondage Russia, but after 1905 this conviction was counterbalanced by a determination to undertake more aggressive action on their own initiative.[22] What was seen as the duplicity or timidity of the liberals brought the Mensheviks to exert an increased amount of energy toward the development of new resources. They also decided to cooperate only with the so-called democratic groups among the bourgeoisie, rejecting altogether the company of conservative liberals.[23] They reached no general agreement on how to deal with this problem, but many Mensheviks emphasized the importance of building a base of socialist strength among factory workers in Russia. Paul Axelrod had conducted seminars in Switzerland in 1904 for the benefit of untutored Russian revolutionaries, and after 1905 he urged Russian Social Democrats to provide proper guidelines for the organization of workers in Russia.[24] Much of this activity was inspired by a growing lack of confidence in liberals and a realization that socialists would have to play a stronger role in a successful revolutionary movement. Even Plekhanov, perhaps the least likely figure to abandon the cooperation strategy, was critical of the "bourgeoisie" in 1905 for adopting a lackadaisical attitude toward the revolution, expecting "miracles in our prosaic times" to destroy the despotism.[25]

The anti-liberal attitudes of the Mensheviks were derived from Marxism and were constantly reinforced by close contact with European Social Democrats in the Second International, especially during the "revisionist" controversy that took place at the turn of the century. In 1889 Alexandre Millerand, a prominent French socialist, accepted a cabinet post in the "bourgeois" government of René Waldeck-Rousseau on the grounds that he could help to ease the burdens carried by the French working people. At the same time the German socialist Edward Bernstein declared that the final demise of capitalism would come after a process of gradual evolutionary change and not as the result of an abrupt political upheaval. Many socialist leaders attacked Millerand

and Bernstein on the grounds that this cooperation with liberals weakened the political power of the European socialist parties and distorted the true message of Marxism. In the quarrels that ensued most Russian socialists found themselves entrenched on the side of those Marxist leaders who were denouncing Millerand and Bernstein.[26] No compromise could be made with those who rejected the doctrines of Marx! The controversy between revisionists and revolutionists came to the surface in Europe before the founding of the Menshevik party, but the future leaders of Menshevism, Martov, Martynov, Dan and Axelrod, all took partisan stands in the quarrel against revisionism and carried their sentiments into the Menshevik party when it began to grow after 1903.

The Russian socialists felt justified in joining the attack against European revisionism, but it helped to make the Menshevik position in Russia awkward. The Mensheviks opposed a strategy of cooperation between liberals and socialists in western Europe, while at the same time they advocated a strategy of cooperation in Russia. Of course, they could easily argue that Russia was very different from western Europe because its people struggled under the lash of the bondage system while Europeans enjoyed the freedom to engage in the combat between the bourgeoisie and the proletariat. It was necessary, therefore, to encourage collaboration between liberals and socialists in Russia, but essential to discourage collaboration between liberals and socialists in western Europe. It could all be explained quite neatly. Unfortunately, the double standard that was easily explained was not easily applied. The Mensheviks quickly found that cooperating with Russian liberals was a very difficult business, especially after the World War broke out in 1914 and most Russian Social Democrats concluded that the greed of liberals lay at the core of the trouble. Hatred for liberals and suspicion for those who were prepared to collaborate with liberals quickly became consistent features in the Menshevik movement, and they could not be easily jettisoned when state boundaries were crossed or sociological circumstances changed. Of course, the Mensheviks could not allow their hostility toward liberals to get out of hand and expect their cooperation with liberals in Russia to amount to more than an empty slogan, but even prior to 1917 virulent anti-liberal attitudes threatened to place all chances for socialist-liberal cooperation in Russia beyond the reach of the Mensheviks. Nothing was done by the Mensheviks to change the clumsy strategic position they occupied, partly because they did not fully recognize its many deep pitfalls.

Following the fall of the Romanovs in February of 1917, the Mensheviks asked all citizens of the new Russia to support the so-called bourgeois government led by the Kadet chief Paul Miliukov. At the very same time, however, they did little to encourage the efforts put forth by the liberal officials of the new government and actually formed a close working agreement with many Social Revolutionary leaders who distrusted the Russian liberals for their own reasons and who supplied a dangerous excess of inertia by adopting much of the Menshevik strategy without really knowing why. The Mensheviks refused to seize power for themselves or in the company of Social Revolutionaries on the grounds that such a step would frighten away the cooperative spirit needed to destroy asiatic Russia. Yet they did everything in their power to restrict the activity of the liberal politicians, because the "capitalists" and the land owners who joined them were not expected to govern in the best interests of humanity. When the revolution broke out the plan to bring socialists and liberals together in a joint effort against the old order had evolved into the contradictory formula coined by the Menshevik journalist Sukhanov: We will support the new bourgeois Provisional Government, only so long as (*poskol'ku postol'ku*) it works to implement our program.[27] Unfortunately, this slogan guided the Mensheviks toward danger.

c) Divisions among Mensheviks

Despite the strong continuity that ran throughout Menshevism on the question of liberalism and revolutionary strategy, this political movement could not be identified by mentioning the name of one man or one faction. Divisiveness within the party was rife and organizational unity, although sought, was never found. Individuals or small groups firmly convinced of the correctness of their own opinions prevented the Mensheviks from enjoying the advantages of unified action. During the events of 1917 internal controversy frustrated attempts to create a cohesive political party and divided the Mensheviks during their efforts to present a consistent program to the Provisional Government; it easily kept the party divided in its relations with the Bolsheviks and the west European socialists. No doubt, imponderous obstacles not of their own making helped to discourage the growth of a unifying spirit among Mensheviks. The imperial police used a series of harsh and clever devices (arrest and exile, police spies and police labor unions) in order to prevent revolutionary organization from growing up on Russian soil, and the Mensheviks were often helpless in their efforts to avoid its watchful eyes. Disagreement might also have been less harmful if large numbers of industrial workers had been lured into the ranks of the movement, but they were not present in sufficient force to coax the Mensheviks onto the path of unity. As a result, the Mensheviks were almost always prevented from acting in unison, and often their strongest weapons were rendered useless simply because party members disagreed on how to aim them.

The early efforts of all Russian Social Democrats were frustrated by this primitive condition, so in 1903 a great effort was made to end divisiveness by founding one disciplined political organization. The sad story of the Second Congress has been told many times. Lenin had control of the agenda. He introduced a series of measures that were aimed at limiting the number of people who could be admitted to high levels of the party and also aimed at preventing extended debate once a decision had been made by the leadership. Once reformed, the party would supposedly be prepared to function well in the face of the imperial police and carry out its mission within Russia's primitive industrial working force. But the Second Congress ended in bitterness and marked the beginning of the famous split between the Bolsheviks and Mensheviks. Lenin tried to assure his success at the meeting first by separating unsympathetic groups from the general body of the Congress and then by forcing his measures on those who remained. His goal was to gain a majority support for a small group of revolutionary leaders who would then direct the party. But the drive to consolidate Russian Social Democrats quickly encountered difficulties. Martov defected from the ranks of the Leninists. He questioned the wisdom of limiting the number of workers who could participate at high party levels and absolutely refused to relinquish his right to protest against decisions made by party leaders. Before the Congress ended Martov had severed his personal ties with Lenin and the Russian Social Democrats were divided into more factions than had been the case before 1903. Lenin finally did obtain support for his measures from a truncated Second Congress, despite Martov's defection, but it was a pyrrhic victory. It did not include the big prize, a unified Russian Marxist party under the strict supervision of a handful of seasoned leaders.[28] Lenin emerged as the leader of a faction of Russian Social democrats that he called the Bolsheviks, while the greater number of Marxists in Russia remained attached to one of the various non-Bolshevik groups

that he branded collectively as the Mensheviks. After 1903, unsuccessful attempts were made to reunite the factions and for a time many
Social Democrats refused to recognize that a wide breach had been
opened. But the split was irreparable and eventually came to include
arguments about revolutionary strategy and tactics as well as party
organization. Personal hatreds were soon woven into the texture of
political disagreements.[29]

The split did little to bring unity and direction to the Mensheviks. In
fact, the bout with the Bolshevik leader brought additional headaches.
During the polemical exchange that followed the Second Congress,
most Mensheviks reacted strongly against Lenin's centralization plans
by emphasizing the importance of free discussion and decentralization.
Indeed, many who had been champions of centralization in 1901 and
1902 and had worked with Lenin to bring about an end to the debating
club atmosphere reigning among Russian Marxists reversed their
argument after 1903. Once Lenin revealed how centralization curtailed
freedom of action, many former advocates of strict discipline recoiled
in horror and began to extol the virtues of decentralization and the
right of each individual to speak his mind. Axelrod was one Menshevik
leader in favor of strong central authority prior to 1903, but who
inclined toward decentralization after the fight with Lenin began.[30]
The chief figure in this drama, however, was Martov himself. Before
1903 Martov had been a close friend of Lenin and a champion of
centralization. After the Second Congress, however, he rejected Lenin's plans as organizational fetishism and in 1904 demanded guarantees that a united Russian Marxist party would never require the sup-
pression of minority opinions.[31] No doubt, he acted in good faith;
Lenin's methods of organization did not attract many people, even
those who found themselves in sympathy with his views on other
matters. But Martov's bitterness and vigilance was typical of the Mensheviks after 1903 when they generally ignored the signs indicating
that a cohesive party structure would be an important asset to their
movement.

Between 1903 and the outbreak of the war in 1914 the divided character of the Menshevik party changed very little. Common experiences
were shared during the revolution in 1905 and in the sessions of the
State Duma, and important issues arose that most Mensheviks agreed
upon, such as opposition to both the Stolypin agrarian reforms and the
Russian war against Japan, but organizational unity remained beyond
their reach. At times, a feeling of comradery seemed to prevail among

the Mensheviks, but the sect-like party structure remained unchanged. From 1908 to 1910 a reformist trend appeared in the Menshevik ranks that increased emphasis on the theme of cooperation with Russian liberals, but the party did not unify around this standard. In 1912 a formal effort was made to unite all Mensheviks. Leon Trotsky, with the help of Plekhanov and A. N. Potresov (Starover), was the central figure in what became known as the August Bloc. The name derived from a meeting that took place in Vienna, called in reaction to Lenin's Prague meeting of Bolsheviks in the spring of 1912. Nobody in Menshevik circles took too seriously the diatribes Lenin delivered at Prague, but the Vienna conference came to nothing. Potresov and Plekhanov renewed their quarrel,[32] leaving Trotsky alone to unify the Mensheviks, a task beyond the talents of all who had tried up to that time and a task that was almost totally foreign to Trotsky's nature.

The outbreak of war in 1914 led to even greater divisiveness among the Mensheviks, although at first it appeared they might unify around the anti-war slogans; only Plekhanov among the best known Mensheviks was prepared to lend support to the Russian government and the Allied cause, postponing the revolutionary effort for the duration of the war. But unity remained only a mirage. By early 1916 the Mensheviks were deeply divided and the party organization totally shattered.

The War Industry Committees used by the liberals to strengthen Russia's military posture were important factors in bringing about fresh divisions. The creation of the Committees was a sign of the growing liberal opposition to the government's alleged incompetence in directing the war effort, and some Mensheviks and Social Revolutionaries were asked to join as representatives of Russia's labor force. At first only a few agreed, but soon others became interested and by the middle of 1916 even a respectable number of Mensheviks from the Social Democratic faction in the Russian State Duma had expressed favorable sentiments toward the Committees.[33] The growing body of opinion that approved of cooperation with the War Industry Committees, however, was not strong enough to dominate and unify the party. Even those Mensheviks who approved of the work of the Committees disagreed over the proper theoretical reasons for entering into such close cooperation with the Russian "bourgeoisie."[34]

Potresov, Maslov, Dmitriev (Kolokol'nikov) and Gvozdev were convinced that a strong defense of the Russian state was absolutely necessary. The military threat posed by the German army jeopardized the livelihood of Russian workers as well as employers, so they advised all socialists to work with the Committees in an effort to protect the country from destruction. Calling themselves self-defensists, they advised industrial workers never to forget the political struggle against the tsarist order but at the same time to remain flexible enough to assist in efforts to strengthen the Russian defense machine. This tactic was certainly well within the scope of traditional Menshevik thinking. Employers and employees had always stood on common ground in their opposition to the tsar. Now they shared a joint interest in the protection of Russia from an enemy invasion. The liberals, of course, sought to gain national expansion from the war effort, Potresov admitted, but the workers and their socialist representatives wanted only an adequate protection of their homeland. In spite of this difference, however, both anti-tsarist forces could and should work together.[35]

Unfortunately, Potresov's views carried no weight for many other Mensheviks who also approved of working in the War Industry Committees. Groups of Mensheviks in Petrograd and Moscow, and many Mensheviks in Siberian exile, realized the benefits to be gained for the revolutionary cause by encouraging cooperation between socialists and liberals, but they were embarrassed by the self-defensist slogans. They agreed to cooperate with the Committees because it presented an opportunity to draw workers into the socialist movement, but they held fast to the conviction that socialists must refuse to support military measures even if carried out solely for defensive purposes. The Siberian Mensheviks, the Petersburg Initiators, and the group of Moscow Mensheviks claimed to be Internationalists and bitterly opposed the protection-of-the-homeland slogan of the self-defensists.[36] They approved of socialist work in the Committees as a temporary measure, but they talked only of an international peace conference and criticized Potresov's pleas to support an energetic defense of the Russian homeland.[37]

Another bloc of Mensheviks absolutely refused to enter the War Industry Committees and condemned those who did, whatever their reasons. They urged all socialists to resist temptation and to shun activities that might prolong the war. They also called themselves Internationalists and saw the war as a gigantic struggle between two bourgeois or imperialist coalitions, but unlike the Siberian Mensheviks and the Petersburg Initiators they saw no benefits in wartime cooperation between socialists and liberals. The chief figures in these groups were Martov, Martynov and Astrov. They were closely attached to the radical European socialist circles that met in Switzerland at Zimmerwald in 1915 and at Kienthal in 1916 and published a manifesto fixing blame for the war on the European bourgeois classes. Martov and his fellow Zimmerwald Internationalists demanded that an immediate end by brought to hostilities and that peace be concluded on terms dictated by radical European socialists. All those socialists who worked in the Russian War Industry Committees were working against a socialist peace, according to Martov, and for the military victory of one of the two bourgeois coalitions. By holding fast to their claims, Martov and his friends not only increased the number of divisions among the Mensheviks, but also added immeasurably to the strength of the anti-liberal sympathies in the movement.[38]

The Mensheviks were not alone responsible for the increasing divisions that appeared in their ranks between 1914 and 1916. Wartime conditions made it difficult for them to iron out many petty differences, and their arch-rival, as usual, did his utmost to keep the antagonists divided. Lenin denounced all those who approved of participation in the War Industry Committees. According to the Bolshevik leader, they followed a policy of capitulation to the imperialists of the world. Distinctions among the Mensheviks who worked with the Committees were meaningless, according to Lenin, and should be dismissed by all serious Marxists. He also harassed Martov and the Internationalists charging that members of their Zimmerwald team were not as enthusiastic about the world proletarian revolution and a socialist peace as they tried to appear. He singled out Chkheidze, the Menshevik head of the Social Democratic delegation in the Russian State Duma, and Paul Axelrod as men who were opposed to the Committees and favorably disposed toward a socialist peace in their public statements while they privately opposed the Zimmerwald program and privately tried to make a compromise with the Russian liberals.[39] Lenin successfully provoked factionalism within the Menshevik party, although the sweetest fruit of his labor was not gathered until the late summer of 1917.

In his memoir, Boris L. Dvinov (Gurevich) wrote that the war had catastrophic consequences for the Mensheviks because it created disunity within the party.[40] This statement was correct, but it implied that the movement enjoyed unity prior to its wartime troubles. In fact, the Mensheviks were not united into a cohesive force prior to the outbreak of the war, and except for brief periods of superficial harmony their history was one of divisiveness and fighting among contending factions. During the events of 1917, the Mensheviks moved toward unity, but then quarreled bitterly over important issues that had no roots in the war period. They agreed, for example, that cooperation between liberals and socialists was required for a successful revolution against the bondage system, and they supported Tsereteli when he implemented this policy in Petrograd, but when the period of crisis opened during the summer months the Mensheviks began to bicker about how the party ought to support the liberals and which politicians truly represented Russian liberals. Deference was rarely shown to one leader or one faction. When the Mensheviks found themselves opposed to Lenin in October and tried to prevent his seizure of power, their efforts were weakened partly by their own inability to work together.

The loose party organization, a strong distrust of liberals and the strategy that aimed at removing the so-called asian way of life from Russian soil were deeply embedded in Menshevism, and in some respects all three factors proved to be sources of great strength in 1917. They brought independence to party members, freeing them from the narrow and tyrannical leadership of one figure. They brought a well-founded confidence and an ability to judge events by one's own standards. And they kept alive a healthy skepticism toward many of the exaggerated claims made by the Kadet party leaders and Alexander Kerensky. They made Menshevism an important source of intelligence and good leadership amidst the confusion and brutality of the revolution. At the same time, unfortunately, they were also the chief causes for the failure of Menshevism, playing a significant part in the turn of events that left Lenin in command of Petrograd in October.

Chapter II
The Revolution Begins

a) The First Days

The uprising that bowled over the Romanov regime at the end of February 1917 was started by Russian workers and soldiers who seized control of the city of Petrograd. Civil disturbances among the working classes had been characteristic of life in the capital during the last months of 1916, and the strikes of late February seemed to be following the usual pattern. On February 27, however, a mutiny broke out among the poorly trained troops of the Petrograd garrisons leaving officers and policemen without sufficient strength to cope with the mobs in the street. The authority of the Romanov government simply disappeared. On the morning of February 28 the city was in the hands of groups of workers and soldiers, and several liberal political leaders took advantage of the disorder by cautiously making plans to form a provisional revolutionary government. On March 2 Nicholas II abdicated, yielding to the revolution without a struggle. The royal family was unable to find a champion. Within two weeks the overthrow was complete throughout the empire.

Although the insurrectionists looked to neither men nor groups for leadership, a focal point did appear at the Taurida Palace, the home of the State Duma. Here the Petrograd Soviet of Workers' and Soldiers' Deputies grew from a small committee that had formed a few days prior to the mutiny. On February 25 a number of Mensheviks in Petrograd, the notable Georgian N. S. Chkheidze among them, had tried to establish a political committee consisting of both the leading Social Democrats in the State Duma and those socialists who were active in the various Petrograd labor organizations. This effort probably would have ended in failure if the action in the streets had been brought under control by the police, but its survival was assured once the revolutionaries gained the upper hand. On February 27 the committee was joined by other socialists who had been liberated from prison. In the evening of February 27 elections were held among the workers and soldiers in various parts of the city to determine who would serve as their official representatives on the new committee. In this manner the Executive Committee of the Petrograd Soviet became an important center of the revolution.

During these first days of upheaval a feeling of joy and triumph overwhelmed the Mensheviks. The long awaited moment of revolution was at hand and the Mensheviks drifted quickly into a short period of delirium: "Hurrah! It has come at last," Skobelev greeted Sorokin with outstretched hand.[1] The moment seemed too great for ordinary partisan prose. The occasion called for something grand: "Clearly, the sun of freedom now shines over our land caressing and warming millions of people, and casting on them a sweet spirit and rosy dreams. The turgid nightmare has passed, the unbelievably heavy load has been thrown from our shoulders."[2] The excitement was universal among party members revealing their fear of the fallen monarch and their great hope for the future. The revolution eliminated the tsar announced *Rabochaia Gazeta*, the daily Menshevik newspaper that now began to appear on the streets of Petrograd. It took its place among the revolutions that had "shaken Asia since 1905 from the Kremlin to the immovable Wall of China."[3] Everybody felt the urge to rejoice. Writing about the Russian revolution from a hypothetical point in the distant future, Vladimir Rozanov declared: "Our children will not believe their ears, listening to our stories about the last tyrant of all Russia, Nicholas II, or our stories of the times of the system of bondage .... When we speak of the old regime, it will seem to them that we speak not of Russia, but of Sodom and Gomorrah."[4] The women were included in the jubilation. "Our sisters, wives, and daughters were with us on this great day. They were with us in joy and grief at the outburst of the struggle."[5] The "asiatic order" had suffered a great defeat, according to the Mensheviks, and it was now in retreat. The new balance in Russia favored "creative forces."[6]

The Mensheviks had more to cheer about than the crushing defeat administered by the masses to the so-called bondage system, because they found themselves occupying the most influential positions in the newly formed Petrograd Soviet and also in the Moscow Soviet that was established a few days later. Even when current Soviet historians denigrate the Mensheviks for failing to fulfill the wishes of the masses during the events of 1917, they readily admit that the Soviet leadership was firmly in Menshevik hands.[7] The leaders of the Executive Committee of the Petrograd Soviet (formed on February 27) were the Menshevik journalist, N. N. Sukhanov, the Mensheviks from the Workers' Group of the War Industry Committees, B. O. Bogdanov and

K. A. Gvozdev, and the Mensheviks from the Fourth State Duma, M. I. Skobelev and N. S. Chkheidze, the President of the Soviet. In addition to their strength on the Executive Committee, the Mensheviks dominated the important Contact Commission, formed to serve as a liaison body between the Soviet and the new Provisional Government. A few Bolsheviks, soldiers, and independent radicals were also on hand, but among these people only Alexander Kerensky had sufficient stature to challenge the Menshevik leadership. The Mensheviks did not supervise the insurrection in Petrograd, but they were soon in a position to direct its energies. Moreover, other developments were taking shape in a manner favorable to them, especially with regard to the new revolutionary provisional government.

During the late February disturbances, several leading liberal politicians in Petrograd began to negotiate with the emperor about the future role of the State Duma. Nicholas had recessed the Duma in February, but it was the only legal institution useful for political dissent and the liberals in the Progressive Bloc were seeking to reopen its doors.[8] Once the great scope of the Petrograd insurrection was realized, however, this group decided to defy the emperor and form a government on its own initiative. Calling themselves the Provisional Committee of the State Duma, the members of this small group enjoyed considerable support from that sector of society the Mensheviks had labelled as bourgeois Russia. Along with the support of the Russian general staff, whose officers were not prepared to defend the imperial government, the Committee enjoyed the confidence of most professional people engaged in the direction of the Russian war effort. It also had close contacts with the banking and finance interests of Russia and with the governments of England and France. The Committee's membership included prominent men from the leading non-socialist political parties that were represented in the Duma, but its greatest energy came from the Kadets P. N. Miliukov and V. N. Nekrasov, the Octobrists A. I. Guchkov and S. I. Shidlovksy, and the Nationalist V. N. Lvov.

The Soviet leaders were understandably pleased to see revolutionary action taken by the Duma Committee. It helped to balance the power of the Petrograd Soviet, an institution of the Mensheviks intended to lead away from the reigns of state power, and it looked like the beginning of the new bourgeois democratic government they planned to support in the first stage of the revolution.[9] In addition, the Provisional Committee was prepared to cooperate with the Soviet; the street mobs were unmanageable, and the liberals were ready to deal through an organized political center that appeared to exercise some influence over the masses. An invitation to discuss the makeup of a revolutionary government was sent to the Soviet on March 1 and the Mensheviks quickly responded. They were as anxious as the liberals to establish order and political stability in the new "bourgeois" in Russia.

The two revolutionary committees met that very evening in the Taurida Palace, the home of both the Soviet and State Duma. The Soviet was represented by the Mensheviks Chkheidze, Sukhanov and Sokolov while the Duma Committee was represented by the scions of Russian society, Paul Miliukov, Alexander Guchkov and George Lvov. Fortunately for the cause of harmony, the Soviet leaders had no intention of preventing the Duma Committee from holding positions of government power and the meeting was quite cordial. The participants took time getting down to business, but finally found common ground by agreeing that the confusion in the city of Petrograd must come to an end before the revolution could consolidate its gains. The danger of a successful reaction against the insurrectionists by the tsar and his friends seemed great, although the prevailing atmosphere was one of confidence. Sukhanov set the tone of the meeting by reminding everybody that the struggle against anarchy was in the interest of the Duma Committee as much as it was in the interest of the Soviet leaders. Agreement was quickly reached on this point and things then moved along easily. The Soviet leaders were disinterested in obtaining government posts, but they did state the conditions required in return for their support of the new government. The Duma Committee responded favorably to the assertion that all citizens must be granted freedom of political agitation in the press and freedom to organize in political parties and trade unions. It was also agreed that the Petrograd garrisons should remain armed, although it is difficult to imagine circumstances in which the troops would have obeyed orders to surrender their weapons. All political prisoners were to be granted an amnesty and civil liberties were to be extended to soldiers on campaign. Finally, the convocation of a Constituent Assembly was to take place at the earliest convenient moment. In return for a government guarantee to protect these rights, Sukhanov, Chkheidze, and Skobelev pledged the support of the Soviet Executive Committee.[10]

Neither the threat of a Soviet seizure of political power nor the possibility that the Soviet leaders might participate in the new revolutionary government were matters of concern during the meeting of the

two committees or during the first six weeks of the revolution. The
Mensheviks intended to cling very closely to their prearranged strategy and the workers and soldiers appeared ready to follow their leadership. But the Mensheviks took no chances, making it clear to their
followers that the Soviet was to serve outside the government structure. The first issue of *Rabochaia Gazeta* undertook a subtle persuasion
campaign. It assumed a patronizing attitude, expressing confidence
that the soldiers and workers understood the tactical position held by
the Soviet leaders and would resist the temptation to seize power.
"The temporary Duma Committee strives to found a Provisional
Government. This government will be decidely bourgeois in character
.... Do not struggle for its removal, do not struggle to replace the
government with representatives from the Soviet ....."[11] Some Mensheviks were less didactic in explaining their plans, but equally as clear:
"The proletariat and the revolutionary army showed their entire
demeanor during the first and most difficult week of the revolution by
their readiness not to split and to conduct the cause of the liberation of
Russia together with the liberal bourgeoisie."[12] These same sentiments
were expressed by the Georgian Menshevik, I. G. Tsereteli, when he
arrived in Petrograd from exile in Siberia: "Having overthrown the old
regime," he addressed the crowd at the Nikolaevsky Railroad station,
"you considered the circumstances from the point of view of the interests of a great people .... You did not force your will on the events at
that time. The power is in the hands of the bourgeoisie ..."[13] Both
O. A. Ermansky (Kogan) and N. N. Sukhanov revealed the same state
of mind in their memoirs. In his usual abrupt fashion, Sukhanov,
wrote: "The power to take the place of the tsar must be only bourgeois. Rasputin and Trepov ought and can be replaced only by the
bosses of the Progressive Bloc."[14]

The Soviet was not to become an instrument of state power, a car-
dinal rule of the Menshevik political strategy throughout the events of
1917.[15] It was an organization of workers that could include soldiers,
sailors and intellectuals. In fact, it could include all friends of the revolution who were ready to destroy the old order while they "guided" the
bourgeois Provisional Government along the correct path. This rule
placed a limitation on Soviet policy and served as evidence of the Menshevik domination of that body. It was Lenin and some Social Revolutionaries who saw in the Soviet a useful vehicle for the seizure of state
power, and it was Lenin who eventually captured the Soviet and
directed its energies toward a *coup d'etat*.[16]

Among Mensheviks outside Petrograd the attitude toward government power was equally firm and equally consistent, as several illustrations from memoir publications have indicated. Following the February uprising in Moscow, workers expected the eight hour working day to be initiated as quickly as possible since it had been one of the chief reforms the revolutionary parties had promised to put into practice. But when the Menshevik-dominated Moscow Soviet discussed the possibility of changing the length of the working day, Boris Dvinov reminded his comrades that the laws regarding the length of the working day had to be approved by the Provisional Government. It did not occur to Dvinov that the Moscow Soviet could usurp the power of the government, even in this peculiarly proletarian sphere.[17] In Vitebsk where Gregory Aronson served in the Menshevik-dominated Soviet, it was assumed that only the Provisional Government had the authority to appoint and to remove officials representing the state. When the Provisional Government did appoint a much needed official in Vitebsk, he was not acceptable to the Soviet leaders and his removal was demanded. The leaders of the Soviet never considered appointing or replacing an official on their own authority despite the fact that Soviet strength and prestige in Vitebsk was far greater than that of the new Provisional Government.[18] According to recent studies by Soviet historians who have examined the outbreak of the revolution, this same general trend appeared wherever the Mensheviks were present in great strength.

Abstention from government power did not mean abstention from political activity as far as the Mensheviks were concerned: quite to the contrary. Now that the tsar had been removed the Mensheviks were anxious to get on with the business of dismantling the old system of bondage and introducing "progressive" institutions similar to those found in western Europe. The first step had been successfully completed. The emperor was gone. But the revolutionary forces had yet to "destroy the old despotic order, *aziatchina*, and slavery, so that out from the debris a new sprout, the regeneration of freedom, could fight its way to the surface."[19] No time was to be wasted. Russia had remained too long in the hands of those who perpetuated the bondage system with its unnatural laws and fashions: "Take away the privileges of *dvors*, priests, merchants, *chinovniki*, and landlords."[20] The Mensheviks would accept no excuse for delay. The tsar was gone, but tsarism remained to be removed. To those who were content to rest with the laurels won during the insurrection of February 27 *Rabochaia Gazeta* issued a sharp warning: "The old gang of satraps that once enslaved Russia is still lurking in dark corners, waiting for a weak moment to strike at the revolution; conditions that will prevent their desire to strike must be quickly created."[21]

Many of the admonitions that came from the Mensheviks were directed at socialists, but the chief target of the impatient demands to sweep Russia clean of the "old system" was the new Provisional Government and the liberal leaders who held its top posts. It was on the shoulders of the Provisional Government that the Mensheviks placed the responsibility of rearranging Russia to suit an image the Soviet leaders held of a modern democracy. It was against the Kadet chief Paul Miliukov and the leaders of the liberal parties of Russia that pressure was applied by "the party of the extreme opposition." *Rabochaia Gazeta* went straight to the point: "The tasks of the Provisional Government are clear and simple; with the support of the people and the army to destroy swiftly and decisively everything that remains of the old order and that interferes with the new one, and create just as swiftly and decisively, everything without which the new order cannot exist."[22] Having long ago abandoned faith in the healing power of the institutions and administrators of imperial Russia, the Mensheviks now wanted these institutions abolished and replaced by something new. Yet irony prevailed in the fact that the new "bourgeois" government would receive little more confidence and respect than the government of Nicholas II. Correct tactics demanded that the liberals occupy the official positions of authority, but the activist strain in Menshevism was already placing strict limits on the leaders of the new government. Even Tsereteli, one of the most reasonable among Mensheviks in his dealings with the liberal political parties in Petrograd, left no doubt in the minds of the people where he stood with regard to the new government: "Should the moment arrive when this government renounces the revolutionary path and chooses the path of compromise and negotiations, then you and I, comrades, will march dauntlessly against this government and together we will cast it into oblivion in the same way as we did the old regime."[23]

On March 3 when the cabinet positions in the new government were announced to the public, Miliukov tried to include a member of the royal family, substantially as a figurehead. The move was immediately and tersely blocked by the socialists and the masses. Miliukov had to withdraw his proposal as quickly as possible lest he become the object of scorn from the very first. During this episode the leaders of the Soviet showed no desire to compromise with Miliukov and no desire to shield the new foreign minister from public ridicule. Cooperation between the Soviet and the Provisional Government had taken legal form, but there was yet little sign of its spirit.

Many writers have discussed these first confusing days of the revolution, and two major explanations have been put forth to clarify the events. One theory emphasizes the spontaneous character of the insurrection. The February revolution and the motives of the Soviet leaders can best be understood without seeking complicated historical roots connected to action that was obviously unrehearsed. According to this interpretation, it makes little sense to look for significance in the party affiliation of those men who played a prominant role in the early days. A "pure" Soviet existed in the first days of March, one writer maintained.[24] It was composed of soldiers and workers, the masses, who were presumably disinterested in both political parties and complicated questions about political tactics. In his book on the Social Revolutionaries, Oliver Radkey used a variation of this thesis. He called the February insurrection and the formation of the Petrograd Soviet "the heyday of independent radicalism."[25] The authors who hold the spontaneous thesis stress the lack of formal political organization among the mutinous soldiers and the part played by the confused clutter of humanity that collected around the Taurida Palace during the early days of the revolution. They write about freedom and high pitched emotions. They de-emphasize the claims of Sukhanov and Ermansky that positions of state power were scrupulously avoided in February by the Soviet leaders for tactical and not emotional reasons. Authors of the spontaneous thesis also de-emphasize the fact that avoidance of state power during the revolution was a key part of the Menshevik strategy long before 1917. The thesis is at its strongest point when it analyzes the genesis of the popular insurrection and the mutiny that broke out in late February, but it does not explain why the Soviet leaders encouraged the establishment of dual power, an arrangement that remained the cornerstone of Petrograd politics until Lenin's victory in October. And by overlooking the strong Menshevik influence in the February uprising, the theory cannot explain why a large number of mutinous soldiers, politically naive and loosely affiliated with the Social Revolutionary party, were easily led through a maze of tactical maneuver by a few civilians, most of whom were connected with the Menshevik circles of the Russian Social Democratic Workers' Party.

Another explanation used to clarify the early events of the revolution is the class struggle interpretation. It is most often identified with the work of Soviet historians, but others hold variations of this view. These authors readily accept the fact that the Mensheviks were the organizers and tactical leaders in the first days of the Petrograd Soviet; the workers and soldiers (the lower classes) were not themselves Mensheviks, but they were easily led by "the petty bourgeoisie." The Soviet historian A. M. Andreev actually maintained that the popular insurrection was inspired by the Bolsheviks, but it was captured by the Mensheviks on February 27, betrayed, and then surrendered into the hands of the liberal "bourgeoisie" on the evening of March 1.[26] According to Andreev, the early course of the revolution was chartered by the Mensheviks whose fault lay in tying their fortunes to the liberals and refusing to seize state power. The strength of the class struggle interpretation rests in its recognition of the decisive Menshevik leadership in Petrograd at the beginning of the revolution, but beyond that point the theory has a serious weakness. It ignores the importance of Russian institutional history (particularly its asian characteristics) as it was studied and used by the Mensheviks (and Lenin) long before 1917. In trying to explain both the motives of the revolutionaries and the course of the revolution solely in class terms, the theory fails to give an adequate description of events that took place in a society in which class hostility of the west European variety played neither the sole nor the dominant role. Soviet historians interpret the relationship between the Petrograd Soviet and the Provisional Government as a capitulation by the petty bourgeoisie to the liberal or big bourgeoisie. But as Marc Ferro observed in his study on the February revolution: "The Soviet placed the Duma Committee at the helm, but in order to direct it at will aimed a pistol at its head."[27] It is a strange sort of capitulation that leaves the "petty-bourgeois" prisoner armed and threatening to shoot his "haut-bourgeois" captor if the captor fails to carry out the orders of the prisoner.

One significant feature common to both the spontaneous and class interpretation theories is that evidence from Menshevik sources is not analyzed on its own merits. The writings of Sukhanov and Ermansky and the editorials in *Rabochaia Gazeta* are often cited, but only to support hypotheses that were not held by the Mensheviks. Why not accept their explanations as an accurate description of how the events unfolded? The Mensheviks considered tsarist Russia to have contained certain asian political and social patterns that needed to be dissolved before Russia could realize full bourgeois democracy, and this progress could be achieved only if the socialists cooperated with the liberals who now correctly controlled the new government. And what's more, the Mensheviks enjoyed a well-deserved reputation for scrupulous adherence to tactics they felt to be based on correct ideology. A Menshevik conspiracy certainly was not responsible for the outbreak of the revolution of 1917, but the Mensheviks were not simply carried along by the tide of events nor did they "sell out" the revolution. Their refusal to take over state power and their determination to monitor closely the acts of the new regime were characteristics of Menshevik thinking and had been for many years. The so-called dual power arrangement that emerged in the first days of the upheaval conformed to a Menshevik vision of revolutionary authority that can be found in the thinking of Plekhanov, Martynov and Axelrod. In the midst of the action in February one Menshevik writer even thanked Plekhanov for his early wisdom and foresight.[28]

b) Balancing the Soviet Foreign and Domestic Policies

Immediately following the establishment of the Provisional Government, the Menshevik leaders turned their attention to the thorny problem of foreign policy. Russia's status as a belligerent power in the European war did not change as a result of the February revolution, but the Soviet leaders certainly intended to change the emphasis on Russia's military effort and to bring hostilities to a close on their terms. Carrying out plans to achieve these ambitious goals, the Mensheviks encountered stiff resistance from the Kadets in the Provisional Government, but they first needed to resolve difficulties among their own ranks.

Prior to the February insurrection, as we have seen, the Mensheviks were divided on the war issue into four major groups. At one extreme stood Plekhanov's faction. It had abandoned the revolutionary effort, at least for the duration of the war, and worked for the defeat of the Central Powers. It stood beyond the bounds occupied by most Mensheviks; in this respect Plekhanov did indeed separate himself from other Menshevik groups. A step to the left of Plekhanov stood the self-defensists whose best known spokesman was Potresov. His faction encouraged socialists to support defensive warfare and all military measures designed to protect Russian borders. To the left of Potresov stood two Zimmerwald groups. The first slot was occupied by the moderate Zimmerwaldists. They were prepared to participate in the Russian War Industry Committees (a form of defensism), but at the same time called for a socialist peace in Europe. To the far left stood the extreme Zimmerwaldists. Their principle figure was Julius Martov who opposed all military measures and all financial or political schemes that might result in continuing military action. He spoke only of concluding a universal socialist peace in Europe. On the eve of the revolution most Mensheviks were to be found supporting either Potresov's point of view or that of the more moderate Zimmerwaldists.

The revolution changed this picture. Both the tsar and the War Industry Committees were swept away by the insurrection, which gave all Mensheviks a substantial stake in the new democratic regime. Many foreign policy issues that had divided the party were now obviously gone, and the chief problem was how to reconcile the former antagonists and to present a uniform Soviet policy. Something had to be done in a hurry because the Provisional Government was already informing the Allies of Russia's official position.

An important meeting of Mensheviks was held on March 3 that was attended largely by moderate Zimmerwaldists and Self-defensists.[29] At the meeting Potresov demanded that the Soviet Executive Committee support a policy of defense of the revolution against foreign aggression, while at the same time the moderate Zimmerwaldists (especially Ermansky) demanded that Potresov and his friends support the socialist peace slogans. A lively discussion followed, but common ground was found when Potresov dropped his objections to the peace aims and the moderate Zimmerwaldists agreed to accept the policy of defense. The two formally antagonistic groups found unity by adding the defense measures advocated by Potresov to the socialist peace goals advocated by the moderate Zimmerwaldists. In the second week of March these views were officially accepted by the Petrograd Soviet and on March 14 they were published in *Izvestiia* as An Appeal to the Peoples of the World.

The Appeal served the cause of both peace and defense. It implored the masses of Europe to rally together in an effort to bring about the immediate conclusion of peace and it accused the "bourgeois" governments of Europe with bringing about the state of hostilities. The sentiments in the Appeal were put forth in strong language: "Refuse to serve as an instrument of conquest and violence in the hands of kings, landowners, and bankers — and by our united efforts we will stop this horrible butchery that is a stain on humanity ...." At the same time, however, the Appeal went beyond a simple restatement of the peace sentiments found in the Zimmerwald Manifesto. The Manifesto (accepted by most Mensheviks before 1917) spoke only of peace and of the evils of imperialism, but the Soviet Appeal of March 14 expressed a determination "to defend the Russian revolution from foreign military force ...."[30] The Appeal embodied the Zimmerwaldist proposal in addition to a warning that the Petrograd Soviet was not led by pacifists. *Rabochaia Gazeta* quickly elaborated on the message in the Appeal. On March 16 the Menshevik newspaper reminded its readers of the editor's opposition to the war, but it also warned that the revolution would defend itself: "Our general goals are not victory for one capitalist over another, but peace among the people who have been cheated. However, we will defend the revolution's freedom from every reactionary encroachment — from within or outside the country. The Russian revolution will not retreat before the bayonets of the militarists ...."[31] On March 17 a Menshevik journalist wrote that "the revolution was a victory over tsarism, but if it is not victorious over the war — all its forces will have fought in vain." But the same author assured readers that "the voice of the revolution will defend its freedom with arms in hand."[32]

The Mensheviks in the Soviet were lucky to find so easily a foreign policy that was acceptable to most socialists in Petrograd, but they had still some concern about criticism from their own radical Zimmerwaldists who objected to military defense in any form. The strong statements in favor of defending the revolution could draw fire from Lenin and even from Martov who would be quick to compare the Soviet foreign policy with the right wing defensist positions occupied by Plekhanov and the German Social Democrat, Phillipp Scheidemann. The Soviet leaders felt obliged to assure potential critics in their own camp that the defense of the Russian revolution required a military posture of a new variety which could not be favorably compared with the policy of national defense. Scheidemann and Plekhanov had joined the bourgeoisie, but the Soviet leaders had not. Sukhanov was outspoken in his support of the new Soviet policy. He had been a member of the radical Zimmerwaldist groups prior to 1917, but in March he became a strong supporter of defense. According to Sukhanov, the Soviet commitment to defend the revolution was free of the bond that tied the German socialists to the imperial government in Berlin. The Soviet policy did not represent another *Burgfrieden*. "Our policy of defense is defense of a proletarian character. It is not defense of the country, not defense of a nation. This defense is of freedom, defense of the revolution from conquest by reaction."[33] Tsereteli also pointed out the important distinctions between the policy of the Petrograd Soviet and the policy of the European socialists: "One cannot compare our defense with social patriotism, with political opportunism or with an indirect support of imperialism," but only with ideas that are in deep contradiction with these entities.[34] The Soviet leaders wanted the support of all socialists, so they emphasized the need to defend the revolution, and they emphasized the gulf that separated the Petrograd Soviet from the Allied powers and the gulf that separated the Soviet from the bourgeois Provisional Government in Russia.

Once the Soviet leaders reached an agreement among themselves and fortified their new stand against criticism anticipated from the left, they turned to face the capable and haughty Paul Miliukov, former college professor, Kadet leader and foreign minister of the Provisional Government. Miliukov's views were not incongruous to most Europeans. He did not like the fact that the war was consuming the strength of his country, but he did feel that peace in Europe and the survival of his government depended on an Allied military victory over the Central powers. Miliukov asked his countrymen to endure the wartime conditions until the defeat of Germany; in fact the new foreign minister may have nursed a theory that the force unleashed in the February revolution was an expression of anger by Russians who were dissatisfied with the tsarist government's direction of the war effort. On March 4, 1917, Miliukov wrote to the Russian diplomatic representatives abroad, giving instructions to his staff. He outlined the Provisional Government's position in foreign affairs: "We will strictly observe the international obligations contracted by the fallen regime. We shall steadfastly strengthen the relations which bind us to the Allied nations .... The government of which I am a member will devote all its energy to the achievement of victory."[35] Miliukov's policy did not free him to take unilateral action. It committed Russia to the war effort as a member of the Allied team. Miliukov pledged his government to coordinate the Russian military efforts with those of the Allies, particularly the English and French who also aimed at achieving peace through victory. Any changes in the Russian diplomatic or military plans, according to Miliukov, would have to be made in step with the Allied powers whose strength and influence in the partnership was likely to be considerable.[36]

Obviously, the Menshevik leaders and their Social Revolutionary allies in the Petrograd Soviet could not adjust to the position taken by Miliukov, and began to open a propaganda campaign against the government. Miliukov would have to bring his policy in line with Soviet thinking. *Rabochaia Gazeta* led the charge. "What does Miliukov really want," the editor asked rhetorically. "By saying that we must destroy the Turkish state, he really wants us to march on Constantinople and rename it Tsargrad; and by freeing the people of Austria-Hungary, he means the annexation of Galicia ... These desires, which are not in step with the will of the people, constitute the real goals of Miliukov ...."[37] The attack continued. On March 15 and again on March 19 the Menshevik newspaper criticized the foreign policy of the Provisional Government. Finally, the editor asked for a guarantee that Miliukov would steer Russia toward the Zimmerwald goal of a general European peace without annexations and indemnities.[38]

When Miliukov moved to defend himself from the socialist propaganda barrage, relations between the Petrograd Soviet and the Provisional Government became seriously strained. He attacked his critics in editorial articles that appeared in *Rech*, the Kadet newspaper in Petrograd, and intensified government efforts to capture the loyalty of the soldiers in the Petrograd barracks. The activity among the soldiers was especially threatening to the Soviet leaders. If Miliukov was successful in persuading the troops in Petrograd to obey officers loyal to the Provisional Government, the Soviet could be quickly reduced as a serious competitor in Russian political life. Sukhanov expressed the concern of the Soviet leaders: "The patriotic bourgeoisie, playing on the foreign peril, is making a conscious effort to wrest the army away from the Soviet and make it subject to the plutocracy."[39] By the third week in March a serious confrontation between the Soviet and the government was unavoidable, and the Soviet leaders began to consider using the garrison in a public demonstration against the Provisional Government. Such an action might kill two birds with one stone. A display of strength by the Soviet may bring the Provisional Government closer to the Zimmerwaldist thinking on the war issue and at the same time it might help to establish an *esprit de corps* around the Soviet leadership. On March 21, Sukhanov proposed that "the Soviet begin a nationwide, systematic campaign for peace and mobilize the proletariat and the garrison under the slogans of peace."[40]

Sukhanov's call for action encountered little resistance until the "tall, lean, ox-eyed Caucasian," Iraklii Tsereteli rose to address a meeting of the Soviet Executive Committee in the late afternoon of March 21. The Georgian Menshevik spoke out in opposition to Sukhanov's plans. His polemic ignored Sukhanov, but questioned the manner in which the Soviet leadership was conducting its relations with the Provisional Government. Tsereteli charged the Soviet leaders with disturbing the political harmony that had to be maintained between the Soviet and the Government: "We ought to refrain from politically irresponsible opposition." Tsereteli did not try to alter the Zimmerwaldist-defense posture adopted in the March 14 Appeal to the Peoples of All the World, but he expressed fear that radical action would endanger the safety of the new "bourgeois" regime. The Mensheviks wished to achieve a socialist peace in Europe (on that point agreement could be reached), but outward hostility toward the Provisional Government would endanger political harmony. Plans to change the foreign policy of the Provisional Government had to be carried out with caution. Tsereteli wanted the Executive Committee of the Soviet to assure the survival of "that unity of progressive forces which were created for the solution of internal problems."[40] He reminded the Mensheviks of their commitment to the strategy of socialist-liberal cooperation during the revolutionary period. Tsereteli felt that uncontrolled street demonstrations and vitriolic propaganda assaults on the Provisional Government would further divide the socialists from the liberals and dim hopes for defending the revolution against internal as well as external enemies. According to Tsereteli, the action recommended by Sukhanov would weaken the stability of the Provisional Government and expose all the revolutionary forces to defeat. A week after his confrontation with Sukhanov, Tsereteli spoke at the All-Russian Conference of Soviets. He touched on a number of issues including the relationship between the Soviet and the Provisional Government: "At the very moment, comrades, when the Soviet of Workers' and Soldiers' Deputies announces that it is entering into a conflict with the Provisional Government and it turns out that one part of the people is supporting the Soviets while the other part is supporting the Provisional Government, then at that moment our national cause will be lost ..."[42]

Sukhanov was embarrassed by the speech of Tsereteli. He realized that the new figure on the scene might push him away from the center of the stage. Sukhanov was a man of intense pride who was devoted to the Marxist cause in Russia, but his intellect suffered from rashness and a certain shallowness. He rarely thought deeply on any subject and was no match for the shrewd and self-contained Georgian.

In 1922 Sukhanov reinterpreted the events of March 21 and decided that Tsereteli's plan differed from his own because it placed emphasis on the defense of the revolution and slighted the cause of establishing a socialist peace in Europe, a reinterpretation of events that is accepted by many contemporary historians. At this later date, Sukhanov also implied that the Petrograd Mensheviks stood behind him by emphasizing the cause of peace over the policy of defense.[43] But the sources from March 1917 support no such reinterpretation. No hostile reactions to Tsereteli were evident on the part of the Petrograd Mensheviks, which may be a clue to understanding why the Sukhanov-Tsereteli confrontation of March 21 received no attention in the Menshevik press. Nor do the sources printed in March of 1917 indicate that Sukhanov even suspected Tsereteli of placing the Menshevik peace plans in jeopardy. In fact, Tsereteli's foreign policy measure was accepted by the Soviet on March 22 co-sponsored by Iurii Larin, a resolute radical Zimmerwaldist; Sukhanov himself revealed this information. It was true that confusion and exasperation filled that Soviet meeting room immediately after Tsereteli's first speech on March 21, but it was quickly dissipated once Tsereteli apologized for his own didacticism; he had just arrived in Petrograd from exile in Siberia had been gruff with some very sensitive people on the Executive Committee.[44]

Sukhanov's questionable reinterpretation of the events of March 21 can be easily attributed to forgetfulness or injured pride, but it has drawn attention away from the important issue. The incident on March 21 revealed that Tsereteli's concern rested less with points of emphasis in Soviet foreign policy and more with holding together the Menshevik domestic revolutionary strategy. Tsereteli was afraid that Sukhanov's street campaign against the Provisional Government would disturb the cooperative spirit between liberals and socialists and jeopardize the safety of the revolution. Those historians who emphasize the foreign policy aspects of the March 21 confrontation expose a divergence of opinion where one did not exist.

After the March 21 confrontation against Sukhanov, Tsereteli made a successful effort to consolidate his power in both the Executive Committee of the Petrograd Soviet and in the Menshevik party. The left Petrograd Mensheviks were willing to accept him, showing no sign of resistance. O. A. Ermansky and V. Bazarov, for example, were avowed Zimmerwaldists who had opposed cooperation between socialists and liberals in the Russian War Industry Committees, but in March of 1917 they accepted the leadership of Tsereteli and were prepared to support his views among other Mensheviks in Petrograd;[45] before the revolution, Tsereteli himself had been a moderate Zimmerwaldist. It was true that Martov and Martynov (the most outspoken Menshevik radical Zimmerwaldists) were still abroad when Tsereteli first consolidated his position, but consistent opposition from these men did not come to the surface until after the failure of the June offensive and serious dissent did not appear until after the collapse of all efforts to bring a socialist peace to Europe.

Tsereteli's leadership was also acknowledged by the Menshevik Self-defensists who promoted the views of Potresov and Gvozdev. Potresov interpreted the February revolution as a crushing defeat for what he called the semi-asiatic despotism in Russia and a great victory for its expanding bourgeois order. Like Tsereteli, he saw the Soviet and the Provisional Government as the institutional bastions of the new order, and wanted their leaders to work in harmony to complete the process of bourgeois westernization.[46] In matters relating to the defense of the revolution, Potresov and those closest to him were pleased with the Georgian's leadership, but their views were not identical. They saw the protection of Russian frontiers as an essential factor in the salvation of the revolution. They stood to the right of Tsereteli, however, in their skepticism about the plans to establish a socialist peace in Europe and on several occasions advised the majority in the Menshevik party to make certain that peace plans not be allowed to threaten good relations between the Soviet and the Provisional Government.[47]

The Mensheviks who stood closest to Tsereteli during 1917 were identified with neither the Self-defensists nor the radical Zimmerwaldists. N. S. Chkheidze, F. Dan, and B. I. Gorev (Gol'dman) were the most important. They believed the words in the Soviet Appeal of March 14, calling for both peace and defense, and they also followed the traditional revolutionary strategy of the Menshevik party that called for political cooperation between socialists and liberals. Unlike the Self-defensists and the radical Zimmerwaldists, this group remained loyal to Tsereteli throughout the first six months of 1917 and fell from power with him after the Kornilov affair. These men represented the center of Menshevik opinion during most of 1917. They have been described by a number of misleading labels, the Siberian Zimmerwaldists being only one of the most inaccurate. Chkheidze, a melancholy Georgian, had not been exiled to Siberia. Before the revolution broke out he led the Menshevik faction in the Russian State Duma. He was a cautious political leader who remained as far away as possible from the inter-party feuds of the pre-revolutionary period. It was through Chkheidže's parliamentary savvy and popularity that Tsereteli overcame some trying situations in the Soviet in 1917. Gorev had been numbered among the radical Zimmerwaldists before the insurrection in Petrograd. He was a professional journalist who helped Tsereteli by serving on the editorial board of *Rabochaia Gazeta*. Dan was much closer to Martov than to Tsereteli in his private affairs, but he worked with Tsereteli in Siberia during the early war years and became attached to the Georgian leader. After Tsereteli's downfall, Dan rejoined Martov's group. He apologized for his stand taken in 1917 and eventually became an important figure in the left wing of the Menshevik emigration.

Tsereteli's support from Social Democrats extended beyond the Menshevik party. The Bundist leader Mark Liber spoke on behalf of Tsereteli in the Executive Committee of the Petrograd Soviet on March 21, a sign of the general drift in Bundist circles toward Tsereteli's stand; the Jewish Bund formally entered the Menshevik party at the May conference of Mensheviks, the same conference at which Tsereteli solidified his position as the official spokesman for the Menshevik party. In addition to receiving the approval of many Bundists, Tsereteli also captured the loyalty of some Bolsheviks. Both V. S. Voitinsky and P. N. Sevruk (Gomel) joined the Menshevik party in March as supporters of Tsereteli.[48] Of course, the reunion of all Bolsheviks and Mensheviks that Tsereteli hoped to achieve did not come about, but in the spring of 1917 many Bolsheviks were reticent in their opposition to the Soviet leadership; it was not until after Lenin's influence over the Bolsheviks grew strong in the summer of 1917 that the Bolshevik party became a strong foe of the Petrograd Soviet.

One of Tsereteli's most impressive gains in March of 1917 was to capture the support of some important leaders in the Social Revolutionary party. It cannot be said that the Social Revolutionaries understood the Menshevik poltical theory. *Delo Naroda*, the Petrograd daily newspaper of the Party of the Social Revolutionaries, was a confusing publication that never seemed to grasp the important role that institutions and classes played in the tactics of Lenin and his Menshevik adversaries. But the Social Revolutionaries were important. When the revolution broke out the party was able to capture the imagination of the soldier rabble, the only armed forces in Petrograd until the autumn of 1917. The loyalty of the soldiers to the Social Revolutionary party did not run deeply, but so long as it existed the Soviet could speak with a strong voice. By gaining the support of Social Revolutionaries, Tsereteli was able to rely, at least temporarily, on the armed garrison in the capital city which gave the Menshevik leaders an authority that far outweighed their slight numerical strength. The close friendship between Tsereteli and some important Social Revolutionary leaders, especially V. Zenzinov and A. Gots, has been stressed recently by a number of contemporary Soviet authors. They considered the friendship to the base of the petty bourgeois coalition that dominated the Soviet from February until October of 1917. The differences between the Mensheviks and the Social Revolutionaries, however, have been given little emphasis in their research, especially the embarrassing evidence that shows the Mensheviks as leaders and the Social Revolutionaries blind followers.[49]

Despite his initial success, however, conclusions about the consolidation of Tsereteli's power over the Mensheviks and over other socialist groups in Petrograd must be drawn cautiously. The events of March gave a deceptive appearance. It was true that the clever Georgian emerged as the central party figure, remaining the chief Menshevik spokesman until the end of August. But the Mensheviks themselves did not unite closely around Tsereteli. They still remained tied in small groups that owed loyalty only to a tactic or to an idea and not to the new party leader or to a unified party structure. As long as these groups agreed to work together, Tsereteli could serve as party spokesman simply because his views coincided with theirs. Thus, as long as the desire to support the Provisional Government was strong among the Mensheviks and as long as the twin goals of revolutionary defense and a socialist peace could be pursued without contradictions, Tsereteli could remain the spokesman of the Mensheviks and the head of the Soviet Executive Committee. But once the small Menshevik groups began to disagree on how to support the Provisional Government and how to conduct foreign policy, Tsereteli would find his support quickly weakening. The same unwritten agreements that kept the Menshevik groups together and behind Tsereteli's leadership also kept the Social Revolutionaries united and attached to the Mensheviks. The Social Revolutionary party did not follow Tsereteli. It was a conglomerate of individuals and groups as independent of one another as was the case among the Mensheviks. The Social Revolutionaries who followed the Mensheviks in 1917 did so in groups or as individuals, following the particular Menshevik leader or the special Menshevik group that was most appealing. If the Menshevik groups lost their unity and broke apart, the Social Revolutionary party would simply follow them into fragmentation. As much depended on the ability of the Mensheviks to work together as on the personality of I. G. Tsereteli.

Tsereteli was born in 1881, the son of a Georgian literary figure. After completing his early schooling, he was sent to the university of Moscow. Here he was drawn toward Marxism. Tsereteli travelled abroad in 1905, and during this period he rejected Lenin's dictatorial plans and joined the Mensheviks. In 1907 he was elected to the Second State Duma as a Social Democratic deputy, but he was soon arrested and sent into exile. He remained in Siberia until the outbreak of the revolution. Tsereteli had valuable gifts that will be envied by any political leader. He possessed a calm personality that enabled him to listen carefully and to exchange views with men of differing opinions, opponents as well as comrades. Tsereteli was one of the few Social Democrats in Russia who moved gracefully among men of varying political loyalties without losing his patience and without losing sight of his own goals. He combined this confident and graceful manner with an outstanding oratorical skill. Standing before an audience with his head turned to his right, he easily captured the attention of listeners. He could develop a complicated argument while speaking, presenting in a clear fashion only that part of his views needed to carry the moment while emphasizing only that part of his opponent's view needed to weaken the opposition. His speech in the Executive Committee of the Soviet on March 21 was an excellent lesson in the art of political oratory. He did not become entangled in a detailed discussion of his own political opinions (a typical trait of revolutionaries), he did not dwell on Sukhanov's rashness nor did he talk at length of his own strong opposition to Miliukov's policies, but he allowed all three themes to pervade a speech that was essentially a restatement of the basic policy of the Menshevik party. The reason for his success on that day can be traced as much to the clever way in which he presented his argument as to the strength of the argument itself.

What motivated our protagonist during his period of leadership in the Petrograd Soviet? First and most important he remained convinced throughout 1917 that cooperation between liberals and socialists had to be maintained for the survival of the new regime. In this respect he followed the traditional Menshevik political strategy. He realized the possibilities of the collaboration strategy in 1905 when he rejected

Lenin, and in 1907 he gained a reputation in the Duma as the champion of united front action among all socialists and liberals in their struggle against the tsar.[50] Part of the speech he delivered to the All-Russian Conference of Soviets on April 11, 1917, is well worth repeating here: "At the very moment, comrades, when the Soviet of Workers' and Soldiers' Deputies announces that it is entering a conflict with the Provisional Government and one part of the people supports the Soviets while the other part supports the Provisional Government, then at that moment our national cause will be lost."[51] Unlike Alexander Kerensky who was also a socialist (of sorts) and who also possessed impressive oratorical gifts, Tsereteli did not rely solely on personal charm and political cunning. He relied on the notion that political cooperation among the "progressive forces" of modern Russia would consolidate the revolution and bring bourgeois democracy to the people of the former tsarist empire. In regard to the war, Tsereteli was also very much within the Menshevik tradition, and associated with neither Plekhanov nor Martov. He wanted to bring hostilities in Europe to a close with a socialist peace. He held the vision of a postwar Europe dominated by socialist politicians who would prevail in both domestic and world affairs. He was convinced that a lasting peace settlement could be concluded and maintained only by socialists. In his analysis, the outbreak of war was the result of bourgeois greed that could be controlled only when the representatives of the proletariat gained the upper hand throughout Europe politics. Tsereteli possessed all the traits of a good Menshevik. He emphasized the division of mankind into two hostile classes, one of which exploited the other according to a natural historical pattern that would work itself out for the better in the course of time. He never harbored any doubts about the ultimate intentions of the Russian liberals, although he emphasized the important role they needed to play if Russia was to free herself from the bondage system. He also maintained a Menshevik perspective of this socialist-liberal cooperation. It was a temporary alliance between class enemies that functioned best when the Kadets served as little more than Menshevik puppets. The liberals were enemies, but they must serve in the revolutionary cause if Russia was to be liberated.

Tsereteli's victory of mid-March reduced Sukhanov's influence in the Executive Committee, but it had no effect whatever on Miliukov whose foreign policy remained unchanged by all the maneuver among socialists in the Petrograd Soviet. The foreign minister of the Provisional Government showed no inclination to limit his ambitions to please Tsereteli any more than he tried to please Sukhanov. Miliukov still saw the direction of Russia's war effort as the business of the Provisional Government and the Allied chiefs of state, and he boldly continued his efforts to capture the loyalty of the troops in the Petrograd garrison. Moreover, he considered the Soviet leaders to be the representatives of a small minority of the Russian people, and hoped their political influence would wane as time passed. His foreign policy statement of March 6 followed closely the line he revealed in his March 4 memorandum. And on both March 9 and 11 he quietly accepted political recognition on behalf of the Russian Provisional Government by the various Allied powers whose support was contingent on Miliukov's readiness to continue the fighting. The Soviet leaders were not pleased with Miliukov's stand, and were expecting Tsereteli to initiate action. He began in late March by preparing a formal statement of Soviet policy. It included statements favorable to both the defense of the revolution from foreign invaders and the establishment of an international peace. It also called upon the Provisional Government to renounce all aggressive designs and to repudiate annexations and indemnities. Supposedly written in the spirit of Zimmerwald, the program was a long way from Miliukov's position. It met with a favorable reception in the Soviet on Friday March 24 (Sukhanov voted in its favor) and was then presented to the Provisional Government by the Contact Commission, the Menshevik-dominated committee established on March 7 to serve as the liaison body between the Petrograd Soviet and the Provisional Government.

Miliukov studied the statement with little enthusiasm, but wary of Soviet strength, especially in the city of Petrograd, he promised to deliver a public statement of his own. The following day Miliukov produced a document declaring that "the obligations undertaken toward our allies would be fully observed," revealing his intention to wage war to its victorious conclusion (or perhaps to the defeat of Russia at the hands of Imperial Germany). Needless to say, the statement was totally unacceptable to Tsereteli and the Soviet leaders. They demanded an immediate change showing once and for all that the Provisional Government was sensitive to the sentiments in the Soviet. Miliukov was reluctant to concede, but he decided to bargain. After some considerable haggling back and forth between the government and the Soviet, Miliukov revised the unacceptable document and, coinciding with a crescendo of abuse raised against him in the socialist press, he made the following statement on March 27: "Defense is not the sole, but the primary aim of the war, and there will be no violent seizure of foreign territory."[52] Tsereteli happily accepted this version of Miliukov's foreign policy as did most other socialists in the Executive Committee of the Soviet. It was considered by them to be a concession on the part of the Provisional Government, "a step away from the foreign policy of the tsarist regime, a step toward peace."[53]

The publication of the March 27 declaration on war aims is usually interpreted as a victory for the Petrograd Soviet, but it is difficult to understand why this interpretation has not been challenged. Despite several revisions made in the unacceptable version of March 25, the declaration still showed little congruity with the views of the Menshevik leaders in the Soviet. By making no direct statement about extending Russia's boundary lines and avoiding use of the terms annexations and indemnities, the foreign minister was obviously rejecting the Menshevik demands in a clever fashion. In addition, the style of the new pledge suggested that Miliukov had not budged from his desire to achieve peace through a military victory over the Central powers. He simply stated most of his former aims without using the popular jargon of the times. It was true that the Provisional Government had taken a step away from the tsarist position, a retreat the Mensheviks hoped to turn into a full scale rout, but the temporary victory hardly outweighed the dour implications that arose from the document accepted on March 27 by the Soviet Zimmerwaldists. As a matter of fact, acceptance brought about the Soviet recognition of several points in the policy that Miliukov was advocating.[54]

The declaration formally accepted by the Petrograd Soviet recognized the English, French and Belgians as Russian allies, compromising the neutrality treasured by the Zimmerwaldists in the Executive Committee. The Soviet leaders were now neutral Zimmerwaldists standing on the Allied side of the barbed wire. It meant that London and Paris would now be entitled to a voice in formulating the socialist plan to restore peace in Europe at a time when the German military threat was ominous. None of the Mensheviks recognized it at the time, but their determination to bring a general peace to Europe while maintaining at the same time balanced relations with the Provisional Government was becoming a most complicated task. Lenin recognized the trap and called for the destruction of the Provisional Government as the first step toward a true socialist peace, but the Mensheviks rejected Lenin's plan as detrimental to the cause of democracy in Russia. The Mensheviks accepted Miliukov's declaration with glee, convinced that their integrity and all their plans were intact, but unforeseen complications were developing that were anticipated by neither defensists nor internationalists.

Nor did the squabble with Miliukov help the revolution fight on the domestic front. The restraint exercised by the Menshevik leaders in early March and the careful planning designed to produce harmonious relations with the Provisional Government while asiatic Russia was being destroyed were offset by the bad feelings that arose during the discussion of foreign policy. Tsereteli wished to maintain harmony between the two power centers in Petrograd, but wrenching the note from Miliukov only made the February leaders in both wings of the Tauride palace deeply suspicious of each other.

Chapter III
The April Crisis

a) The Confrontation

After the publication of the Declaration of War Aims on March 27 a great deal of the tension that had built up in Petrograd since the insurrection was released. A short quiet period and a feeling of optimism prevailed in Soviet quarters. The masses had accepted the revolutionary leadership, it seemed at the moment, and outward appearances suggested that the Soviet and Provisional Government were entering an era of cooperation, despite the inevitable tugging and pulling that was bound to occur between two centers of authority. "No more thunderous Marseillaises were heard in the Tauride Palace," Sukhanov recalled, and "the columns of the newspapers were liberated from the burden of endless resolutions on 'dual power,' ... on loyalty to the Government and to its slogan of 'war to the finish'."[1] The general calm was reflected in the pages of *Rabochaia Gazeta* whose writers now seemed blasé about the relationship between the Soviet and the Provisional Government. Leading articles were devoted to minor social and economic organizations and to the May Day celebrations that would fall on April 18 in revolutionary Petrograd. Occasionally the calm was broken by the quarrels taking place between various political leaders, especially in the area of foreign policy and as a result of statements made by visiting socialists from France, particularly Albert Thomas who arrived in Russia on April 9. The calm of pre-revolutionary Petrograd was never restored, of course, but early April was perhaps the only time throughout 1917 when the Mensheviks felt that the revolution was secure and that a victory over the bondage system was in sight.

During this short-lived period of political tranquility Tsereteli, Chkheidze, and Gvozdev, representing the Executive Committee of the Soviet traveled almost 500 miles to Minsk to attend the All-Front Congress. The Congress was composed exclusively of military delegates, mostly rank and file soldiers, and its convocation gave an important opportunity to the Soviet leaders who rarely lost a chance to strengthen their support among the soldiers. The Menshevik leaders spoke to the Congress at great length, assuring the troops, and themselves, that both a general peace and defense of the revolution were being pursued simultaneously by the Provisional Government working in cooperation with the Soviet of Workers' and Soldiers' Deputies. They also advised the Congress delegates that the Soviet leaders could be relied upon to protect soldiers from the many brutalities and indignities of the past and even encouraged soldiers to exercise the same rights enjoyed now by the civilian population of Russia. The delegates at the Minsk Congress expressed their approval of these sentiments, and the favorable reception raised still further the optimism of Soviet leaders, especially that of Tsereteli who felt socialists had found a natural and strong ally in the rank and file of the Russian army.[2] But things were far from being as calm as Soviet leaders hoped them to be.

On April 3, soon after an uncomfortable trip across Germany in a "sealed train," an exasperated and ambitious V. I. Lenin arrived in Petrograd. He was greeted at Petrograd's Finland railroad station by a delegation from the Soviet, headed by Chkheidze himself, but as soon as the Bolshevik leader set foot on the platform he read his April Theses, attacking socialists for concluding an alliance with the Provisional Government. The alliance was a mistake from the beginning, according to Lenin, and he called upon socialists to destroy the Provisional Government and to transfer all political power to the Soviet. The alliance was not an agreement forged by the leaders of two institutions to combat the remnants of tsarism, but a clever trick used by bourgeois liberals to enslave the Russian people to the interests of capitalism. Were the Chkheidzes, Tseretelis, and Steklovs fools or were they worse than fools? Lenin left the question unanswered. The argument put forth in the April Theses was directed against the Menshevik strategy in domestic affairs and it bore a remarkable consistency with the views Lenin held in 1905 when he published *Two Tactics of Social Democracy in the Democratic Revolution*, the polemic against Martynov; the outbreak of war in Europe had not changed Lenin's mind on this subject. Much of the April Theses was devoted to a discussion on the war, but aside from announcing his general displeasure with the policy followed by both the Provisional Government and the Soviet, and repeating charges against world imperialism, he did not make clear how he intended to conduct his own foreign policy. Lenin was opposed to concluding a separate peace with Germany, but he dodged the question of how the new revolutionary state should maneuver in the international arena. His first concern was "to explain to the masses that the Soviet of Workers' Deputies is the only form of revolutionary government...." The use of the army to defend the revolution from foreign invaders might be justified, according to Lenin, but only if the Provisional Government was overthrown and revolutionary defensism became the foreign policy of a Soviet government.[3] He expressed these same ideas at a meeting of the Bolshevik party on April 24-27.

The Mensheviks responded quickly to Lenin's attack, but not forcefully. They reminded Lenin of Russia's peculiar institutional development, the non-socialist mentality of its peasants, and that plans for a socialist seizure of power were based on assumptions no less free of illusions in 1917 than they had been in 1905. Worst of all, his bad behavior now "could not render a better service to reaction."[4] But there seemed to be no reason to be overly concerned about Lenin in early April. After all, even most Bolsheviks showed little enthusiasm for his outlandish plans while other politicians in Petrograd could hardly believe that Lenin was speaking seriously.[5]

Lenin's arrival in Petrograd revived the old and bitter rivalry that had been brewing since 1903 between the Mensheviks and the Bolshevik leader and it produced the only important challenger to the Menshevik leadership in the Soviet. The argument that separated Lenin from the Mensheviks had started over the question how the Social Democratic party was to be organized and it gradually extended to include almost every point of contact between the two Marxist factions; in many cases the rivalry released intense personal hatreds. Some Mensheviks might have thought Lenin was ready by April 1917 to acquiesce in the general spirit of unity prevailing among socialists, but they were quickly sobered once their old antagonist opened a campaign to lure workers, soldiers and anarchists to his banner. Lenin badgered the Mensheviks throughout 1917. He organized demonstrations designed to embarrass Tsereteli and the Soviet Executive Committee, preached sedition among the masses of the city, disrupted the June All-Russian Congress of Soviets with demands that the Mensheviks seize state power, and in July placed his name at the head of groups of rioting sailors and workers who were calling on the Menshevik leaders to change Soviet policy. Lenin's efforts met with limited success during this last battle between himself and the Mensheviks until the Kornilov revolt gave the Bolshevik leader a good opportunity to destroy both the Mensheviks and the leaders of the Provisional Government.

On April 8, Victor Chernov, the most outstanding figure in the Party of the Social Revolutionaries arrived in Petrograd and was immediately installed on the Executive Committee of the Soviet. His presence at its meetings was not particularly significant and the Menshevik leaders around Tsereteli continued to control policy, despite the popularity of the Social Revolutionary leader among his fellow revolutionaries and among the soldiers. But at Chernov's arrival came the beginnings of the first great shock to the stability of the Provisional Government, a shock from which it never completely recovered.

When the Soviet delegation returned to Petrograd from the All-Front Congress at Minsk on April 11, Chernov indicated that the Allies were under the impression that Russia still intended to wage war until the defeat of the Central Powers. The Soviet leaders were surprised, but following a discussion of the information revealed by Chernov they decided to request of the Provisional Government a foreign policy statement coinciding in content with the domestic statement of March 27, in which the Government supposedly declared its intentions to pursue a general peace without victor or vanquished. The Executive Committee did more than simply suggest that Miliukov meet this latest demand. At this time the Provisional Government was trying to procure Soviet approval to float the Liberty Loan to assist in financing the war effort. The discussion concerning the loan was on the agenda of the Soviet for April 16 and had been assured an easy passage by Tsereteli, but in light of Chernov's information the Soviet leaders decided to link the loan to the foreign policy issue. The Provisional Government was abruptly informed that approval to raise the money would be given immediately following the arrival of the foreign policy statement in London and Paris.⁰ The story that Tsereteli reluctantly allowed the Soviet to confront Miliukov a second time on the foreign policy issue is not substantiated by the evidence.

Miliukov had no intention of directing a purely defensive war unless it was forced upon him by military necessities, and, furthermore, he had no intention of subordinating his will or changing the foreign policy of the Provisional Government to suit the demands of the Soviet leaders. His views should have been clearly recognized by the Executive Committee when it became known that the March 27 Declaration was published solely for domestic purposes. But the Soviet leaders remained cautious and decided to give Miliukov an opportunity to issue the declaration of March 27 in the form of a foreign policy statement. Miliukov responded to the Soviet demands, and also to pressure applied within the cabinet of the Provisional Government, by sending the declaration to the Allied capitals on April eighteenth, but he included with it an addendum that made his ultimate intention quite clear: "It goes without saying," the supplement read, "that the Provisional Government, while defending the rights of our mother-land, will fully observe the obligations taken with respect to our allies ..." The statement also noted that Russia had complete confidence in the victorious conclusion of the present war.[7] It now seemed obvious that Miliukov expected to respect treaty agreements made among the Allies at the time Russia was ruled by the imperial government. It also appeared that Soviet influence exerted on the foreign policy of the Provisional Government had been overestimated by the Executive Committee.

When the Soviet leaders received their copy of the note they were angered by what they considered Miliukov's treachery and descended into a rage. Immediately left-wing members of the Soviet, led by radi-cal Mensheviks and Bolsheviks, demanded street demonstrations be organized to protest against Miliukov. "Now is the time for the masses to step in," Yurenev declared excitedly. "Now we ought to answer the government's provocation by appealing to the masses." Bolsheviks joined in the applause for this statement, but so did many Mensheviks, even some of Tsereteli's close supporters whose first inclination was not to wonder why Miliukov had ignored Soviet wishes but to club the "bourgeoisie" into submission.

Tsereteli, however, maintained his reserve during the meeting, declaring that a call to the masses would result in street demonstra-tions that could easily get out of control and lead to a civil war the Soviet leaders had good reason to avoid. He suggested that the Execu-tive Committee of the Soviet interpret the Government's foreign pol-icy note as an error in judgment on the part of Miliukov and request that a new note, or a revision of the old note, be sent to London and Paris, a note that would be more in line with the Soviet views;[9] if this move failed to yield results, then the masses would be asked to step in. By urging the use of tact and pointing out the danger of public demon-strations, Tsereteli once again reminded the Executive Committee that copperation with the Provisional Government was in its best interest as long as cooperation was possible. He quickly swayed a majority of his Soviet colleagues to his side, and the Provisional Government was given yet another opportunity to alter its strategy and bring the whole matter of foreign policy to a quiet close.

It seemed for a short time that this latest moment of tension would pass quietly, but suddenly everybody was reminded that power struggles among political leaders cannot always be confined to a space limited by the four walls of a committee meeting room. The wrangling over foreign policy had led to the release of Miliukov's note to the press, probably the work of Kerensky,[10] precipitating the riots and destroying the calm that had prevailed in Petrograd since early March. On April 20 the Finland regiment, massed behind the puzzling figure of F. Linde, advanced down the Nevsky Prospect then moved along the Moika until it surrounded the Provisional Government at its new quarters in the Marian Palace. The rioters were soon joined by other groups of soldiers, calling for the resignation of Miliukov: "Down with Miliukov," "Down with the Provisional Government," "Down with Annexations and Indemnities." Later in the day and again on April 21 shooting occurred several blocks toward the northeast on the banks of the Neva River where rioting workers from the Viborg District of the city, making much the same demands as the soldiers, encountered demonstrators rallying in support of the Provisional Government. The scope of the rioting and street fighting went far beyond the control measures at the disposal of civil authorities.

The Menshevik leaders tried to restore calm. Chkheidze, Skobelev, and Gots, the Sovial Revolutionary leader, risked their lives to quiet the regiments, while Liber, Gvozdev and Bogdanov spoke as best they could before irate workers, trying to reassure the crowds; despite their efforts many people were killed, most of them by gunfire. General Kornilov, commander of the Petrograd garrisons, tried to use military action to restore order on behalf of the Provisional Government, but was frustrated when Soviet leaders ordered his troops to remain in their barracks. Viewing the April disturbances from the midst of the city of Petrograd, one could easily have concluded that Russia was on the brink of civil war, but suddenly the rioters ceased their activities, apparently in response to a Soviet appeal that was published in most Petrograd newspapers on April 22. There were some demonstrations in other cities in Russia as well as in Petrograd. Moscow, Kiev, and Kharkov were troubled, but incidents there were mere reflections of the action in Petrograd, and were not generated by any local power struggle nor connected to the rural disturbances that became grave in the fall of 1917; in all the provincial cities the riots started at least a day after the Petrograd disturbances, on April 21 or in some cases even later.

The Mensheviks were not pleased to see the outbreak of violence, but they could hardly be expected to denounce the Petrograd riots. It was, after all, the masses protesting against the government of the bourgeoisie and especially against Miliukov, the *bete noir* of Russian socialists. In fact, the Mensheviks announced, it was Miliukov who brought the popular protest down upon himself by "delivering the Russian democracy a stab in the back," and it was Miliukov who now would have to assume all responsibility for any bloodshed in the streets of Petrograd; the Menshevik conduct since the beginning of March had been, as usual, monotonously correct. Yet the Mensheviks quickly recognized the serious danger awakened by the disturbances, and urged that the Soviet, not street mobs, take immediate action in the matter of Miliukov's note. *Rabochaia Gazeta* condemned Miliukov, but allowed itself room to take a stand against the riots by "emphatically opposing the kindling of civil war by the followers of Lenin."[11] Even Sukhanov, who energetically condemned Miliukov and his supporters for "betraying trust," expressed some wariness about the presence of mobs in the street.[12] Once the riots became worse and had obviously gotten out of hand, the Mensheviks came close to panic. On April 22 *Rabochaia Gazeta* and the more radical *Novaia Zhizn* printed the Soviet plea for public order on their front pages; *Rabochaia Gazeta* followed it on April 23 by printing a similar plea written by the Petrograd town Duma; neither the Soviet nor the Duma pleas appeared in the pages of *Pravda*. On April 23 an editorial entitled "The Lessons of Two Days," clearly revealed the feeling of the Menshevik leaders. It frowned upon the individual character of the street demonstrations and regretted that "this protest had not come in the form of an organized performance."[13] The Mensheviks, alleged proponents of spontaneity and individual freedom, quickly found that supporting spontaneity in abstract form was far easier than supporting it in national politics once it was transformed into ugly and unmanageable mobs deaf to all appeals to reason. The Mensheviks, needless to say, were relieved when the riots ceased. Less serious concern about the riots was shown by the Mensheviks in Moscow, largely because activity there had been far milder than in Petrograd. But I. A. Isuv, the chief Menshevik leader in the Moscow Soviet, suggested that the Moscow Soviet issue a declaration condemning participation in unorganized street demonstrations.[14]

The April riots were a reflection of the power struggle that had been brewing since February between the Soviet Executive Committee and the Provisional Government, and they gave an indication of the tenuous grasp that the socialists held on the loyalty of the masses. The slogans carried on the placards by the rioting soldiers and workers, and the sudden halt brought to the disturbances after the Soviet expressed its displeasure, supports the conclusion of most observers and historians that the riots were spontaneous, and directed toward the defense of the Soviet leaders against Miliukov. The people rioting in the streets on April 20 and 21 had focused their attention on the domestic political conflict among revolutionary leaders, despite the fact that the issue of foreign policy touched off the street action. The placards called for the resignation of the foreign minister and for the resignation of the Provisional Government, and the slogans dealing with the war called for the renunciation of annexations and indemnities, not the conclusion of peace. These demands had become identified with Soviet policy during its fight against the Provisional Government. The masses supported the Soviet leadership but not necessarily the substance of the Soviet demands. Only some contemporary Russian historians find strong indications of anti-war sentiment and, incidentally, demands for a Soviet seizure of all government authority in the April riots. In an anniversary year article and in his recent book on the revolution, I. I. Mints noted the appearance of placard slogans calling for the fulfillment of Lenin's program: "All Power to the Soviet," and "Down with the War."[15] No doubt a few such slogans were to be found among the crowds during the rioting on April 21 and 22, but only *Pravda* placed emphasis on their appearance.

The Soviet negotiations with the Provisional Government about a new note defining foreign policy aims were initiated in the midst of the anxiety and tension caused by the riots. Further concessions were made by the Provisional Government over the protests of Miliukov who was being badgered by men in both the cabinet and his own political party as well as by the socialists in the Soviet. A new foreign policy statement was published on April 22 which was more in tune with the domestic note of March 27, assuring Russia's allies that defense was Russia's primary reason for continuing in the war. The majority in the Soviet Executive Committee accepted the content of the new note, despite objections from the members of its left wing who pressed for further concessions. Tsereteli announced to the Soviet on April 23: "The Provisional Government has carried out the demand of the Executive Committee. It has communicated the text of its declaration repudiating annexations to the governments of the allied powers...." He then continued with what must have been ambivalent feelings as visions of the April mobs still crowded in the back of his mind: "The unanimous protest of the workers and soldiers of Petrograd brough it to the attention of the Provisional Government as well as to all the peoples of the world that the revolutionary democracy of Russia will never reconcile itself to a return to the purposes and methods of the tsarist foreign policy...."[16]

b) The Mensheviks Reject a Coalition Government

The April disturbances subsided, but the unruly and independent character of the crisis made it obvious to everybody that the Provisional Government needed additional political support in order to maintain order. A much more active part now would have to be played within the formal structure of government by the Soviet leaders. The disturbances provoked by the political struggle between the Provisional Government and the Soviet reopened the question of government power, a problem that appeared to have been neatly solved in February. After the April street fighting, most of Petrograd felt that the cause of political stability now required that Mensheviks in the Soviet assume some share of responsibility for government actions. Thus began a week and a half filled with discussions, threats, and declarations of faith that resulted in the Mensheviks being reluctantly drawn into a coalition government with the Russian liberals.

The Mensheviks faced the ominous signs by quietly reminding everybody that their earlier convictions had not and would not be changed. The party would not seize power. On this point there could be no compromise! It was true, of course, that the masses had given no significant signs of expecting or demanding a Soviet seizure of power, but Bolshevik agitators had brought forth the suggestion boldly announced by Lenin in the April Theses. The Mensheviks were reasonably certain, however, that "the Soviet would not give way to the irresponsible instigator who suggested it take power into its own hands."[17] This reaction was no different than it had been in February of 1917 or during the revolution of 1905 when Menshevik pamphlet writers argued that a socialist seizure of government power during the Russian bourgeois revolution would bring failure to the revolutionary movement. By removing the liberals from government positions, a seizure of power would have divided the revolutionary allies and weakened "progressive" forces. A civil war would follow and then a restoration of the bondage system, because the conditions sustaining that system had not yet been removed by the successful insurrection. In April of 1917 the Mensheviks did not justify their position on state power by a lengthy reappraisal of this strategy, and there is merit to asking how many party members could have explained it in detail, but the idea was so thoroughly ingrained that it was referred to by Dvinov as the party's "grand design." On April 22 the editors of *Rabochaia Gazeta* only reminded readers of their stand with a superficial summary: [Russia] has experienced a bourgeois revolution .... It is not time for the socialist revolution: there still are not the economic conditions in Russia, there is still not [sic] the level of culture and political development in the majority of the population. Following this reasoning, democratic workers should not tie their hands to the management of the state."[18]

The Menshevik leaders now realized, however, that public statements explaining their revolutionary strategy would not strengthen the Provisional Government. Immediately, they began to suggest changes of a practical nature designed to release the pressure applied to the Soviet leaders. First, they discussed Chernov's suggestion that the whole mess might be immeasurably improved if Miliukov resigned as Minister of Foreign Affairs and took up the less important post of Minister of Public Enlightenment (Education); after all, Miliukov had been a college professor. Unfortunately, Miliukov had no intention of accepting a lesser cabinet post, and nobody really thought that such a step would improve matters very much. The editors of *Rabochaia Gazeta* then proposed an even more radical move by suggesting that Russia's foreign policy be conducted by the Soviet leaders, leaving only domestic affairs in the hands of the "bourgeoisie."[19] This proposal had a particular attraction for the radicals in the party, especially Sukhanov, but it did not enjoy majority support. Finally, in a last ditch effort to avoid a serious discussion about state power, the Liberty Loan for the support of the war effort was given an enthusiastic review in *Rabochaia Gazeta*, praised in the Executive Committee and approved in the Soviet with considerable fanfare. Obviously, the Mensheviks felt these makeshift plans and palliative measures would extricate them from the dilemma they faced at the end of April.

But the Mensheviks had arrived at an impasse they could not surmount by following the tactics of 1905, by redistributing portfolios among liberal ministers or by approving government requests for war credits. One important reason can be traced to the Kadets, the embattled liberals and so-called political allies of the Mensheviks. When the revolution broke out in February, the "bourgeoisie" was quite willing to direct the affairs of state without Soviet interference. In fact, it seemed happy to do so and might well have tried to prevent ambitious socialists from entering into any but the least important cabinet positions. But this situation did not prevail after the April riots. The moderate and left elements in the Kadet party were in favor of a closer working arrangement with the Soviet leaders and their influence was growing stronger at the higher levels of the party. Once the riots revealed the impotence of the government, many more liberals became outspoken in their demands that Soviet representatives hold important cabinet posts.[20] Kerensky served as a catalyst in this transition by using the influence of his cabinet post to encourage a coalition government between liberals and socialists. Kerensky himself was a socialist, of course, and his contention that all members of the Provisional Government "unanimously decided to obtain, at all costs, the inclusion in the cabinet of representatives of the Soviet ..."[21] was an overstatement (both Guchkov and Miliukov remained opposed to the presence of socialists in the cabinet), but it is certain that by late April all but a few government figures, in addition to many high ranking army officers, expected Tsereteli or Chkheidze to accept a post in the cabinet.

Other changes also took place in Petrograd that effected the question of state power. In February the soldiers and workers supporting the Soviet were willing to let the Mensheviks and the Social Revolutionaries establish contact with the Provisional Government and reach whatever agreement suited their fancy. They showed no serious interest in the structure of government and even less interest in the socialist interpretation of the Russian revolution. By the end of April, however, this posture was changing, especially among those soldiers and workers who had been drawn toward the center of political action. The soldiers and workers easily recognized the weaknesses of the Provisional Government in the face of the aggressive strength of the Soviet Executive Committee. They watched the Menshevik leaders in the Soviet openly usurp government functions at both Shlisselburg and Kronstadt when the Provisional Government proved unable to cope with the disturbances that broke out at these places; in his discussion of the April Crisis, Stankevich wrote: "Not the government, but the Soviet gave the orders in Petrograd."[22] As the Mensheviks and Social Revolutionaries continued to use their authority to prevent the collapse of the new regime or, as in the case of Kornilov, to curtail its activities, they were unintentionally encouraging the soldiers and workers to look for greater Soviet participation within the official structure of government.

The socialist anti-government propaganda of the previous month brought about the same result. When *Rabochaia Gazeta* and the Menshevik pamphleteers warned soldiers and workers in the spring of 1917 that the revolution might be in danger of betrayal by certain figures in the Provisional Government, they were discrediting the government in the eyes of the masses and inviting many politically active elements of the population to demand that a greater effort be made in the protection of their interests. Troops in the Petrograd garrisons came to expect solid guarantees that they would be protected from punishment, especially courts-martial and front line duty. The masses certainly did not call for a seizure of power by the Soviet in April, as Soviet historians like to imply, but a growing number among the rank and file were looking for the Mensheviks and the Social Revolutionaries to play a direct role in government affairs. After all, if the government could not be trusted, then why not install Soviet representatives in the cabinet to assure honest proceedings.

Even within the Menshevik party the April Crisis brought signs of sympathy for a coalition government. It cannot be said that Mensheviks of any faction showed enthusiasm for entering what was theoretically the bourgeois government, but the growing realization that the Provisional Government might be too weak to withstand a shock similar to the April Crisis brought the question up for discussion. Stephan Ivanovich (Portugeis), writing in the right wing Menshevik daily, *Den*, dealt with the subject of coalition on a speculative plane even prior to the April Crisis. He stated that Soviet recognition of the Provisional Government constituted in itself a form of participation.[23] Once the April Crisis passed, however, the right wing of the party began to call for active socialist participation. A. I. Kantorovich discussed the weaknesses of the Provisional Government and the state of instability in Petrograd as serious threats to the revolution.[24] An editorial in *Den* published on April 25 went further by tying the question of participation in the cabinet to the Menshevik strategy of socialist-liberal cooperation. The collaboration strategy employed by the Mensheviks now demanded that all socialists help the bourgeois intelligentsia by founding a temporary emergency government made up of both socialists and liberals.[25]

The masses were beginning to show more interest in the mechanics of government, and most liberals in the cabinet felt the time had arrived for the Soviet leaders to assume cabinet posts, so no one was surprised on April 26 when Prince Lvov, President of the Provisional Government, made a public request that Chkheidze bring the matter of coalition before the Soviet Executive Committee. Lvov addressed a personal note to Chkheidze on April 27, telling the president of the Soviet: "The Government will renew its efforts to widen its circle by asking for the participation in the responsible work of government of those actively creative elements of the country who have not until now had a direct part in the government of the state." Lvov went on to ask Chkheidze to be "good enough to bring this matter to the attention of the Executive Committee of the parties represented in the Soviet ..."[26]

The politely phrased request from Lvov clearly indicated the degree to which the liberals in the Provisional Government expected Soviet participation. They were not requesting mere token representation by minor Soviet figures, nor did they invite the Executive Committee to take all state authority into its own hands, an offer the Mensheviks would have rejected. The Provisional Government looked to the Soviet to assist in forming a cabinet that would contain both liberals and socialists in sufficient number to restore badly needed political stability. They wanted to reorganize the cabinet and tighten the bonds holding the Executive Committee of the Soviet to its alliance with the Provisional Government. They wanted the official center of political authority strengthened by the presence and cooperation of important Soviet leaders in the cabinet, a step that was expected to reduce the prestige of the Soviet as an institution and lessen the antagonism between the government and the Soviet.

But the Mensheviks were still not ready to enter the government, even at the invitation of Prince Lvov. The party leaders in the Executive Committee were not yet as fearful as the editors of Den about the weakened condition of the Provisional Government. And they easily understood that entrance into the cabinet would limit the usefulness of the Soviet as a hide-out from which they could sally forth to intimidate the government. As cabinet ministers they would be in a certain sense captives of their liberal allies. "So long as we maintained this position (in the Soviet)," Tsereteli cleverly concluded, "we could ... exercise real influence upon the government, since the government and the middle classes which back it are greatly impressed by the power of the Soviet."[27] If they made the mistake of assuming cabinet posts, Soviet leaders might even end by attacking their old friends because a "bourgeois" government would be naturally hostile to the proletariat: "Carrying on responsible activity in government," *Rabochaia Gazeta* fearfully surmised, "socialists would not only prohibit a rising in the process of revolutionary social conflict, but soon would summon their interests to force the disorganization of revolutionary elements."[28] And what about those masses that had been listening to Mensheviks warn about the dangers of the bourgeois government? What would they think? The friends of spontaneity expected them to be quite confused: "Appealing to the masses as a representative of the Soviet," Skobelev told the Executive Committee on April 27, "I was trusted by them and usually succeeded in making them submit to democratic discipline. If I were now to appear before them as a minister, might they not tell me that they know how to talk with Skobelev, Vice-Chairman of the Petrograd Soviet, but not with Skobelev, the cabinet minister?"[29]

In the Menshevik circles further to the left of the Soviet Executive Committee the reaction against entering a coalition cabinet was even stronger, indicating that differences within the party, checked since February, had not been dissolved. The hostility of the Mensheviks toward the liberals had always been strong, and in radicals like Sukhanov and Ermansky it even was stronger than it was in moderates like Potresov or Tsereteli. We need not take the moderate Menshevik Woytinsky literally to realize the truth in his statement describing the moods of his left wing comrades: "They were accustomed to look upon government, courts, coercion, police and other attributes of authority as evils."[30] Stankevich brings to our attention the same phenomenon: "They instinctively and habitually held a negative attitude toward the authorities which always seemed wicked, soiled, and destroyers of the principles of purity ...."[31] Sitting on such a perch, the radical Mensheviks could not think seriously about cooperation. Only under unusual circumstances were they ready to consider a coalition government. If the liberals guaranteed that a coalition government would carry out the Soviet program in both foreign and domestic policy, if they promised to liquidate the war, quickly taking further steps away from the European hostilities, and if they introduced the socialist program in domestic policies, Sukhanov would consider entrance into the Provisional Government a progressive step.[32] Otherwise the Mensheviks had no business to conduct with the Provisional Government and Lvov's note should be flatly rejected. Sukhanov concluded his summary of the situation by advising the Mensheviks to follow the advice of the socialist conferees who gathered at the International meetings in Amsterdam (1904) and Paris (1900) who voted to refrain from entering "bourgeois" governments; Sukhanov did not mention that by 1917 most of the living members who attended those conferences either had entered "bourgeois" governments or had cooperated closely with "bourgeois" ministers.

The meeting that was convened to draft a formal reply to Lvov took place on the evening of April 27-28 in the apartment of Skobelev. The Executive Committee was joined at the session by members from the Moscow Soviet. Several people spoke at length, indicating their own opposition to coalition on specific points, and, moreover, a general spirit against coalition was revealed during the discussions. Bogdanov reported that the most advanced workers in the party, "the elite," who were closest to the thinking of the Menshevik party were opposed to coalition. Liber, Dan, and the right Menshevik Gvozdev also spoke against joining a coalition government as did the members of the Moscow Soviet. In the name of the Soviet Executive Committee, the Mensheviks rejected the invitation sent by Lvov. Chkheidze summed up the matter very nicely: "Whether such an attitude toward the government is right or wrong, it is rooted in the psychology of those elements of the democracy that are rallied around our organization."[33] Even news of the probable resignation of Miliukov, the Soviet's implacable foe in foreign policy, did not influence the April 28 decision against entrance into a liberal-socialist coalition government. There was no indication that the decision made in Skobelev's apartment was unacceptable to the majority in the Menshevik party.[34] There were indications that sympathy for coalition was much stronger among the Social Revolutionaries, but the Mensheviks led the way.

c) The Mensheviks Join a Coalition Government

The Menshevik leaders made their sympathies known to the public and hoped to wash their hands of the whole mess, but they were not going to avoid a coalition government so easily. The notion that Soviet leaders should enter the cabinet became very popular in Petrograd by the end of April. The "Left press ... also took up the idea of coalition," Sukhanov observed, indicating an increased interest among the workers and soldiers for socialist presence in the cabinet. On April 26

Kerensky published a letter in the Social Revolutionary newspaper *Delo Naroda* announcing again his desire for a coalition government. In typical Kerensky fashion, the popular hero threatened to resign his post as Minister of Justice if the Mensheviks did not comply with his wishes.[35] To add additional weight to the argument in favor of a coalition, the Soviet leaders were told by officers of the general staff that many soldiers at the front were showing signs of favoring Soviet participation in government; the necessity of maintaining the loyalty of the army made this revelation a delicate matter.

Of course, many right wing Mensheviks continued to favor a coalition cabinet as they had even before the delivery of the Lvov note. Potresov, for example, published an article on April 28 in *Vlast Naroda* (*The Power of the People*) expressing his views in favor of coalition. "Social Democrats ought to send their representatives to the Executive Committee. They are obligated to help it in these difficult times. This is the imperative of history. This will call forth that order which alone will save the country and the great revolution."[36] And on April 30, N. Cherevanin (Lipkin) wrote an article in *Rabochaia Gazeta* rejecting Lenin's call for a dictatorship of the proletariat and the rural poor and discussing other alternatives open to Social Democrats. His argument did not veer literally from the Menshevik line of reasoning, which excluded the proletariat from of a Russian bourgeois government, but he suggested that during a transition period the proletariat could participate provisionally through its representatives.[37] Cherevanin realized that his suggestion did not coincide with the will of the party, but he made it clear that he would not be opposed to some forms of coalition government. The fact that the article was published in the official Menshevik newspaper indicated that sympathy for coalition had started to spread beyond the right wing of the party.

On April 29, 1917, Alexander Guchkov dissolved all serious resistance against the formation of a coalition government when he resigned his post as Minister of War. Sick, extremely pessimistic about the future of the revolution, and angered by the harsh resistance met by Miliukov, he resigned without giving advance notice. He blamed the Soviet leaders for the country's troubles, especially those involving the deteriorating relationship between the officer corps and the elected soldier committees. Everybody recognized that the resignation of Guchkov made the government immeasurbly more unstable than it had been. Miliukov and Guchkov did not represent the majority will of Russian liberalism, but they were the strongest implacable foes of the

Soviet leaders. Now they were gone. How could a government made up exclusively of liberals survive without them? On May 1, Prince Lvov spoke to Tsereteli on the impact of Guchkov's resignation, assessing the situation as extremely critical and stating that the Provisional Government could no longer stand without the active participation of the Soviet leaders. Tsereteli was now faced with the task of deciding how to strengthen the government. He was forced to re-examine an alternative impalatable to himself and his Menshevik colleagues. Everybody anxiously awaited Tsereteli's next move.

Tsereteli decided to accept Lvov's second invitation to found a coalition government made up of socialists and liberals. "Under these circumstances," he stated, "it was plain that there was no longer room for palliative measures to solve the crisis. Another rejection of the coalition by the Executive Committee could only bring about the collective resignation of the government and an aggravation of the crisis."[38] Chkheidze put the proposal on the agenda and the Soviet Executive Committee voted to reverse their decision of April 28 and join the Provisional Government. The Petrograd city Conference of Mensheviks endorsed the decision on May 4, although the vote was very close (59 against 55).[39]

Why did Tsereteli finally decide to enter the government? Surely Guchkov's resignation by itself did not motivate him, nor did the pruning of Miliukov from the cabinet of the Provisional Government, nor Kerensky's threat to resign unless the bond between liberals and socialists was strengthened. Certainly public opinion was not the determining factor that brought the Georgian Menshevik to agree to the formation of a coalition government on May 1. But all these factors taken together convinced the Menshevik leader that a coalition was the only way to avoid civil war. Tsereteli was afraid that continuing instability would lead to armed conflict, separating completely the socialists from the liberals and bringing destruction to the revolution. Civil war was equated in the mind of Tsereteli and the Mensheviks with the demise of the revolution and the continuation of the bondage system under a dictator, possibly the Romanov family itself; some Mensheviks actually interpreted Guchkov's resignation as the first step taken against the revolution by its enemies. Only when confronted with the spectre of civil war did Tsereteli make his move to increase socialist participation in government affairs. The Menshevik leaders were not coaxed by money, fear of Allied pressure, or by public opinion. Potresov had earlier advocated coalition government because it was the only step "that would save the country and the great revolution." In order to "save the country from civil war," Tsereteli initially used the government power when he frustrated Kornilov's attempts to quell the riots of April 20.[40] The chief Menshevik charge against Lenin's program was that it would bring about a state of civil war, the division of democratic forces and the destruction of the revolution. If the Soviet had not joined the government, B. Gorev assured his readers, revolutionary forces would have gone down to defeat in a civil war.[41]

When Tsereteli and Skobelev joined the first coalition government, the Mensheviks swallowed a bitter pill, but the compromise was not as extensive as one might think. The Mensheviks held back. Coalition brought Menshevik leaders closer into formal government affairs, but it did nothing to end the hostility between liberals and socialists. The formation of a new government was not to be construed as a truce between the classes, as had come about in West European countries since the outbreak of the war. The Provisional Government was to continue as a liberal "bourgeois" government while the socialists remained in command of the Soviet of Workers' and Soldiers' Deputies without losing any of their staunch anti-bourgeois character. The Mensheviks who entered the government were not to become part of the "class" that controlled the government; the "solution" to the state power problem in May brought socialists into the cabinet, yet ever promising to oppose the directives issued by that cabinet. The Mensheviks tried to force the head side and the tail side of the coin face up at the same time. Skobelev assumed the portfolio of Minister of Labor in which post he really served as the champion of the Soviet interests, and Tsereteli entered the Ministry of Posts and the Telegraphs; Lvov created the position of Minister of Posts and Telegraphs just for Tsereteli and both agreed that there would be no bureaucratic responsibility attached to it.[42] Tsereteli was to carry on as the central figure in the Executive Committee of the Soviet. A May 4 article in *Rabochaia Gazeta* explained this ambiguous position. The author insisted that neither the Menshevik party nor the Soviet had given their prestige to the new Provisional Government other than to announce their moral support in very general terms. Only individuals who shared a joint responsibility to the Menshevik party and to the Soviet of Workers' and Soldiers' Deputies entered the cabinet, but the Soviet and the party were not to be held responsible for their behavior as ministers. And, of course, neither the party nor the Soviet were to be responsible for the many mistakes the Provisional Government was sure to make.[43] Thus, we have the Menshevik interpretation of the May coalition.[44]

But the Mensheviks dared not toally separate themselves from the new government, lest they induce among the masses the same lack of confidence that made the coalition necessary for political stability. The decision to enter the government was not popular within the party, and some Mensheviks refused to support the move, but party leaders realized that too reserved a stance might invite a return to the same predicament from which they had just escaped. Finding themselves on the horns of a dilemma, the same writers in *Rabochaia Gazeta* who had extricated the party from all government responsibility also urged people to support the new government. B. Gorev recognized that the entrance of two Mensheviks into the government was undesirable, but expressed regret when a small number in the party announced itself against the coalition. This act, according to Gorev, would undermine the good influence socialist ministers might exercise and embarrass them in the bargain.[45] And while M. C. Panin urged readers to have no fear of criticizing the new government he also stressed that the party must support it.[46]

By May 6, the editors of *Rabochaia Gazeta* recovered sufficient poise to make what might be called an official party statement on the coalition. The writer of "Trust the New Government" admitted that the party was opposed to a coalition, but announced that the time had come to give it wholehearted support. Toward the end of the article readers were reminded that criticism, although a duty of all Mensheviks, need not be antagonistic or destructive criticism. Even the matter of Soviet and party responsibility for the acts of the government was left hanging in the air; the writer suggested that such a matter deserved careful study.[47] As the dust was settling, the Menshevik-Bundist orator Mark Liber tried to analyze the crisis for a Moscow audience. The whole nasty business was the fault of the Provisional Government due to its failure to carry out the process of dismantling the old regime in the manner ascribed by socialists; the Russian masses too had to assume a small share of the blame for their apathy. Obviously, according to Liber, unsolved problems had caught up with the liberals. At that point the masses responded with riots, weakening the government beyond the point where it could function effectively. The Soviet was called upon to assist, and it did, although assisting in the governing process was not the task of the Soviet. Future success now depended to some degree on the ability of the masses to recognize what had been done in their behalf.[48] Party approval for the entrance of Menshevik comrades into the bourgeois government came on May 9, the opening day of the All-Russian Conference of the Russian Social Democratic Workers' Party. The conferees agreed to support the new government and acknowledged that Soviet leaders had entered it, but declined to accept responsibility for the acts of Tsereteli, Skobelev or the Provisional Government itself for any error in judgment that might be made.[49]

Most of those on the far left of the Menshevik party remained opposed to the coalition government. The left leaders joined their fellow Mensheviks in rejecting Lenin's bid to seize power from the liberals, but they were convinced that the ties between Russian liberals and the world bourgeoisie were too strong to free the Provisional Government from the clutches of the London-Paris clique. The leftists had no program of their own to put forth and did not organize any opposition to Tsereteli at this time, but they did publish a statement rejecting the coalition and insisting that the Provisional Government "liquidate" the war.[50]

Lenin's reaction to the Menshevik decision to enter the cabinet was one of unsurprised irritation, and it remained quite consistent with his earlier views. The Mensheviks did not understand, according to Lenin, that the only significant forces in Petrograd in 1917 were the "proletariat," the masses, and the "bourgeoisie," the liberals; one force naturally stood behind the Provisional Government while the other stood behind the Soviet. The Mensheviks had abandoned this perspective for one reason or another, and wrongly thought they could maneuver between the two forces, coaxing both to work together with sufficient harmony to save the revolution. Such action was doomed to failure, according to the Bolshevik leader. The formation of a coalition government only served as evidence that the Mensheviks were being drawn into the camp of the bourgeoisie where they would be serving the interests of world capital.[51] The bourgeoisie that Tsereteli thought he could trust, or at least supervise, was not to be trusted and could not be controlled unless the Soviet held all power, according to Lenin. Only those who understood these "truths" were properly prepared to lead the masses. This interpretation has remained a mainstay of Soviet historiography, even surviving the changes introduced during the reign of the late J. V. Stalin. It has brought Soviet analysts to label the Mensheviks as "conciliators." In a recent and most impressive history of the revolution, I. I. Mints made use of Lenin's analysis to interpret the April crisis and the formation of the first coalition.[52] This interpretation will survive as long as one ignores the pressure the Mensheviks exerted on the Provisional Government and as long as one assumes that the great mass of Petrograders thought like Lenin, even though not quite as clearly.

Discussions between the Soviet Executive Committee and the rump cabinet of the first Provisional Government took place in the Tauride Palace and in Prince Lvov's study on Teatranaia Street. After days of discussion, tension, and bickering the coalition was formed. Stankevich has given us a priceless description of the grand finale. "But the situation was becoming more and more hopeless with every minute. All conceivable combinations were exhausted. Every proposal entailed an already familiar cycle of difficulties and objections. Everyone was obviously marking time. The nervous tension had reached its highest limit and gave vent to extreme agitation and irritation. Questions were not even discussed any longer; everyone was simply speaking — or, more exactly, shouting — from his corner. Chernov, disheveled and infuriated was attacking little Peshekhonov, who was squeezed in a corner. Gvozdev was pronouncing some final words of indignation on the confusion of everything that was going on ... Even Tsereteli lost his equilibrium, in spite of my fervent appeals for calm; he was shouting, I think at Chkheidze ... when all of a sudden Kerensky rushed in and announced that a solution had been found. The combination announced by Kerensky was, practically speaking, far from new and there was much to be said against it. But all were glad to be swayed by his mood. They no longer wanted to listen to objections; the dissatisfied were forced to stop speaking."[53]

On May 5, 1917, revolutionary Petrograd received its first news of the composition of the cabinet as well as an account of the aims of the coalition government. The new cabinet included Prince Lvov as Minister-President and Minister of the Interior, and the popular A. F. Kerensky as Minister of War and the Navy; the Kadets with portfolios were M. I. Tereshchenko, N. V. Nekrasov, and A. I. Konovalov as Ministers of Foreign Affairs, Transport, and Trade and Industry respectively. The Social Revolutionary intellectual Victor Chernov was to serve as Minister of Agriculture, and the Mensheviks I. G. Tsereteli and M. I. Skobelev as Minister of Posts and Telegraphs and Minister of Labor. The platform of the new government reflected compromise between the cabinet of the first Provisional Government and the Executive Committee of the Soviet. In foreign policy, where no compromise was really possible, the Soviet policy was simply added to

Miliukov's. The new government called for "general peace ... without annexation and indemnities," but set the stage for the June offensive by promising to work in concert with the Allies, using "both offensive and defensive" military measures. The government further promised to wage a "resolute struggle against economic disorganization" by introducing additional "government control of production, transportation, exchange, and distribution ..." Labor, the platform authors assured the population, would be protected by the new administration, and a democratic financial reform, including the imposition of higher taxes on "excessive war profits" was to be introduced. Self-government was to be encouraged by the coalition (the statement did not specify where it would be encouraged and where it would be discouraged), and "at the earliest date practicable," the Constituent Assembly would be convened. The most obscure planks in the platform were unfortunately in the area needing the most detailed and resolute attention — land reform and grain deliveries. They reflected the mental anguish of the authors, but produced nothing solid. The wordy statement left all land tenure questions in the hands of the Constituent Assembly and promised to ensure the "greatest possible production of grain."[54]

Induced by the power struggle between the Soviet and the Provisional Government, the April Crisis ended with the foundation of a coalition government and the opportunity for the Mensheviks to revise their revolutionary strategy. Much could have been learned from the disturbances, if the Mensheviks had been practical politicians. By rioting in the streets, the masses of Petrograd showed the revolutionary leaders that quarrels between the leaders of the Provisional Government and the Soviet could easily get out of hand and that cooperation between liberals and socialists was essential if political stability was to be maintained and civil war avoided. In early May the revolutionary leaders had enough time to save the Provisional Government from destruction and certainly enough warnings to arouse an alert political leader whose interest rested primarily in maintaining security. In addition, the turmoil on the Russian countryside that developed to troublesome proportions by the late summer of 1917 had not started, nor had the problems of labor and transportation reached the point of confusion they did in September. In early May the Mensheviks received a warning and they still had time to make an adjustment.

The Mensheviks did not recognize the challenge or the opportunity presented by the April Crisis and continued to follow their old strategy, further weakening both the Provisional Government and the Soviet while Russia moved closer and closer toward calamity. The Mensheviks entered a coalition government, but they did not strengthen the government by taking this step, even though some right-wing party members were hopeful that an era of good feeling between socialists and liberals was at hand.[55] The Mensheviks simply moved the center of the struggle against the liberals from the Executive Committee of the Soviet where it had been since the insurrection to the cabinet of the Provisional Government where it remained until the Kornilov affair. The policy of *poskol'ku postol'ku*, fashioned by years of conflicting intellectual traditions, remained unchanged. Ideology came first and practical politics came last, if it came at all.

Chapter IV
Russian Patriots or Beleaguered Utopians

a) The Diplomatic Offensive

After the formation of the coalition government in Petrograd on May 4, the foreign policy goals of the Menshevik leaders crystalized and for a short time received the serious attention of the European powers. Working through both the Soviet and the Provisional Government, the Mensheviks aimed at concluding peace throughout Europe as quickly as possible without claims for annexations or indemnities and with national self-determination for all peoples. While these ends were being sought, all factions in the party were determined to maintain an adequate defense of the Russian revolution because success in foreign policy depended on the ability of the new regime to protect itself from a German and Austrian invasion.

The aims of this ambitious policy were to be achieved by following an uncharted course filled with hidden dangers. From the start, progress depended on receiving full cooperation from west European socialists and also from many European leaders who were not socialists. Reinforced with this aid, the Mensheviks hoped to generate an atmosphere in diplomatic circles that would permit the restoration of the International. Further success would then depend on the outcome of a proposed conference at Stockholm during which European socialists would be urged to break free from their bourgeois governments and create a new social and political order.

How could these plans be carried out? Non-socialist politicians in the west would be understandably reluctant to cooperate in such an enterprise, and even socialists could not be expected to show much enthusiasm. Relations between the socialists from France and England and those from Germany and Austria had deteriorated since 1914, and, moreover, these people had aims of their own which they fully intended to impose on the Mensheviks. Furthermore, Russia was still officially at war with Germany and Austria, so solid contacts between the Soviet leaders and the socialists from the Central Powers would be next to impossible to arrange. The case in favor of class unity and an international peace conference would have to be argued strongly and almost exclusively before the socialists from the Allied countries who came to Petrograd in the spring of 1917 not to talk of peace but to create a more favorable attitude among the Russian socialists and working men toward the war.[1]

The Allied socialists arrived and were temporarily charmed by the prevailing spirit of revolutionary openness. Albert Thomas, the French Minister of Munitions, arrived in Petrograd on April 9; the Belgian socialist Emile Vandervelde, whose countrymen were living under the rule of the Kaiser's army, arrived on May 5, and Arthur Henderson, Labor member of the British war cabinet, arrived in Petrograd on May 20. These visits were followed by those of other socialists from western Europe. An American mission to Russia followed that of the Allied socialists. It included Charles Edward Russell and was headed by former Secretary of State Elihu Root; the American party reached Petrograd by way of Siberia on May 31. Although the expressed purpose of these visits was to discuss Russia's military effort, the barriers that had hampered all previous discussions between the Soviet and the Allies quickly dissolved in a spirit of comradery. Albert Thomas who was sent to negotiate for the French in place of the proud Maurice Paleologue derived such emotional satisfaction from the political climate in Petrograd that he permitted himself to drift into reminiscences about his own role in the French railroad strike of 1911. At one point his confidence in the Russian revolutionary spirit led him to state: "The whole strength of the Russian democracy lies in its revolutionary fervor."[2]

For their part the Menshevik leaders greeted the guests with the utmost cordiality. They were flattered when the Europeans expressed enthusiasm toward the accomplishments of the revolution, and quickly entertained the notion that the Allied socialists were still members of the International and still representatives of the working masses. Many Russians harbored reservations and were pessimistic about the Menshevik plan for a general peace, but only the Bolsheviks and a few radical Mensheviks disrupted this initial euphoria, meeting the visitors with scorn and asking rhetorical questions designed to embarrass both the visitors and the leaders of the Petrograd Soviet.[3]

The early exchange of pleasantries was encouraging, but in a short time the major issue came to the fore and with it a strong indication that antinomies stood between the Mensheviks and the Allied socialists. In an early interview, the French socialists Lafont, Cachin and Moutet came quickly to the point, asking if the Soviet leaders intended to restore the fighting capacity of the Russian army and to maintain a strong front against the German army. The Soviet Executive Committee assured the French that this step was being taken, but largely in keeping with the Soviet policy of defense, designed to protect the revolution from the caprices of enemies outside Russia.[4] While reassuring the French, Tsereteli spoke in the name of the Soviet and the Provisional Government, further explaining the Russian peace program as the Soviet leadership had designed it. The Russian democracy, he stated, wanted national self-determination realized in Europe and would expect all socialists to join in opposing any settlement of the war that would result in the *status quo ante-bellum*. He repeated the Soviet demand for peace throughout Europe, peace without victor or vanquished and without annexations or indemnities.[5] Tsereteli's response to the French socialists was emphasized on April 25 when the Petrograd Soviet adopted the resolution put forth by Feodor Dan. It stated that the Soviet itself would take the initiative in calling an international socialist conference "to assure the success of the cause of peace;" the conference would necessarily include "all parties and groups comprising the International."[6] Naturally, all national delegations to such a conference would participate on an equal footing.

While the western visitors encouraged all efforts to strengthen the Russian armies, and were ready to discuss the cause of peace, in a general sense, they remained cool toward the idea of an international conference of socialists. Who would attend? What topics would be included on the agenda? Would the decisions of the projected international conference be binding for all socialists? These questions were only a few of those troubling the west Europeans. The main points of estrangement between the Soviet and the representatives of the European countries began to emerge, and they were clearly reflected in the views of Tsereteli and Albert Thomas that came out during a private conversation in early May.

Albert Thomas was willing to make a number of concessions to the inflexible Tsereteli in return for full Russian military support. In fact, he agreed to hold a post-war plebiscite in Alsace-Lorraine to assure self-determination, but the Frenchman could not concur with Tsereteli's opinion that a revival of the old International would be a step toward peace. In any case, Thomas insisted that the prerequisite for French attendance at an international socialist conference must be the promise of fulfilling the practical goal of bringing closer the military defeat of Germany. Thomas would be overjoyed at the prospect of holding a conference at Stockholm if the delegates at such a conference denounced German militarism and if German Social Democrats accused themselves of encouraging the outbreak of war by concluding a political truce (*Burgfrieden*) with the German bourgeoisie. He placed war-guilt on all Germans, praising the political behavior of his own French socialists in the immediate pre-war period who, according to Albert Thomas, successfully prevented the French bourgeoisie from starting the great conflict. France was the land of democracy and freedom, Thomas reminded Tsereteli, while Germany was the home of militarism. "To revive socialist unity in order to struggle for a democratic peace," Thomas declared, "it would be necessary to proceed only after a public condemnation of those political acts which are personified in Philip Scheidemann and his supporters." Germany was responsible for the war, Thomas concluded, and German socialists were not exempt from the guilt.[7]

The Georgian Menshevik refused to be a party to a denunciation of Germany or of the German people. War guilt, according to Tsereteli, was shared by all imperialists, and could not be bound within the confines of any one nation. "The Allied socialists must recognize the common responsibility that all capitalist governments share for the imperialist rivalry and the arms race which itself created the grounds for this present war." Tsereteli strengthened his argument by reminding the French Minister of Munitions that the renowned French socialist Jean Jaures himself considered the Russian order for full mobilization of the army in 1914 a major factor leading the people of Europe into war. The only solution to the problem of the war, and future wars, according to the Menshevik leader, was to destroy the power of imperialism, not to direct socialist hostilities toward a group or a nation that would include a great majority of workers and only a handful of imperialists. At an international conference, such as the meeting he was trying to organize, Tsereteli felt that all socialists could unite on an equal footing and participate in harmony to mount a single great assault against the bourgeoisie. The International would be revived and the "socialist majorities of all belligerent countries could break away from the political activity of their governments." Such an act would give great moral assistance to all oppressed peoples suffering under the yoke of arbitrary governments. But if the Soviet took the position suggested by Albert Thomas, if it sided with one coalition in a life or death struggle against the other, it would betray the oppressed peoples of Central Europe who could not be held responsible for the arbitrary acts of their autocratic and imperialist governments.[8]

Thomas promptly dismissed Tsereteli's arguments as "Zimmerwaldist illusions." Under no circumstances would he entertain the thought of attending an international socialist conference where German Social Democrats would be admitted as equals to the French unless a public confession of guilt was signed by Scheidemann. As to the socialist and democratic convictions of the German Social Democrats, Thomas could envision "Scheidemann in the role of the Roman Pope or Apollo Belvedere, but not in the role of a revolutionary striving for a democratic peace."[9] In his attempt to draw the Georgian Menshevik toward his side, Thomas compared the French and Russian socialist parties favorably (a comparison designed to be a great compliment). He pointed out that both functioned in democratic societies, that both sent representatives into their country's war cabinets, that both supported the policy of defense, and that both discouraged the imperialist strivings of their own national bourgeoisie. How are we different, the French Minister of Munitions asked rhetorically? Only in the fact that we entered the government to seek a general peace without annexations and indemnities, replied the shrewd Menshevik.[10]

After his discussion with Thomas, Tsereteli turned his efforts toward the English labor leader Arthur Henderson, but he was no more successful in his attempts to persuade Henderson than he had been in earlier talks with Albert Thomas. Henderson did show a willingness to attend a socialist conference at Stockholm but only if the German socialists denounced their alliance with the Kaiser. Unless this condition was met, Henderson felt he should abide by the decision of the British Labour Party which had voted in January of 1917 to postpone the revival of the International until the defeat of Germany on the field of battle. In his usual candid fashion, the former ironmoulder told the Georgian revolutionary that only the destruction of Prussian militarism would lead to a true peace. When Tsereteli told Henderson that he had been prejudiced in his views toward Stockholm by the English ambassador George Buchanan, Henderson replied: "I speak to you not as a representative of the English government, but as Secretary of the Labour Party. English workers are not prepared to meet with the German socialist majority nor do they wish their representatives to meet with Scheidemann and his friends." As to Buchanan's wicked influence over him, Henderson reminded Tsereteli that Buchanan was his subordinate and he assured the Soviet leader that if the English socialists did decide to go to Stockholm: "The pleasure of meeting with the Germans will be mine, not Buchanan's."[11]

Henderson and Thomas seemed to stand rather close in their rejections of the Soviet proposals, but this factor did not hold true for all the western socialists. The most inflexible opponent of the Menshevik scheme for a general peace without victory was the Belgian socialist Emile Vandervelde. Eventually the English and French softened their stand to some degree (although not nearly to the point that would have satisfied the Mensheviks and long after the time when anything could have been salvaged from the Stockholm plan), but the Belgian refused to budge one inch. His homeland was occupied by German troops. It had been the location of the first hostilities when its neutrality was violated in 1914 once the German request to enter France through Belgium was rejected. Vandervelde had absolutely no sympathy for the Stockholm plan and was even critical of Henderson and Thomas for their "flexible hostility" toward the Soviet proposals. The Belgian socialist leader felt confident that the arguments he put forth in Petrograd enjoyed the unqualified support of the Belgian workers. He remained firm, with his colleague de Brouchere, in complete opposition to peace talks with "the Scheidemanns, the Davids and the Noskes."[12]

Unwilling to meet at an international conference under the conditions proposed by the Soviet leaders and beginning to grow uncomfortable with the unreliable nature of politics in Petrograd, the Allied socialists sugested that the Soviet leaders attend an Allied socialist gathering scheduled to convene in London later in the year. Once they assembled in London, the Allied socialists could help to determine the conditions for attendance at a future all-socialist international conference. The London proposal was put forth by Arthur Henderson who was anxious to prepare carefully for any future meeting with the German Social Democrats. Meeting in London, Henderson and his socialist colleagues would have steady control over such items as the discussion agenda, the invitation lists, and the location of future conferences, items they could not control in Petrograd. Henderson himself was especially wary of the Soviet leadership ability in international diplomacy, feeling that the level of business and political training of the Menshevik leaders was far below the standard of competence usually required for high positions. He would feel a good deal more secure once formal business matters were removed from the hands of the Soviet leaders.[13] Henderson's proposal enjoyed the support of all the Allied socialists when it was presented to the Executive Committee of the Soviet in early June of 1917.

But the Menshevik leaders refused to compromise even after it became clear that an agreement with the Allied socialists, so important for the success of their scheme, was not going to be reached on exclusively Soviet terms. In the name of the Executive Committee, Tsereteli refused to participate in the Allied conference at London. An exasperated Vandervelde asked Tsereteli if refusal to attend the London conference signified the Soviet Executive Committee's intention to ignore the Allies and to pursue its own altogether different course. Tsereteli dodged the question by replying that the Soviet would approach all socialists in the role of arbitrator rather than as a partisan in one of the two belligerent coalitions. Playing this role, the Soviet would have to insist, Tsereteli continued, that the same standards be applied to all socialists not only to those coming from the Central powers. So strongly did Tsereteli hold this conviction that when Vandervelde refused to attend the Stockholm conference, the usually calm Menshevik leader became emotionally upset.[14]

In spite of the fact that an impasse had been reached, the visits of Thomas, Vandervelde, and Henderson ended in friendship. Each side agreed to a number of superficial compromises aimed at salvaging something from the situation. Vandervelde spoke to the first All-Russian Congress of Soviets before his June departure, praising the "peculiar psychology" and "idealism" of the Russian soldiers and workers. He spoke with great sincerity and feeling. On his part, Tsereteli agreed in the name of the Petrograd Soviet to send an observer (not a participant) to the Allied socialists conference at London. After a brief tour of the front lines Albert Thomas departed, speaking words of encouragement and friendship. Henderson and Tsereteli were photographed together at the request of the English labor leader on the last day of his visit to Russia. The departure of the Allied socialists produced a nostalgic sentiment in Tsereteli.

Contacts made between the Soviet leaders and the socialists from the Central powers were not as extensive as those made with the Allied socialists, but the signs that came from these quarters were not encouraging for the success of the Menshevik peace project. The German Social Democrats made contact with Soviet leaders through Frederic Borgbjerg, a Danish Social Democrat, who arrived in Petrograd in the middle of April. On April 23 he presented the conditions under which Philip Scheidemann and other German socialist leaders would be willing to discuss a general peace in Europe. The Mensheviks felt that the nature of the conditions transmitted by the Germans was nebulous, but they were quite willing to use them as the beginning point for discussions. They made it clear that the German socialists were an important part of their plan and that the Germans had to stand as equal partners with the Allied and Russian socialists at a restoration of the International.[15] Unfortunately, Borgbjerg's reception in Petrograd was cool. Russia was officially at war with Germany and the appearance of any person who might represent the interests of the Central powers created an awkward situation. But more important than the cool reception was the lack of evidence in his report that the German Social Democrats were ready to help the Mensheviks impose a socialist peace on Europe. A desire for peace and a willingness to compromise were evident, but like the Allied socialists the Germans were far from accepting the Menshevik peace plan.[16]

The lack of enthusiasm from the Allied socialists and the sparse contact with the socialists of the Central powers did not discourage the Mensheviks who plunged forth on their own initiative. On May 21 the Petrograd Soviet published an invitation in *Izvestiia* asking all European socialists to meet as equals at Stockholm to discuss the cause of peace;[17] the first plan for opening a peace congress in Stockholm had been drawn up by Scandinavian socialists and Camille Huysmans, but the Mensheviks abruptly seized the initiative and tried to reshape it to suit their fancy. By April 27 the Petrograd Soviet had already passed the resolution of Feodor Dan, giving the Executive Committee permission to send a Soviet delegation to prepare for a peace conference; the Soviet delegation included the Mensheviks Paul Axelrod (already in Stockholm), V. N. Rozanov, I. P. Goldenberg, G. M. Erlich, and A. N. Smirnov, and the Social Revolutionary N. S. Rusanov. The Soviet statement of May 21 was issued as an official invitation designed to give the Stockholm venture greater international notoriety and to weaken the Allied socialists' resistance to this phase of the project. Unfortunately, it had a negative effect. Thomas, Henderson and Vandervelde objected to the unexpected appearance of the invitation in the public press. They had not agreed to meet on equal terms with the Germans and were further troubled to learn that Lenin and other radical socialists had also been invited to attend.

The invitation on May 21 marked a high point in the Soviet effort to use the European socialists in the cause of a general peace, but the hopes for a Stockholm meeting were doomed before that date. Failure would result not because of action taken by the German Social Democrats, who could do little on their own to make an all-socialist European congress a reality. Neither was Lenin to blame, although he caused headaches for the Menshevik leaders; he refused to attend any socialist congress unless its membership was restricted to those who met his particular requirements! Nor were the Allied governments responsible for the plan's failure; it was true that the final hopes for holding the congress at Stockholm were not completely extinguished until the Allied governments refused to grant passports to those socialists who finally did decide to attend, but the governmental action of mid-August was taken only after all the reasonable possibilities for success had passed and the place of Soviet prestige in international relations had sunk to a very low point. The plan foundered when the Mensheviks refused to compromise with the Allied socialists. Without full cooperation between the Soviet leaders and the Allied socialists, a restoration of the International at Stockholm was out of the question.[18]

It certainly cannot be said that the Soviet plan was without merit. By seeking to achieve a peaceful international order administered by moderate socialists, the Mensheviks showed cognizance of many problems that Europeans faced but seemed unable to resolve. They could see that the burdens of war would bring no reward for most of the people living in the belligerent countries and that a military victory won by either the Allies or the Central powers would soon lead to a renewed outbreak of fighting.[19] They also saw that nations living without political freedom would be restless and that efforts to control them would lead to turmoil and tyranny. They wanted to put an end to the misery and to reduce the danger of war in the future. Unfortunately, the Mensheviks helped to weaken their own diplomatic efforts. They were uncompromising and expected success quickly without giving careful thought to the motives of the people whose voluntary cooperation was necessary for success. Lenin was celebrated for his revolutionary sectarianism, but in 1917 the Soviet leaders were imbued with the same spirit. The Stockholm plan contained the germ of a fair peace but in the hands of amateurs and impatient revolutionaries it lost much of its value.

b) The Menshevik Party in the Spring of 1917

As the revolution deepened and the Mensheviks came to play an increasingly significant part in the foreign and domestic operations of the new Russian regime, the good health of the party organization became an important stabilizing factor in Petrograd politics. If the Mensheviks could prevent party factionalism from weakening the support behind Tsereteli, Dan and Chkheidze, the Soviet leaders could continue to speak with authority to both the Kadets in the Provisional Government and the Allied socialists. And if the Menshevik organization could strengthen its influence among the workers and soldiers of the city, its leaders could gain popular support in their battle to prevent Lenin and the anarchists from gaining the upper hand in revolutionary politics.

In the first six weeks after the emperor was overthrown the Mensheviks did nothing to anticipate the ruinous effects that a long tradition of factionalism might make on their organization, nor did they take steps to increase the party's influence among the masses. These factors simply were not expected to count heavily in the political life of the new Russia. The removal of the tsar was supposed to dissolve serious differences among all Russian Social Democrats from Lenin to Plekhanov who were now sure to unite into one strong political force. And, indeed, signs of unity among Social Democrats could be found everywhere during the first months of the revolution. The Petrograd Menshevik organizations quickly drew together around the new journal *Rabochaia Gazeta* and the leadership of Tsereteli. In Moscow both the defensist Mensheviks who wrote for *Delo* and the anti-defensists from the Initiator groups came together to form the Provisional Committee of the Moscow Mensheviks and began to publish the daily journal *Vpered!* The same pattern of unity also appeared in Kiev and seems to have appeared among the small Menshevik organizations in Kharkov, Rostov-on-Don and Nizhni Novgorod.[20] The Menshevik leaders in the Executive Committee of the Petrograd Soviet reaped the benefits of this unifying trend, and there seemed to be little reason to anticipate trouble by trying to iron out old differences or by creating a new structure of leadership. This same complacency prevailed in the attitude held by the Mensheviks in their early dealings with the masses. Both *Rabochaia Gazeta* and *Vpered* discussed the importance of including worker organizations in civic politics and the key role the Mensheviks ought to play in creating a cohesive workers' movement, but this prodding was aimed more at gaining popular support for the Soviet leadership and less at increasing the numerical strength of the Menshevik party. Some way, working people were now expected to rise above the mundane level of party politics and support "the democracy."

Some Menshevik neighborhood committees met during the early weeks of the revolution in Petrograd and Moscow, but they were poorly attended and in many cases admission was restricted to registered party members. Some strictly Menshevik activity could also be found taking place in most of the large cities of Russia, but it lacked enthusiastic leadership and forward planning. There is no doubt that the smooth course run by the revolution during March and early April helped to lull the Mensheviks into a lackadaisical mood, but their grand strategy was also a contributing factor. It was the bourgeois revolution and the Mensheviks were most concerned with monitoring the bourgeoisie. The focus of attention was not on party politics but on the relationship between the Petrograd Soviet and the Provisional Government and what Sukhanov called "high politics."

It was Lenin who jarred the Mensheviks into taking action at the lower levels of politics and caused them to tighten discipline in their own ranks.[21] He bitterly attacked the Soviet leaders in his April Theses, quickly dispelling all hope of Social Democratic unity while at the same time he opened a campaign to capture the support of the soldiers and workers in Petrograd. Lenin also encouraged dissension among the Mensheviks and met with considerable success, especially after the formation of the coalition government. The Mensheviks responded to Lenin's action by launching a propaganda campaign of their own and undertaking organizational activity. They quickly tried to strengthen party cohesiveness and to increase the number of contacts between the party and the masses. On April 13 the first Menshevik faction was formed in the Petrograd Soviet (not until June were Menshevik groups established among the soldiers at the front), and in mid-April the Committee of Petrograd Mensheviks began to tighten its bonds with both the Jewish Bund and the smaller Menshevik neighborhood committees throughout Petrograd.[22] This activity reached its first high point at the convocation of the All-Russian Conference of Mensheviks that met in Petrograd from May 7 to May 11.

The meeting was called by the Menshevik Organizational Bureau, a body of men selected from among the old Menshevik Organization Committee, the Committee of the Petrograd Mensheviks, the Central Committee of the Jewish Bund, the Central Committee of the *Mezhduraionists* (a group of Social Democratic cells on the left fringe of the Menshevik movement), and the Social Democratic faction from the Russian State Duma. The presence of both the Bundists and the *Mezhduraionists* in the new Organizational Bureau, and the invitation sent to

Plekhanov's *Edinstvo* group, reflected an attempt to include all Social Democrats who could be expected to support the Soviet leaders and oppose the aggressive policies of Lenin. The Mensheviks from the Moscow Soviet were also invited to attend the Conference as well as Menshevik representatives from provincial areas within a short distance of Petrograd. The Conference would obviously be dominated by the Petrograd Mensheviks (both the Petrograd Committee and the leaders in the Soviet).[23] They were the best known figures in the party and also those who felt the full brunt of Lenin's attack. It was fully expected that the Conference would support the Soviet policies of Tsereteli and Chkheidze; in fact, one Soviet historian has suggested that the May Conference of Mensheviks was brought together principally to strengthen Tsereteli's grip on the party.

A long speech delivered by Tsereteli opened the sessions of the Conference on May 7.[24] The address was designed to defend the policy of the Soviet Executive Committee and set the stage for its quick endorsement. An outspoken opposition had developed since the decision had been made to join a coalition government, and the Menshevik leaders in the Soviet wanted to discourage infighting within the party. Tsereteli apologetically explained his reasons for entering the Provisional Government. He knew only too well the uncomfortable feelings endured by the Mensheviks because they were tied so closely to the "bourgeois" government, but the risk of civil war in Russia had grown too great, he explained, to expect the liberals to stand alone in government positions. Now that the new cabinet had been formed, however, he hoped the Conference would give its support to the government's efforts especially those aimed at concluding a general peace. Tsereteli's speech was followed by the strong endorsements of M. I. Skobelev and Nicholas Chkheidze. A resolution in favor of the temporary participation of socialists in the cabinet of the Provisional Government was placed before the delegates and passed. It was similar to the resolution passed at a meeting of the Petrograd Mensheviks on May 3, although the tally of May 3 had been very close.[25]

The Soviet Menshevik leaders then brought forth a resolution in support of the foreign policy of the new Provisional Government. It was presented by Feodor Dan and quickly became the center of a lively debate. The Dan resolution began with a general statement about the causes of the war and the tasks that lay ahead for those socialists who wished to work for peace. It was a capitalist war, the resolution declared flatly, taking place in the "era of class war." The task of all socialists was "to prepare the proletariat in the coming battle to destroy the bourgeoisie, and to struggle in all countries for peace without annexations or indemnities." The resolution went on to suggest that all Mensheviks work together by encouraging the convocation of an international conference to which socialists of all nations would be invited to attend. Discussing the need to maintain a strong defense of Russia while peace negotiations were in progress, the resolution then went on to denounce fraternization at the front as "ineffective" and called upon all Mensheviks to support the coalition government's effort to keep together an efficient fighting force.[26] G. Batursky (Boris Solomonovich Tseitlin) supported the resolution, but realized the problems that Dan's proposals might create within the party. He wrote an article in *Rabochaia Gazeta* designed to make the resolution agreeable to all Mensheviks. "The Dan resolution stands for the convocation of an international conference of socialists and an intense struggle for peace among the international proletariat, a peace without annexations and indemnities." Batursky also pointed out that "It shows that the path to peace does not rest in the victory of one coalition over another." Approaching the question of military preparedness on the Russian front, Batursky warned the Conference "that the downfall of the revolution would be a blow to the world proletariat ... because destruction of the revolution would be death to the cause of peace. Thus, the revolution cannot ignore its outer danger .... It must not allow the army to become disorganized." By relating the matter of military preparedness to the safety of the revolution, Batursky hoped to lead the Mensheviks toward acceptance of a program designed to maintain a strong defense while efforts were being made to conclude peace.[27]

The presentation of the resolution on the war gave the Menshevik opposition an opportunity to speak out for the first time. O. A. Ermansky, an editor of *Rabochaia Gazeta* and supporter of the Menshevik leaders in the Soviet until May, favored an intense struggle for peace in Europe and the convocation of an international conference of all socialists, but he now claimed that an energetic struggle for peace would be cancelled by overt acts of militarism. He opposed the strengthening of the Russian front lines, a key part of the coalition government's defense policy. The two actions were contradictory. By strengthening the front lines at this time, Russian socialists would aid the Allied cause and work against a general peace without the victory of one coalition over the other. What are we doing, Ermansky asked. "If we support the present drive for strong military preparedness, we will lead the party and the revolution in the wrong direction and away from a general peace."[28] Astrov (Isak Sergeevich Poves) joined Ermansky and warned his comrades of the dangerous policy presently being implemented by the Soviet leaders: "Do not become tools of the Anglo-French chauvinists whose ultimate goal is the liquidation of the Soviet and the reduction of Russia to the status of a colony of western imperialism."[29]

The complaints of Astrov and Ermansky were dramatized at a big rally held by the Vasilevsky Island *raion* Menshevik committee. Before this time the *raion* committee had not enjoyed a particularly significant history, but this meeting developed into a lively demonstration led by Larin, Binshtok and Ermansky, three important names in the camp of Tsereteli's Menshevik opposition. Fifteen hundred people supposedly called upon the Menshevik party to reject Soviet participation in a coalition government and speak out against efforts to strengthen the front lines.[30]

Few of the delegates at the Conference were convinced by the arguments of the dissenters, and were quick to tell Ermansky, Larin, and Romanov (from the Moscow group) that matters could not rest where they were standing. Strong measures had to be taken to protect the frontiers of Russia if a general peace in Europe was to become a reality. The right-wing Mensheviks Cherevanin (F. A. Lipkin) and I. N. Kubikov (I. N. Dementev), both from the Petrograd Committee, struck Ermansky in a vulnerable spot. Without an active defense of Russia, Kubikov argued, Germany would probably win the war, and bring about the victory of one coalition over the other. This would be a disaster. If victory came to the German empire, the world would not see peace on the basis of the national self-determination of all peoples. The struggle for peace was not possible, therefore, unless the Russian revolution maintained a strong defense, the only assurance against a German invasion.[31] If the Provisional Government neglected to strengthen the front, the Mensheviks would actually be working toward a separate peace, as well as annexations and indemnities. War in Europe was a fact of life the Mensheviks must accept, Cherevanin continued. The German, English, and French workers were fighting one another. Should Russia follow the advice of Plekhanov and join the horror? Absolutely not! Cherevanin would have Russia join no coalition, but play the role of the savior of Europe by reviving the International and awakening workers' consciousness in all countries. In order to accomplish these ends, he advised the Conference to support the Dan resolution that called for a strong military effort. This action would protect Russia and help maintain the military *status quo* in Europe until final peace was achieved.[32]

Tsereteli was supported by the Menshevik journalists who wrote in *Den*, a Petrograd newspaper that soon came under the complete editorial control of A. N. Potresov and that small number of men who called themselves Self-defensists before the insurrection. In April, these Mensheviks were among the first to favor participation of socialists in the Provisional Government. They wanted the Conference to give whole-hearted support for strong defense measures, and feared that an opposition bloc in the party might lower the morale of the troops. Even before the Conference began, an article appeared in *Den* warning the Mensheviks who opposed Tsereteli that they served neither the revolutionary cause nor the cause of world peace. A strong army was an essential prerequisite for peace and even offensive action might be needed to secure defensive goals.[33] During the Conference, Kantorovich and Potresov gave further support to the Menshevik leaders Tsereteli, Chkheidze and Dan. Kantorovich wrote in *Den*, reminding the Conference of the party's obligation to support the individual initiative of the proletariat. The Russian proletariat was presently in favor of the military action, so those who opposed the Dan resolution did not reflect the mood of the working class.[34]

After a lengthy debate on the war, the Mensheviks went on to discuss the nationality and land questions, but the attack of Tsereteli's opposition was broken by the passage of the Dan resolution. In fact, the May 6 approval for participation of socialists in the Provisional Government was a sign that the Conference delegates would not seriously challenge the policy of the Menshevik leaders in the Petrograd Soviet. The vote in favor of socialist participation in a coalition government was 44 against 11 with 13 abstentions: the approval of the Dan resolution on the war was 47 in favor, 5 opposed and 11 abstentions;[35] the margin of victory for Tsereteli at the Menshevik Conference was more secure than the 59 against 55 tally taken among the Petrograd Mensheviks on May 3 prior to his entrance into the coalition ministry. Factionalism had not been destroyed, but it had been beaten back.

At the close of the Conference the party leaders could also rejoice at other signs of unity. An opposition group had come to the surface and the center of its strength was obviously in Petrograd, but *Rabochaia Gazeta* proudly announced that 127 different Social Democratic groups had joined the party, including the Jewish Bund; Plekhanov's *Edinstvo* group refused to join and continued to call for an Allied military victory.[30] The Conference delegates elected a new seventeen man Organization Committee to serve as the guiding force in the party, although in typical Menshevik fashion its authority was weak. Tsereteli was not on the Committee, but it did include his close supporters Dan, Gorev, Bogdanov and Isuv. Only Ermansky and Romanov appeared on the committee to represent the left opposition. *Rabochaia Gazeta* naturally fell into the hands of the Organization Committee and would continue to support the views of the Soviet leaders.

In May of 1917, few Mensheviks were swayed by the arguments of Tsereteli's opposition, but the party majority tried to harass its opponents. Loyal supporters of Tsereteli and Chkheidze on the editorial board of *Rabochaia Gazeta* limited the amount of space the left Menshevik fringe could use to express its opinions, and they criticized those opinions that found their way into print. On May 14, for example, when Ermansky's article criticizing the Dan resolution on the war appeared, the new editorial board of *Rabochaia Gazeta* felt obliged to add a note: "Comrade Ermansky expresses the opinion of only a small number in the party." On May 12, Tsereteli expressed surprise that the Soviet line was meeting with opposition in the editorial office of *Izvestiia*, the Petrograd Soviet's daily newspaper. Tsereteli's surprise discovery was followed by a meeting of Menshevik leaders and new editors were placed on the editorial board of *Izvestiia*. These included the Menshevik majority men Dan, Goldenberg and Woytinsky;[37] Woytinsky considered his own position on the political spectrum as being "somewhat to the right-of-center of the majority of the Executive Committee." The purge of the opposition was effective. Articles critical of Tsereteli no longer appeared in the official newspapers *Rabochaia Gazeta* or *Vpered*. Ermansky, Astrov and Martov were driven to establish their own journal in Petrograd, *Letuchii Listok*, which appeared only twice during 1917. On many occasions the Menshevik party opposition published articles in *Novaia Zhizn*, a radical Marxist Petrograd newspaper supposedly edited by Maxim Gorky. Outside the city of Petrograd, the opposition also had to establish separate journals on its own initiative, finding itself unable to use the publishing apparatus of the local soviets because they were controlled by the party majority. Needless to say, the purge of the opposition in the Menshevik party increased the influence of Potresov and Ivanovich, the former Self-defensists.

Further explanation needs to be given about the opposition in the party, because its strength and size grew (especially after the July uprising) and because its intellectual roots drew on sources of European thought that were new to the Russian socialist tradition. It should first be understood, however, that although the opponents of Tsereteli adopted the name Menshevik Internationalist, the term must be used with caution. No Russian Social Democrat considered himself limited by national prejudice and even Plekhanov's *Edinstvo* carried on its masthead the famous motto: Proletarians of All Countries Unite. In addition, it needs to be pointed out that those Mensheviks who regularly used the internationalist label prior to the Russian revolution (to separate themselves from the socialists who supported national defense) were not necessarily the same ones who joined the opposition against Tsereteli in late May. Most Mensheviks who called themselves internationalists before the revolution joined Tsereteli in 1917 and promoted the policy of coalition with the Kadets. Those who counted themselves among the Menshevik Internationalists in May represented a small number of radical party members who were even unable to attract the loyalty of the pacifist, Paul Axelrod. Their stand was justified almost exclusively by the conviction that imperialism had brought major changes to Russian politics and economic life.

With only one exception, an emphasis on the notion of imperialism can not be found in Menshevik literature before the revolution. To be sure, the word itself had been used, and some mild forms of the idea appeared from time to time. In addition, by 1917 the west European literature on the subject was well known to the Mensheviks. But the theory was not considered germane to the Russian scene. Potresov, for example, doubted that an imperialist system of any sort had yet made a strong appearance in Russia.[38] It was through Martov, who arrived in Petrograd from Switzerland in May, that the theory began to gain a place in the thinking of radical Mensheviks, and both Martov and Lenin were the heralds of its grand entry into Russia. Both had studied J. A. Hobson and Rudolph Hilferding, the best known proponents of the theory in western Europe. The assumptions made by Lenin in *Imperialism: the Highest Stage of Capitalism* gave abundant evidence of his dependence on the idea, and Martov's wartime writings were filled with signs that he relied on it heavily to explain the cause of the world war.[39]

It its roughest form (the form in which it appeared in Petrograd in 1917), the theory presents a vivid picture of a world in slavery divided by and dependent on the whims of two great centers of investment banking. According to Martov, these banking enterprises (one located in Berlin and the other in London and Paris) had weakened or destroyed all the old institutional and intellectual barriers that formally separated classes and nations. The imperialists, in fact, had created a new era in history by drawing all the peoples of Asia and Africa out of provincial isolation by subjecting them to the industrial machinery now owned by either the Berlin bank or the London-Paris clique. The Russian imperial government was drawn into the service of London and Paris at the time of the Balkan wars, and in 1917 its place was simply taken up by the Kadet liberals who appeared in the Menshevik Internationalist literature as little more than agents of the Allied banking enterprise. Imperialism, it followed, was the number one enemy of mankind. The war was started by each of these banking houses with an eye to destroying the other one, and victory in war would enslave all mankind to the winning center. The Russian revolution was the last hope of the world and all its energy should be used to destroy imperialism.[40]

Unfortunately, the theory of imperialism was lethal to Menshevism because it implied that Russian socialists ought to reject the Russian liberals altogether. It even made the Menshevik guarded policy of *poskol'ku postol'ku* with its ambiguity toward the Kadets seem counterproductive. It forced the Mensheviks toward a socialist revolution in Russia that would, in turn, inspire an anti-imperialist revolution throughout the world. Of course, the theory was tailor made for Lenin. He had always placed the Russian liberals in treasonous roles and marked them as targets for extinction. His adoption of imperialism required no important change in strategy and even brought him a fresh catch of ideas and slogans for use in political combat. The Mensheviks enjoyed no such advantage. If they accepted imperialism, even the mildest form, cooperation with the Russian liberals would have to be abandoned and the asian character of Russian society as a moderating factor in their strategy would disappear. It would eliminate most of the important differences that separated the Mensheviks from Lenin. The refusal of most Mensheviks to embrace imperialism in 1917 and the tortuous path followed by those who tried were revealed in the person of Martov.

Julius Martov was one of the best known figures among all Russian Marxists, and in many ways his public life was typical of the men and women in the revolutionary movement. Alienated from all the tradi-

tional institutions of tsarist Russia, he wandered about in exile, attended an endless number of conspiratorial meetings, maneuvered amidst
the intrigue of emigre politics, and spent many hours in the study of
socialist theories. This life suited Martov.[41] He had a knack for speculative thinking and a strong streak of individualism. But Martov's
thought had neither the logical structure nor the respect for institutional history that gave lasting qualities to the work of men like Plekhanov and Marx. His writings were journalistic. They reveal a brisk
intelligence and a good understanding of contemporary events, but
very little creative strength. Martov's revolutionary activity was much
like his activity as a thinker. He was deeply involved in the revolutionary movement and he played an important part in the birth of Menshevism in 1903, but he was not a natural political leader. He lacked
presence, a keen sense of timing and the recklessness that brought
political success to Lenin.

Although Martov's weakness as a political leader was evident after
his return to Petrograd in 1917, his most serious problem was intellectual and not personal. Martov relied heavily on imperialism to explain
the outbreak of war and revolution. He saw the Russian Kadets as
mere agents of London and Paris bourgeois investors, and for that
reason opposed Soviet cooperation with the Provisional Government.
At the same time, however, Martov could not support Lenin's seizure
of power. In this respect he still retained vestiges of the traditional
Menshevik school of thought. Like Tsereteli, Martov still stood in the
long shadow of Plekhanov. He had accepted as correct the view that
the old Russian order could not be destroyed by socialists alone and
that help could be found only within the liberal camp. He was not a
petty bourgeois vacillator, as Lenin called him, but a Europeanized
Russian intellectual who held two theories that called for contradictory
political tactics. The path to be followed by this man of courage was
clear but painful. He rejected the Mensheviks and their policy of cooperation with the liberal tools of imperialism and also rejected Lenin for
organizing a socialist revolution in an asian country unready for socialist rule. He stood alone with a handful of comrades who gained
nothing for themselves, but who soon reduced the confidence of many
Mensheviks supporting Tsereteli's leadership.

c) The June Offensive

Despite the holding action executed against the Internationalists at the
party Conference, Tsereteli was well aware that the Soviet peace

campaign still faced discouraging obstacles. The Allied socialists were not ready to join the Mensheviks in this righteous cause. On the contrary, they seemed to be leaning more than ever before toward military victory as the only realistic solution to the international stalemate. The masses in Petrograd and the troops in the army seemed to hold no special enthusiasm for the socialist peace scheme, and by late May serious signs of disloyalty could be detected in both these quarters. Finally, there was the ever present threat of any enemy that could be expected to take advantage of a weakened Russian army. As the party majority had correctly pointed out to the Internationalists, a German and Austrian invasion of Russia would bring a quick end to whatever hopes the Soviet had placed in a general peace. Under these anxious circumstances, the Soviet leaders were brought to consider and then to accept military action by the Russian army as a necessary means of keeping their plans alive and themselves in positions of power.[42]

Oddly enough, the ill-fated attack that finally took place at the end of June was not planned by the Petrograd Soviet, much less by the Menshevik party. It was in fact a legacy from pre-revolutionary days. The tsarist government had agreed to strike at the Central Powers in conjunction with attacks that were to be made by the French and British armies. The Russians had launched a successful military drive against the Austrians in the summer of 1916, the famous Brusilov offensive, so new plans for joint action met with general approval at the Petrograd Inter-Allied conference in January of 1917. But the February revolution left the matter unsettled. The rapid decline of morale among Russian army officers (probably as a result of staff changes instituted by Guchkov), the shortages created by transportation problems, and the Zimmerwaldist posture of the Petrograd Soviet caused the cautious Commander-in-Chief, General Alexeev, to postpone the attack. The French and English prodded both Alexeev and the leaders of the Provisional Government, hoping to induce action on the eastern front while Nivelle and Allenby were attacking in the west, but the Russians could not be moved. Despite the warlike reputation suffered by the first Provisional Government, Miliukov and Guchkov did not force the hand of the Russian General Staff by setting a date for the attack. Matters temporarily rested in this state.

At first the Mensheviks pretended to ignore the tactical and strategic aspects of military life, despite the fact that government plans for a full military campaign could not have been completed without their approval. They concentrated on political matters and seemed more interested in the Russian army as a bastion of Soviet support than as an instrument of warfare. During March and early April, common soldiers were urged to form their own clubs or committees for protection against the abusive power of the officers and to ignore regulations thought to be a part of the outmoded bondage system. The General Staff was left to defend the frontiers of Russia using whatever means it deemed necessary as long as these did not subvert Soviet authority. The Mensheviks were not responsible for the publication of the notorious military Order Number I,[43] which did nothing to strengthen the defense of Russia, but they considered it to weigh in favor of the socialist leadership and defended the record of the free soldier committees.[44] In these early weeks of the revolution, as far as the Mensheviks were concerned, the key question regarding the army was how to prevent domestic political enemies from using their power against the Soviet.

After mid-April things changed gradually and the Mensheviks began to walk down the path leading to aggressive military action. They pricked up their ears when a Russian defeat on the Stokhod River gave the Germans an important military advantage.[45] What good would the revolution accomplish if it fell victim to an external military force? Concern continued to grow, and by the end of the month the party leaders were wondering how the army would fare against a full scale attack. The gradual improvement in weather conditions made a German offensive a stronger possibility with each passing day and stories about the deteriorating state of the Russian army were common gossip in Petrograd. At the end of April the Menshevik leaders in the Soviet were apparently rethinking their earlier posture, because they made no effort to stop the high command from changing the slogans in the trenches from Defense to Offensive. They still certainly hoped to stop short of an all-out military assault, but the permissiveness of March was now gone. By early May soldiers were being instructed that a strong bond linked together correct military bearing and the success of the revolution.[46] In early June a detachment of Kronstadt sailors was punished for disobedience and the Soviet leaders made no effort to protect them. Quite a different response from the ones seen in March and early April.[47]

It was not until late May that the Mensheviks passed the point of no return in their drift toward accepting offensive military action as a necessary measure for defending the revolution, but even at that time they hoped to avoid what seemed inevitable to others. (It is simply not true that the Mensheviks accepted military action as a condition to forming a coalition government with the liberals in the first week in May). On May 17 *Izvestiia* coyly stated that preparation for future military action did not necessarily mean that such action would take place, but the writer left little doubt that Soviet resistance to the offensive had eroded considerably since March. It asserted that military action may be needed for the defense of the revolution and that the Soviet leaders would allow the General Staff to determine if and when the proposed attack would begin.[48] Soldiers would be expected to obey orders to go forward. Not until May 28 did *Rabochaia Gazeta* finally break its long silence on the subject. It discussed the weakening condition of the Russian army and the need to restore correct discipline if the revolution was to protect itself and bring peace to Europe.[49] In the first week in June at the All-Russian Congress of Soviets the Menshevik leaders requested and received the approval of the delegates to support the pending military action. When last minute preparations were being made at the front in mid-June all the Menshevik newspapers in Petrograd and Moscow from *Edinstvo* on the right to *Novaia Zhizn* on the left supported the attack to be launched by the Russian armies. Despite their hostility to Tsereteli and their cries about the evils of imperialism, the Menshevik Internationalists supported fully the June attack.

Criticism of the Mensheviks for their involvement in the June offensive has been widespread. It began with Lenin, and the number of critics multiplied rapidly once the failure of the action was found to fit comfortably into the hypotheses of those who rely exclusively on hindsight and who measure political movements solely in terms of success and failure. Lenin's views were consistent with those he put forth in the April Theses. He thought a successful military offensive would bring the Soviet and the Provisional Government to work closely together. He was against this development. He wanted to divide the forces that were loyal to the February revolution, destroy the Provisional Government and use the Soviet as the sole institution of authority in Russia. In the polemics exchanged prior to the military action, he again dragged out his theory about the petty bourgeois Mensheviks vacillating between the proletariat (Lenin) and the bourgeoisie (the Provisional Government). The Mensheviks had been duped, according to Lenin, and were now carrying out the orders of the imperialists who controlled the wealth of Russia and the world. Lenin was not successful in preventing the offensive from taking place (although he tried), but its failure helped to keep alive his explanation of the events. After the October revolution the theory was again used by the "old" Bolshevik Shliapnikov who repeated Lenin's argument, but did not leave the Mensheviks with the immunity of stupidity. He accused them of consciously conspiring against the revolution.[50]

In recent years, Soviet Russian historians and some others have repeated and embellished Lenin's interpretation of the June offensive. According to a recent version, the military offensive had the dual purpose of destroying the revolutionary movement in Russia as well as aiding the Allied imperialists.[51] The domestic phase of the offensive was planned by the leaders of the Provisional Government with the full knowledge of the Petrograd Soviet. Successful military action at the front was expected to revive patriotic fervor in Russia and help quiet the forces of disruption in the army and in the capital city. The offensive was part of the counterrevolution, and the French historian Marc Ferro went so far as to conclude that the "authorities" also hoped to use anti-semitism, nationalistic sentiments, and the Church to support this campaign.[52] The evidence will not support these exaggerations even though some individual political figures harbored such motives. Nor will the evidence support the contention that the Soviet leaders expected the offensive to bring about an Allied military victory.

Still other writers have criticized the Soviet decision to accept military action, pointing out that the Russian army was not fully prepared to undertake an offensive. Military action should have been postponed or even cancelled for these practical reasons.[53] This criticism has its reasonable aspects, but it is based largely on hindsight and ignores the fact that there were no alternative choices available. If the offensive had been postponed or cancelled, no substantial improvement would have occurred in either the military or the diplomatic picture. Dan, Cherevanin and Batursky presented this logic to the Menshevik Internationalists at the May Conference hoping that Martov and his friends could resolve the dilemma, but they could not. The campaign to secure a general peace in Europe would have been doomed if the Soviet appeared unwilling to defend the frontiers of Russia. The Allied socialists, already far from accepting the Stockholm plan, would not have cooperated with Petrograd if the Russians allowed their armies to fall apart. Nor would postponement or cancellation of the military action have helped in domestic politics. Idleness had weakened the fighting capacity of the army, leaving Russia open for an invasion, and desertion had already begun to disrupt life behind the lines. Without military action these hazards would have grown worse, but a limited display of military activity would have helped keep alive hopes for a general peace and given some stability at home. The Mensheviks reached this conclusion, as did Lenin, Martov, Kerensky, Miliukov, and Generals Brusilov and Ludendorff.

In 1917 the Mensheviks in and outside the Soviet were committed to bringing about a peace in Europe based exclusively on their terms. They would not take steps toward a separate peace with Germany nor would they make a deal with the Allies (including Russia's liberals). A righteous desire to avoid what they saw as the pitfalls of the past and to achieve their own political ends as quickly as possibly brought them to see opportunities in military action, and criticism that ignores these ambitions is not very helpful. In June of 1917 the Mensheviks came to see that it was not a matter of emphasizing defense rather than peace, but that without an adequate defense there would be no general peace and perhaps not even a Russian bourgeois revolution. If they are to be criticized for failure, the criticism should focus in the area where the Menshevik leaders could have improved their chances for success, and that area rested in their relations with the Kadets. A closer working agreement with the liberals was open to the Soviet leaders in the late spring, if they were prepared to compromise with the "bourgeoisie." They were not.

Chapter V
July

a) Downfall of the First Coalition

The Russian government founded in March of 1917 was provisional in more than simply its name. Everything about it had an air of impermanence and weakness. Before the ink was dry on the decree creating the new power, its pessimistic ministers realized only too well that directives issued in its name could not be enforced in many parts of the capital city of Petrograd let alone throughout the vast territories once ruled by Nicholas Romanov. The formation of the coalition government in May was supposed to correct most of these deficiencies, but it did little to improve the situation.

The major causes of weakness were both the centrifugal forces that battled against the centralizing efforts of the new regime and the internal quarrels that divided the revolutionary leaders in Petrograd. The centrifugal forces throughout the country limited the sources of energy flowing to the new government, while the quarrels between socialists and liberals in Petrograd created a division of purpose at the nerve center of the revolution. After the April Crisis it was the second factor, divisions between socialists and liberals, that brought about the downfall of the revolutionary government. In early July the collapse resulted from a combination of both centrifugal forces and internal quarrels. In July of 1917 the centrifugal force was nationalism.

Oddly enough, it was on the question of nationalism and the national minorities that the socialists and liberals in Petrograd had much in common. Both the Menshevik leaders in the Soviet and the liberals in the Kadet party recognized the need to introduce strong local self-government in the new Russia, and both sides wanted the new local power to be organized along natural geographic or economic lines and not along cultural or religious lines. At the same time, both liberals and socialists discouraged the national minorities from taking the path toward outright separation from Petrograd and both also wanted to delay all decisions on the question of national autonomy until the meeting of the Constituent Assembly, a body that would surely favor the centralizing efforts of the new Russian state.[1] When various nationalist leaders tried to wring concessions from Petrograd, the Soviet and the Provisional Government stood together in opposition to the political demands of non-Russians. Muslim groups were largely ignored when they tried to gain the attention of the Soviet leaders Tsereteli and Chkheidze, and the Finnish Seim finally declared its own autonomy, much to the disapproval of the Mensheviks and the Kadets. When the Ukrainian issue arose in May and June, Petrograd hoped that discussions with Kiev could be delayed at least until the end of the war.[2]

The Ukrainians refused to wait and by June their national leaders had gained enough self-confidence to make demands on Petrograd. Composed of representatives from several Ukrainian political organizations, the Rada announced on June 10 that it was ready to assume extensive local autonomy; "People of the Ukraine, we are forced to create our own destiny .... If the Russian Provisional Government cannot introduce order into our land, if it does not want to initiate with us a great work, we must undertake it ourselves." The announcement did not declare complete separation from the new Russian state, but it presented the Ukrainian Rada as an equal with the Provisional Government in legal and administrative affairs. It declared the Rada to be the only government of the Ukraine and insisted that its autonomy be recognized by Petrograd at once.[3]

Both the socialists and liberals in Petrograd agreed that the Ukrainians had gone much too far. *Rabochaia Gazeta* questioned the legal and popular grounds on which the Rada could claim to represent all the people of the Ukraine, and *Rech* spoke of the ease with which the Germans could take advantage of a semi-independent Ukraine. The Provisional Government itself took a less harsh stand than either of the two party newspapers, but it too implored the Rada to postpone all action until the meeting of the All-Russian Constituent Assembly. The Provisional Government sent a note to Kiev on June 17, stressing the need for cooperation and unity in this contemporary time of troubles. When the Rada ignored the note, the Provisional Government took an additional step. It sent a cabinet delegation to Kiev that included Tsereteli and Tereshchenko in hopes of persuading the Rada to curb its ambitions. The delegation from Petrograd was joined by the cabinet ministers Kerensky and Nekrasov after it arrived in Kiev on June 28; none of the ministers who travelled to Kiev were selected by the Kadet party.

At first the delegation met with success, but the end result was a disaster. A compromise solution was found in Kiev after concessions were made by both the representatives of the Provisional Government and the leaders of the Rada, but when the new agreement was later presented to a full cabinet meeting in Petrograd it was rejected. The Kadets in the cabinet were angry and unwilling to accept the concessions surrendered to the Ukrainians by Tsereteli, Tereshchenko, Kerensky and Nekrasov. They claimed that the agreement granted too much autonomy to the Ukraine, and that it was not based on action taken in the Constituent Assembly. They pointed out that the cabinet delegation sent to Kiev exceeded its authority by recognizing the strong legal position of the Rada and by denying the right of the Provisional Government to predetermine the mutual relations among the various parts of Russia. The Kadet ministers threatened to resign if the agreement signed with the Rada leaders was not quickly abrogated.

Tsereteli was anxious to save the first coalition from extinction and tried to discourage the Kadet ministers Shingarev, Manuilov, Stepanov and Shakhovsky from resigning. First, he cleared the air by insisting that the Provisional Government was not being presented by the delegation with an ultimatum, as the Kadets indignantly insisted, but with a fair compromise that represented the best solution that could be reached under the circumstances. He reminded the Kadets that a compromise had been made in February to establish the Provisional Government itself, and again when Petrograd faced the Finnish demands for autonomy. He then went on to point out that the Rada withdrew its most unpalatable demands, and was now preparing to issue a statement that would reflect the concessions made on all sides.[4] But his attempt to prevent the dissolution of the government was unsuccessful. The Kadets had reached the end of the rope. They reviewed the entire record of the coalition government, again complaining that the Mensheviks in the Soviet had joined forces with Miliukov's enemies in the liberal camp to force their will on the Russian people. The Kadets announced that they could no longer serve in the cabinet and resigned on July 2, 1917.[5]

There have been a number of provocative interpretations of the Kadet resignation. Leon Trotsky, for example, maintained that the Ukrainian issue was a mere pretext used by Miliukov to withdraw the Kadet ministers, while the real cause was suggested by "the collapse of the offensive—not yet officially acknowledged, but no longer a matter of doubt to the well informed. These liberals considered it expedient to leave their left allies (the Mensheviks) face to face with defeat, and with the Bolsheviks."[6] But Trotsky's interpretation is open to serious doubt. Both Lenin and Sukhanov, among the best informed men in Petrograd, did not mention military failure in their accounts of the Kadet resignation. Surely, neither of these two gentlemen would have allowed such an excellent opportunity to escape their attention. Nor does Trotsky's interpretation explain how Martov could write an article in *Novaia Zhizn* on July 2 condemning the Provisional Government for taking unfair advantage of the successful (!) offensive.[7] Finally, of course, Trotsky does not explain the fact that the Kadets resigned on July 2, but the German counteroffensive against the Russian forces did not even begin until July 6.

Lenin viewed the Kadet resignation as further evidence of an unfolding international class struggle. He scoffed at the suggestion that the Kadets viewed the nationality issue from the lofty perch of loyalty to principle. He concluded, in an article published on July 3, that the Kadet exit from the cabinet was a move calculated to present Tsereteli with the alternatives of steering the Provisional Government either with or without the aid of "world-wide Anglo-American capital." As a member of the "vacillating petty bourgeoisie," Tsereteli would be frightened into yielding to the wishes of Miliukov, according to Lenin.[8]

Both Lenin and Trotsky left important questions unanswered in their treatments of the late June events, but the interpretation presented by the Kadets and also by Tsereteli was easily supported by the available evidence. The Ukrainian issue was indeed a real point of contention, according to the chief antagonists, but it also served as a pretext. The relations between the socialist and liberal ministers were not good even when the government was initially formed in May, and they grew steadily worse as time passed; the resignation of A. I. Konovalov, the Kadet Minister of Trade and Industry, on May 19 and the harassment of A. A. Manuilov, the Kadet Minister of Education, in June can be traced directly to the pressure exerted against the government by the Soviet leaders. At the end of June the Kadets were ready to leave the government, once it became clear that the socialist ministers were ignoring their wishes. The Ukrainian affair was perfect for the occasion. Despite general agreement on the nationalities issue among Kadets and socialists, some differences did exist and these differences proved to be important in late June. The Soviet leaders, led by the Mensheviks, expected the national minorities to await the Constituent Assembly before settling legal matters between Petrograd and the border lands, but the Soviet was prepared to make exceptions to this rule. For example, both the June Soviet Congress (Mark Liber's declaration) and the Menshevik editors of *Den* urged the Provisional Government to recognize the legal presence of the Rada in Kiev, even if the most outlandish Ukrainian demands had to be rejected.[9] According to the Mensheviks, recognition of the Rada would be greeted as a sign of Petrograd's good faith among all the minorities of ther former empire and strengthen the hand of the Provisional Government in the long run. The Kadets did not agree. They intended to practice exactly what they preached to the nationalities.[10] They discouraged the Provisional Government from discussing the question of national autonomy with non-Russians and insisted that the Constituent Assembly was the only legal body with the power to settle the issue. Until it was convened everybody had to accept the sovereignty of Petrograd. This shade of difference between the Kadets and the Mensheviks was important because it entered the picture at exactly the time when relations between the socialists and the liberals in the cabinet had reached the breaking point. The Kadets resigned from the cabinet when the Kiev delegation by-passed the cabinet instructions and recognized the Rada.[11] Recognition of the Rada was a concession only the Mensheviks and Kerensky were willing to make. Once the delegation returned, the Kadets concluded that Tsereteli's conscience could live more comfortably with a compromise in Kiev than with a compromise in Petrograd.

After the Kadet resignations, Tsereteli was faced with the complicated problem of forming a new government in Petrograd, made more difficult by his own determination to eliminate the chief Kadet politicians from the new cabinet. Tsereteli and his comrades in the Soviet and in the Menshevik party had not lost faith in the traditional tactics of liberal-socialist collaboration, but they were exasperated and began to despair of working in harmony with the best known and most influential liberals in Russian political life. The failure of the first coalition at the end of June shifted the center Soviet leadership opinion temporarily to the left. Unfortunately, the establishment of a well-balanced liberal-socialist cabinet without Kadet ministers in key offices and without the cooperation of Miliukov operating behind the scenes would require great skill. The Kadets were the only major organized liberal group in Petrograd and Miliukov was still their strongest leader. They fully expected to maintain a strong place in the Provisional Government, and they could be expected to work against Tsereteli's wishes. In addition, the appearance of a cabinet without important

Kadets would be a big step toward the formation of an all-socialist government, a political arrangement that was close to Lenin's plan and unacceptable to the Mensheviks themselves. Time was now needed to resolve the whole problem, so Tsereteli delayed by placing the task of forming a new government in the hands of the Central Executive Committee of the All-Russian Soviet of Workers' and Soldiers' Deputies; the Central Executive Committee was a body elected by the delegates to the First All-Russian Congress of Soviets that met in Petrograd in early and mid-June. It was a pliable tool of the shrewd Georgian Menshevik who now appeared to hold the fate of the revolutionary regime in the palm of his hand. It required at least three weeks for the Central Executive Committee to assemble, and Tsereteli hoped to use this time to master whatever difficulties lay ahead. Unfortunately, unexpected trouble arose in Petrograd during the first week in July and the entire picture changed rapidly.

b) The Confusion of July

The disturbances that marked the period known as the July days began late in the afternoon of July 3 and lasted until late in the evening of July 4. They were evidently started by political agitators in and around the First Machine Gun Regiment. The difficulties then spread to many of the workers' districts in suburban Petrograd. The most destructive activity took place on July 4. Rebellious soldiers and workers from Petrograd were joined by a contingent of sailors that made its way to the capital from the Kronstadt naval base located on an island about 20 miles from the city. The mobs marched into the center of the city, causing only superficial damage to property but turning the town into a state of anarchy. Some shooting occurred, causing the deaths of a number of citizens. The mobs occupied several locations in the city, but eventually the focus of attention became riveted on the Taurida Palace, the meeting place of the Soviet Workers' and Soldiers' Deputies. Many Soviet leaders were fearful for their lives. On the evening of July 4 demonstrators came very close to kidnapping V. M. Chernov, who no doubt would have been murdered if not rescued by his courageous comrades. The slogans carried by the rioters denounced the Provisional Government and demanded that the Petrograd Soviet seize state power, but the mood of anarchy and the lack of direction prevailing among the mobs made questionable just how determined these men were to realize such ends. The Bolshevik Central Committee reluctantly and belatedly declared itself as the political leader of the strange forces roaming the streets of Petrograd, but Lenin and his "conscious vanguard of the proletariat" enjoyed no more success guiding this enterprise than the Menshevik champions of spontaneity had in their efforts to bring the riots under control. The force of the disturbances reached its peak in the evening of July 4, and then began to run out of energy. By July 5 most of the soldiers had returned to the barracks and the sailors to the naval base. The disturbances were over. Loyal troops collected by the Soviet for the protection of the city appeared only after the whole business had run its course.

Despite the fact that Lenin was unhappy about the timing of the riots and the lack of direction among those who participated in the demonstrations, Sukhanov's observation that the July 3-5 riots came as a result of Bolshevik and Anarchist agitation in the barracks was partly true.[12] The Bolsheviks and the Anarchists had been trying to encourage the growth of an anti-government spirit among the troops throughout May and June while preparations were getting under way to launch the military offensive. The Provisional Government and the Petrograd Soviet took only mild measures to distract the soldiers from the agitators. As a result, this radical activity led to an attempted street demonstration on June 10, and considerable evidence of Bolshevik propaganda appeared among the soldiers who marched in a Soviet-sponsored parade on June 18. It seems that the July disturbances were sequential to this June agitation. The political radicals, especially in the First Machine Gun Regiment, had decided to riot in the streets of the capital as early as July 1, a decision they reached prior to the cabinet crisis and long before any news of a military failure arrived in Petrograd from the front lines.[13]

On the other hand, the rioters were not carrying out Lenin's plans even though Bolshevik agitators helped bring the pot to a boil. Rumors were spreading about government attempts to disarm and disperse some of the regiments as part of the preparations for the offensive. The soldiers were worried that front line duty and disciplinary action were in store for some of them, although these fears were founded on rather shaky evidence. Frightened by rumors and prodded by radical orators, the First Machine Gun Regiment burst upon the city. Others followed. Thus, the riots did show the influence of Lenin's propaganda and that of the Anarchists as well, but a great deal of the energy behind the July action rested in the desire of some soldiers to keep the regiments together in Petrograd and away from front line duty. This self-centered motivation among the demonstrators caused Lenin to have grave doubts about the "character of the movement," the words used by Sukhanov to describe Lenin's interpretation of the events.[14] In any case, the riots were quite limited in scope. Only a small percentage of all the soldiers in Petrograd participated in the disorders while most others remained neutral and eventually helped to protect the Soviet leaders and the Provisional Government. Outside Petrograd and Kronstadt there were no appreciable disturbances. An attempt by the Moscow Bolsheviks to start trouble ended in a mouse-like demonstration.[15]

The first reaction to the July uprising by the Soviet Executive Committee and the Menshevik leaders was to prevent the rioters from overthrowing the Provisional Government, such as it was. *Rabochaia Gazeta* and *Izvestiia* used persuasion, hoping that rhetoric might distract troublemakers and convince most people that mob action at this time was an "incorrect form of struggle." The editors implored citizens to remain at home and not to join in the street activity. People were urged to ignore the Bolshevik demagoguery and to remain loyal to the leaders of the Soviet of Workers' and Soldiers' Deputies. The population was reminded that street riots and armed demonstrations were declared illegal by the government after the April Crisis. The use of manifestos and oratory to discourage the riots included courageous public denunciations of mob action by the Menshevik leaders and an outright refusal to discuss the demands made by rebellious soldiers and workers: "No kind of ministry can be formed under the view of machine guns."[16] The Mensheviks stood firmly, and it was not until the Soviet leaders were on the verge of being dragged into the pages of history at the end of a rope that they considered using force to stop the disturbances; in fact, the trouble was over by the time reinforcements arrived on the scene.

Once the riotous activity subsided, both the Soviet officials and the leaders of the Menshevik party staunchly reminded the people of Petrograd that the Soviet would not under any circumstances seize government power. The Mensheviks had grown even more conservative in their determination to prevent a Soviet government from being installed in revolutionary Russia. The harried editors of *Rabochaia Gazeta* and *Den* answered the demands of those supporting the Leninist slogans with an emphatic No! They explained again that the Soviet was a non-government organization representing only a small minority in the vastness of the Russian population. Such a small minority could possibly seize power, but doing so would bring the country to ruin. In the event of a socialist seizure of power, the "dark forces" of the counterrevolution would easily incite the masses of Russia to rise up against the Soviet and destroy the revolution. "If the Soviet took power into its hands there would remain the difficult task of uniting the majority of the people around the Soviet ...." A struggle would ensue between the Democracy and "all organized bourgeois elements," which would lead to civil war and counterrevolution.[17] The Soviet did in fact have temporary command of the city of Petrograd, since the Kadet resignations left a socialist majority in the cabinet, but a new coalition would have to be formed in order to restore power to the "bourgeoisie." The coalition must be revived, the Mensheviks declared, if democracy was to survive in Russia. And if there was any lingering doubt about the close connection between the Mensheviks and Plekhanov on this score, it was dispelled in July. Plekhanov's daily newspaper *Edinstvo* stood with the Menshevik and other Soviet leaders, determined to prevent a Soviet seizure of power. Plekhanov used the same arguments supported by the same evidence as the editors of *Rabochaia Gazeta* and *Den*.[18]

This political response of the Mensheviks to the demands of the July mobs was not molded solely by the circumstances of the moment. It was drawn from the same intellectual sources that inspired the February and April action. The Mensheviks were excited about changing the face of Russia as quickly as possible, but a government controlled by the Soviet would be much too "progressive" for semi-asiatic Russia where a weak bourgeoisie and a small proletariat were still struggling to dismantle the old asiatic system. The economic and social patterns followed by the Russian people were still far from those ways that allowed democracy to flourish in capitalist Europe. The Russian mind had not yet been conditioned by hours of work in factories or by years of activity in craft guilds and trade unions. Mentally and institutionally, according to the Mensheviks, Russia was still part of Asia. Russian society had not been permitted to organize, leaving its dispersed masses, especially in rural areas, in an "uncivilized" state and susceptible to any kind of anti-socialist propaganda. *Rabochaia Gazeta* appealed to its readers in much the same way that Axelrod and Martov did when they appealed to Lenin prior to 1905: "If the senseless attempts of the Bolsheviks had succeeded, if they had succeeded in overthrowing the Provisional Government by force of arms and in thrusting power upon the Soviet ... at bayonet point, the cause of the revolution would have been lost."[19]

The determination to prevent the Soviet from taking over all Russian political life brought the Mensheviks to intensify their own propaganda activity among the masses of the city. In early July the Mensheviks launched a bitter campaign against Lenin and his friends. Lenin had now been unmasked. He was a bad shepherd, using tactics that would bring about the inevitable collapse of the revolutionary effort. He put forth dangerous and demagogic slogans that made no theoretical sense. He claimed to be an ally of the Soviet, but in fact he was opposing the will of the Soviet itself by calling for a seizure of power. Lenin was beneath contempt. He represented only a small band of adventurers who were ignoring both the aspirations of the masses and the laws of historical development; Lenin claimed to be a Marxist, but had not Marx himself recognized the differences between Europe and Asia? The Menshevik pamphlet writer Gorev charged Lenin with trying to disrupt the political stability of Petrograd and block the peacemaking efforts of the Soviet to boot.[20] Stephan Ivanovich (S. O. Portugeis) directed his attack at Lenin's allies, the Anarchists, who had been active in Petrograd politics since May. He traced their ideological origins to the bourgeoisie and not the proletariat and explained how they could bring only harm to the revolutionary forces. He advised workers and citizens to exercise self-discipline and to reject leaders who prescribed the prompt dissolution of all government as a cure for human ills.[21] In this propaganda activity against Lenin and the Anarchists, the Menshevik majority leaders in Petrograd enjoyed the full support of the Menshevik organizations in Moscow.

The campaign undertaken against the Bolsheviks and the Anarchists in July even included police action. Some Bolshevik leaders were arrested and their headquarters, formally the home of the dancer Kshesinskaia, were captured by forces loyal to the government. At the same time the Anarchists were driven from their stronghold in the Durnovo villa. Loyal troops stationed some miles from the city and in the city itself were mustered and used to disarm the regiments that participated in the riots. The police measures were criticized by Martov and the Menshevik Internationalists who considered them a limitation of political freedom (which they were) and saw in their execution ominous signs for the revolution. Most Mensheviks approved of the police operations, although some had reservations when they wrote their memoirs. On July 4, when troops loyal to the Soviet appeared at the

Taurida Palace and restored the balance of authority in favor of the Executive Committee, Dan "was so filled with glee that he tried without success to conceal it ... by assuming a balanced expression."[22] Woytinsky later wrote that the Mensheviks were struck by guilty consciences when the police measures were taken against the Bolsheviks, but the measures were taken. One further step was also considered after the July riots. Tsereteli suggested that the coming meeting of the Soviet's Central Executive Committee take place in Moscow, away from the explosive atmosphere of Petrograd. But this proposal was withdrawn after a storm of abuse was showered on Tsereteli from the left; Martov maintained that such a transfer would place the treacherous scheming of the bourgeoisie beyond the watchful eye of the proletariat.

The meekness with which the police measures were carried out, however, did not meet the same ruthless standards set by those who ruled Russia before February and after October. Tsereteli and some of his closest associates were ready to use even sterner measures in an effort to protect the Provisional Government (so he said in his memoirs), but many Mensheviks were reluctant to punish Lenin too severely. They still expected Lenin to become "reasonable" and still looked for the greatest danger to the revolution to emerge "on the right.". They still regarded the Bolsheviks as comrades, regardless how misguided and childish. No serious effort was made to capture Lenin. Measures to prevent the Kronstadt sailors from once again pouncing on the city were not taken, and the process of disarming the disloyal regiments was never completed with the kind of devotion needed to finish the task properly. The outbreak of more disturbances on July 8 brought a temporary halt to the official action against the Bolsheviks.

The police measures and the anti-Leninist propaganda campaign were expected to help restore public order in Petrograd, but the Mensheviks realized that a new cabinet had to be formed at once if the revolutionary leadership was to retain the confidence of the people. It was not going to be a simple matter. Negotiations between the Soviet leaders and other groups had been in progress since July 2, but concrete results were delayed by the turbulence of the riots and by Tsereteli's desire to avoid making a compromise with the Kadets. Of course, not all Mensheviks wished to exclude the Kadets from a new government, and Tsereteli was meeting with resistance on this very issue.[23] Right-wing Mensheviks were especially dubious of a Russian bourgeois revolution without the bourgeoisie, and in addition to negative reactions from the right wing of his own party, the Menshevik leader had yet to deal with Alexander Kerensky, a man whose presence could no longer be ignored.

Kerensky was a remarkable man. He was one of the few politicians in Petrograd who was capable of administering to the affairs of state on the highest levels; he might have become an important figure in contemporary Russian history if the Provisional Government had survived. He was shrewd. He understood the importance of dealing with the Petrograd Soviet, the Allied leaders and the Russian liberals all at one and the same time. In addition, Kerensky certainly possessed the oratorical gifts needed to command a devoted public following, a requirement for success in twentieth-century European politics. Nor was Kerensky burdened with the Mensheviks' problem of embracing one's own political tactics as a religious creed. He was flexible and ready to enlist the services of anyone who wished to put Russia on a stable footing. Kerensky was not without shortcomings. He was convinced that once the Provisional Government fell into his hands the great questions that separated the Mensheviks and the Kadets could be resolved. He was under the illusion that in his personality most Kadets and Mensheviks would find the one correct leader and bury their differences long enough for Russia to be brought, by Kerensky, to better days. Exactly how far Kerensky thought his own strength and cunning could carry the burden of office in troubled times is not easy to ascertain. He had too much confidence in his own powers of persuasion, but unlike most Mensheviks he did recognize when the cause of the democratic revolution was lost. He fled Russia after Lenin's seizure of power.

Kerensky was nominally a Social Revolutionary and a member of the Petrograd Soviet of Workers' and Soldiers' Deputies, but he ignored his duties in the Soviet and began to build his power in the Provisional Government. He secured the position of Minister of Justice in the first cabinet and then Minister of War and the Navy in the coalition government of May and June. His influence grew during the spring of 1917 as the Soviet and Kadet leaders busily struggled against one another. His rising star was evident in the steadily increasing importance of the cabinet positions he held and in the popular following he enjoyed in the capital city. By the time the May coalition was formed, one could speak seriously of a Kerensky faction in the cabinet. It included Nekrasov and Tereshchenko, both Kadet party rivals of Miliukov. The group was held together more by the promise of Kerensky's

political future than by the mystical bonds of masonry or a great concern for the masses that some suspect served as the cohesive strength
of the partnership. Kerensky's strategy to advance his faction to the
top government posts was quite simple and quite traditional — *divida et*
impera! He first linked his fortunes to the Soviet leaders Tsereteli and
Chernov as the Kadets were being forced to relinquish the center of
the stage, but once he assumed the post of Minister-President he used
the Kadets to keep the Soviet leaders in check. He launched his political offensive in early June before the Ukrainian issue had come to a
head. At that time Nekrasov and Tereshchenko were working closely
with Kerensky and the two men approached Tsereteli with the Keren-
sky-inspired suggestion that the Menshevik leader use his influence to
dissolve the first coalition. A new government would be established in
its place. Nekrasov briefly described the new leadership as a type of
"English war cabinet," consisting of five members who would be
invested with "extraordinary powers in order to deal most effectively
with the affairs of the government." Although Nekrasov did not mention the names of the five members, it was clear that Nekrasov and
Tsereteli would hold important posts, and that Kerensky would be the
Minister-President. Had the plan gone into operation, it would have
temporarily eliminated the Kadets as contenders for the highest posts
in the government. But in June Tsereteli discouraged further speculation on the plan. He was well aware that Kerensky's ambition might
upset his own tactical scheme of continuing the socialist-liberal alliance
between the Kadets and the Soviet. In his memoirs Tsereteli wrote
that he rejected Nekrasov's proposal, giving Kerensky's lack of organizational talent and absence of political convictions among the reasons;
the Menshevik leaders did not trust Kerensky.[24]

The effects of the July riots turned the tide in favor of Kerensky's
quest for power. The Menshevik leaders around Tsereteli were more
exasperated than usual at the Kadets, thinking for a time that the
influence of Miliukov and his closest associates could be eliminated
from the cabinet. Moreover, the unrest in Petrograd made the Soviet
leaders anxious to establish as quickly as possible a government that
enjoyed popularity among the masses in the streets. Kerensky's moment had arrived. Both the Menshevik prejudice against the liberals
and his own reputation as a forceful and popular revolutionary leader
made him seem like a good candidate for head of the government. He
must have presented a version of Nekrasov's June proposal to Tsereteli
immediately after returning to the city from the front lines on July 6.

At that time Tsereteli did not have several alternatives from which to choose and was ready to accept a Kerensky government. He and Kerensky must have agreed on some compromise version of the June plan, but before Kerensky could be installed it was necessary to remove Prince Lvov, the last of the moderate liberals, from the post of Minister-President.

Prince Georgy Evgenevich Lvov was a kindly old man who somehow managed to remain aloof from the political infighting that character-ized relations among the politicians in the Provisional Government; he was selected to fill the chief government post by Miliukov in February, perhaps because of his political naivete, but he was counted among those liberals who remained in the cabinet after the Kadet exit on July 2. He could be counted upon to cause Kerensky trouble, so his removal from office became essential; besides, he occupied the post Kerensky wanted to hold for himself. Pressure was applied to Lvov by both the Soviet leaders and Kerensky. The Soviet leaders led the attack They demanded that the government institute certain reform measures that were bound to provoke the Prince who, like most liberals, felt that the Soviet should not dictate national policy. At the same time Kerensky carried on a campaign against Lvov. He emphasized the need for a strong government, speaking in a pathetic tone about the mild manner of the Prince which left no doubt in the minds of listeners the point Kerensky was trying to make: "His gentle manner of governing is not suited for these very difficult times. It is necessary to use more firm-ness in dealing with people, more coercion is necessary in our govern-ment."[25] Kerensky pushed on one side and the Soviet leaders pushed on the other, so it was not long before Lvov did resign. He was hustled along his way by an editorial in *Rabochaia Gazeta* that accused the old gentleman of being narrowminded because he balked at implementing a "true bourgeois program." After Lvov's resignation, the remaining ministers offered Kerensky the head post in the government. Keren-sky accepted.

Was the Soviet reform program rejected by Lvov designed as a guide for reform in Russia or was it primarily used as a device to eliminate the old man from the cabinet, as Paul Miliukov thought? The question is important. The program later became known (in a slightly revised form) as the July declaration. It included a statement of land reform (supposedly a guarantee to the peasants that land would be distributed to them in a fair manner), a measure for the dissolution of the State Duma and the State Council, promises of tax reform in industry and finance and, finally, a proposal to declare Russia a Democratic Republic. On the face of it the program was supposed to increase the strength of the government, giving it a more permanent character by usurping prerogatives previously reserved for the Constituent Assembly. It was also expected to appeal to a great many Russian peasants and workers. In September of 1917 when the democratic revolution was running out of steam, Dan, Martov and Tsereteli pointed all the way back to the July declaration citing it as evidence of their early vigilance and concern over the many serious difficulties faced by the Provisional Government, and in his memoirs Tsereteli praised the July declaration. Its adoption was absolutely essential because "everybody" was convinced that "great strides" had to be taken by the Provisional Government as soon as possible. Tsereteli even stressed the special importance of the sections dealing with rural Russia, leading his readers to assume that he was more sensitive to the peasant problem in Russia than in fact he was;[26] Lvov, in fact, was accused by the Mensheviks of rejecting the July program simply to protect his estates in rural Russia. But after the establishment of the Kerensky government on July 8 the so-called reform program was changed. The sections dealing with land tenure were abridged and the measures dealing with the State Duma and the Democratic Republic were deleted altogether. In fact, the program that brought about Lvov's resignation reappeared after his resignation in a form that Lvov himself might well have accepted. Perhaps the need for reform was not as great on July 8 as it had been two days earlier, or perhaps the program was indeed designed by the Soviet leaders to serve in the conspiracy against Lvov.[27] The evidence in support of the latter conclusion is quite strong.

During the night of July 7-8 the Second Coalition was formed. The new cabinet contained no Kadet ministers. According to the Mensheviks, it was still not a socialist government. The necessary "bourgeois" component was represented by I. N. Efremov, the leader of a small group of liberal radicals that had severed ties with the Kadets. The cabinet also included Tsereteli and Chernov. Kerensky was the Minister-President. The new government possessed "extraordinary powers," and its program was outlined in a watered-down version of the proposal that had brought about Prince Lvov's resignation. The new ministry had an ephemeral aura. Tsereteli's title was Temporary Minister of the Interior. The government reflected the ambitions of Kerensky and the impatience of Tsereteli with both the Kadets and the mobs in the streets. The public announcement about the new government came with the unhappy news that the German armies had inflicted a severe military defeat on the army of the Russian democracy. The signs of a brewing storm were facing the new temporary government, and things were going to get worse before they improved.

No sooner had the formation of the new cabinet been announced when fresh disturbances broke out on the streets of Petrograd, throwing the Provisional Government into confusion and forcing the Menshevik leaders in the Soviet to reexamine the July 8 agreement made with Kerensky. The exact cause of the second wave of disturbances is rather obscure, but it was different in many respects from the upheaval of July 4. The military element was not as great as it had been earlier, and the mobs bore a strong anti-semitic and anti-socialist character; they were quite destructive. There was no conspiracy connected to the disturbances, but the Soviet leaders were convinced that responsibility for the trouble could be traced to anti-socialist and anti-foreign groups, especially those known as the Black Hundreds. There is little doubt that those who participated in this second wave of disturbances were angered by the news of Russia's military defeat at the hands of the German army and by stories that linked Lenin to German espionage activities. The disturbances started on July 8 after the ominous calm that followed the regimental uprising and continued for almost a week. They stopped gradually.

The Mensheviks again placed the blame for starting the trouble at the feet of the Bolsheviks. The riotous activity was a sign of mass displeasure with the policies of the Soviet, according to *Rabochaia Gazeta*. It was induced by the Bolsheviks whose extremist acts had frightened many people to the mistaken conclusion that the revolution was evil. Lenin had foolishly unleashed the people of Russia who were politically immature and ignorant. He had touched the roots of "barbarism and *aziatchina* in Russia."[28] The failure of Lenin to recognize the important differences between the capitalist society of western Europe and the asiatic society of Russia again brought trouble to the revolution. "From the stone cast by the Bolsheviks into the turbulant sea of Philistinism now radiate wide pogromist and anti-semitic waves." Lenin succeeded in "setting the masses against the Soviet and against the socialists." According to the Mensheviks, the Bolsheviks had opened the door to the counterrevolution, the door the Mensheviks had kept locked by exercising caution and by maintaining some cooperation among liberals and socialists.[29]

The Menshevik leaders and their allies in the Petrograd Soviet dug in to meet this latest threat. Kerensky was again out of town, so the

effectiveness of the defense depended on the courage of the Mensheviks and their skill as journalists; there was little hope that the restless
regiments could be used to quell the disturbances. On July 11 *Rabochaia
Gazeta* carried one of its few banner lines of the year 1917: THE REVO-
LUTION IS IN DANGER. The eight page issue used almost every inch of
space, calling on all organized and enlightened forces "to form a united
front against the rising head of counterrevolution." All those in Petrograd who were not part of the "turbulent sea of Philistinism," "revolutionary organizations and enlightened workers and soldiers must give
vigorous rebuff to the pogrom agitation no matter where it occurs. All
efforts must be exerted to establish revolutionary order ...." Even the
Bolsheviks could be useful on this occasion, except troublemakers.
Everybody was called upon to support the July 8 government. The editors of *Den* stood beside *Rabochaia Gazeta* and *Izvestiia*, calling for an extra
effort from all those who were sympathetic to the goals of the revolution; Potresov even suggested that the services of the Kadets be
enlisted for the defense of the revolution.[30]

Like the earlier July riots the new wave of disturbances took place
only in Petrograd, but unlike the regimental uprising the mid-July riots
caused the political pendulum to swing to the right. The Mensheviks
knew that they had suffered a loss of political prestige during the riots
of mid-July and also realized that the stature of the Soviet of Workers'
and Soldiers' Deputies had been reduced considerably in the eyes of
the city population. The appearance of a mob that possessed a strong
anti-semitic direction was a serious blow to the Mensheviks, a great
many of whom came from Jewish backgrounds. In addition, the quickly
spreading rumors of Bolshevik treason damaged the reputation of the
Mensheviks and other Soviet leaders. Tsereteli, Dan and Chernov had
been identified by many Russians as advocates of a policy of compromise with the Germans, despite the efforts made by the Soviet in June
to assure the success of the military action at the front. Anger and
frustration accompanied the defeat of the Russian armies and the
news from Stavka about disorderly retreats by the so-called revolutionary army created terror among the population in areas near the
front. The Soviet now appeared to some people to be one of the causes
of this disaster and the anti-socialist newspapers in Petrograd fanned
the flames by blaming the Soviet leaders for creating all the turmoil.

Nobody was more aware of the Menshevik troubles and the setbacks
dealt to the Soviet during the mid-July riots than the Kadet party
leader Paul Miliukov. He did not instigate the acts of hoodlumism, as

some Menshevik Internationalists charged, but he was not nearly as upset nor as surprised as the Mensheviks. His first response was to capitalize on the anti-socialist atmosphere prevailing in Petrograd to regain political strength for the Kadets, just as the Mensheviks had capitalized on the anti-Kadet sentiments that prevailed during the July 4 uprising. Miliukov counterattacked and pushed the Soviet leaders onto the defensive.[31] He first blamed Soviet meddling in the affairs of the Provisional Government and the Mensheviks' general incompetence for bringing about the disorders of early July. He then pressed his advantage by explaining that the July 8 "deal" between Tsereteli and Kerensky was now totally unacceptable. The program of the new government was purely a socialist program, according to Miliukov, and he wanted no part of it; it could serve as neither the foundation nor the roof of any government in which he and his associates played a substantial part. If the mid-July riots now forced the Mensheviks to look for assistance from the Kadet party, Miliukov would insist that the July 8 declaration be critically edited and that the first duty of a new government would be to protect the frontier from the advancing German army. Miliukov would have pressed his advantage even further, but he had to deal with Kerensky as well as with the Soviet leaders.[32]

Kerensky travelled a great deal during the months of June and July, especially between the front lines and the city of Petrograd, but he returned quickly when his presence in the city appeared essential for his own gain. He returned from a visit to the front on July 14 and immediately opened private discussions with Miliukov. Both men were ready to make a compromise, despite Miliukov's personal animosity toward the popular hero. Kerensky recognized, as did Miliukov, that a compromise between them was essential if the revolution was to be protected from anarchy and the centrifugal forces that had played such havoc in the last month. Both men apparently agreed that yet another government should be formed (as quickly as possible) and that it be free of direct Soviet control. They also agreed, however, that it should contain cabinet ministers from both the Soviet of Workers' and Soldiers' Deputies and the Kadet party. It was clear that Kerensky would occupy the most important post in the new government and that Miliukov would not participate directly; Chernov was to be excluded because of his devotion to a rapid and radical land reform. The agreement was satisfactory to Kerensky who maintained his position as Minister-President of the Provisional Government and to Miliukov who could now counterbalance the power of the Soviet. The agreement set the stage for a reduction of Soviet influence within the Provisional Government, but its successful execution still depended on the cooperation of the Menshevik and Social Revolutionary leaders in the Soviet.

The mid-July disorders had forced the Mensheviks and their close allies into a corner, but they were as yet in no mood to compromise with the Miliukov-Kerensky combination. The survival of the February revolution now depended on reaching an agreement with the Kadets, but the Petrograd Menshevik organization served notice that none of Miliukov's latest demands would be met. When the city newspapers speculated that the latest crisis would force the Soviet leaders into a retreat, *Izvestiia* denounced the reports as falsehoods: "Minister of the Interior I. G. Tsereteli has categorically declared that the city newspapers ... are engaged in irresponsible activity."[33] The Social Revolutionaries who were close to the Mensheviks also joined in the assault, insisting that the Kadet agitation against Victor Chernov and his land reform program would not bring about the dismissal of this well known agrarian socialist. It seemed that most Mensheviks and their allies were ready to fight to the end. "If the representatives of the bourgeoisie block the way, brush them aside—at least do not yield to their position. Retreat not one step—hold your ground."[34] They still intended to avoid Lenin's solution to the problem of state power (seizing all control and establishing a Soviet government), but they still hoped to arrange an agreement that excluded the Kadets. The Mensheviks could again use "that narrow strata of the bourgeoisie willing to walk the path of the revolutionary democracy." *Rabochaia Gazeta* sugested that I. N. Efremov, A. A. Baryshinkov and other non-socialist radicals were still available to fill in the bourgeois complement in the cabinet.[35]

The determination of the Mensheviks and other Soviet leaders to stand against the tide seemed particularly strong, because the Menshevik Internationalists now launched their first all-out propaganda offensive against the Kadets. The Menshevik Internationalist resistance to Miliukov was vicious and implacable; at one point early in July, Martov even called for a temporary Soviet seizure of state power. In the opinion of the Menshevik Internationalists, the Kadets were not only indirectly responsible for the troubles that faced the Soviet, but they had ignited the fiery anti-semitic uprising of July 8 in order to force the Soviet into capitulation. In two articles published on July 16 and July 18, Martov urged that every effort be made by the Soviet to eliminate the Kadets from the Provisional Government, and he even hinted that their arrest would be a progressive step. According to Martov, "all strata of the bourgeoisie were now incapable of participating in the further development of the revolution," and Martov was becoming suspicious of many of his own comrades in the Menshevik party. The troubled situation in Petrograd called for a government similar to the Committee of Public Safety that ruled in Paris under Robespierre in 1793 and 1794. The new government should be made up of representatives from all groups, organizations and political parties that were sympathetic to the Soviet. Hastily constructed and designed only for temporary use, the new government would restore a balance of authority in Petrograd more favorable to the revolutionary forces. Once the Kadet counterrevolution had been forced into retreat, the temporary government, or committee, would be replaced by a government more in keeping with the traditional political alliance favored by the Mensheviks.[30] Martov took pains to explain the differences between his plan and Lenin's demands for a permanent Soviet government, but on this point Martov now separated himself from the core of Menshevik opinion and tradition.

c) The Mensheviks "Compromise" a Second Time

For a short time, the jacobinism of the Menshevik Internationalists, and especially of Martov, made the anti-Miliukov efforts appear quite ferocious, but it was questionable how long the moderate socialists in Petrograd could reject a compromise and exclude Miliukov. The Soviet was on the defensive. Its leaders had been frightened by the second wave of riots, fearful that the "barbarism" of *aziatchina* was on the verge of upsetting their carefully laid plans. A Soviet government or a Soviet dominated committee of public safety that pretended to incorporate Russia's political liberals was not going to work; it was now opposed by the Bolsheviks as well as the Kadets and it would have been obeyed by nobody, except perhaps Martov.

Once again inspired by the conviction that a socialist regime could not create a democratic society in Russia, the Soviet leaders began to subdue their anti-Kadet spirits. Even the combative resolution released by the Organization Committee of the Menshevik party on July 18 showed clear signs of compromise. The resolution began on the customary frantic note, pointing to the "dark cloud of counterrevolution" and to "certain bourgeois circles" that were taking advantage of the temporary setback in the fortunes of the Soviet, but it concluded by calling for a new coalition government. The fiery rhetoric was typical of Menshevik and Soviet announcements during 1917, but the document made no insulting statements about Miliukov and did not expressly exclude the Kadets as potential partners in a new coalition government. It was signed by most of the party leaders who had been elected at the May Menshevik Conference and its appearance indicated that the great body of Mensheviks had turned away from Martov as well as Lenin.

As the readiness to compromise became more obvious, the Mensheviks began to make sharp criticisms of Martov's views. Of course, many right-wing Mensheviks had opposed Martov since May and had been hostile to him throughout July. On July 16, Potresov rejected Martov as a dangerous agitator and leader of a fringe element in the party. He criticized the Menshevik Internationalists' program as being too heavily influenced by Lenin and urged his comrades to come to terms with the Kadets;[37] of course, Plekhanov rejected the Menshevik Internationalists. In the latter days of July, however, the rejection of Martov became stronger even among the party leaders aroung Tsereteli. The July 16 meeting of the Petrograd City Menshevik organization (a center of Internationalist sympathy) rejected Martov's resolution to establish a Soviet government, and by July 18 the criticism of Martov in the official party newspaper was commonplace. Ivan Kubikov actually criticized Martov for abandoning the entire Menshevik concept of the Russian bourgeois revolution. Kubikov cleverly compared Martov's typically Menshevik approach to Russian politics during the revolution of 1905 to his near Leninism of 1917. Why had Martov denounced Lenin in 1905, Kubikov asked, but adopted views quite similar to those held by the Bolshevik leader in 1917?[38]

By July 20 the Menshevik resistance to Kadet presence in a new government had crumbled, but an agreement between the Kadets and the Soviet was still far from view. The Soviet flirtation with bourgeois democracy without the bourgeoisie had ended, at least temporarily, but the problem of achieving harmony and political stability in Petrograd was yet unsolved. There were some encouraging signs, but not enough. Both parties realized that leadership of the revolution had slipped from their grasp in early July, but neither protagonist was willing to surrender much ground in order to recapture the initiative.

Miliukov was ready to yield to the extent of accepting Kerensky, a socialist, as the head of the Provisional Government, while the Mensheviks were ready to cooperate by isolating that body of Soviet opinion that was flirting with Leninism. But the two camps could come no closer together. Each one wanted to retain the upper hand in the new government, and the Mensheviks wanted to retain it without serving in the cabinet. Another impasse seemed to be in the making and yet another crisis when Kerensky's shrewdness and verve saved the day.

On July 21 Kerensky resigned. He withdrew his belongings from his office and wrote a dramatic letter of resignation that was equal in scope to the tension generated in Petrograd by the action of July. Of course, nobody really thought that Kerensky had quit once and for all, but everybody realized that his feigned resignation could easily rekindle the flame of anarchy and revolt. The only alternative now available was for all moderate parties in the liberal and socialist camps to reach an agreement during a face to face confrontation. Kerensky's "resignation" forced the Soviet and the so-called bourgeois leaders to meet and remain together until a political compromise could be found. A meeting was called immediately and it took place in the Malachite Hall of the Winter Palace.

During the tense gathering a number of proposals were put forth by both sides and were quickly rejected for one reason or another. Then Nekrasov spoke to the assembly. He presented a formula that really contained nothing new, nor did it come as a surprise to the men gathered at the Palace, but it seemed likely to meet with less resistance than those suggested earlier in the evening. Nekrasov opened his monologue with remarks that were designed to establish Kerensky's leadership by placing both the liberals and the socialists on the defensive. First he scolded the Soviet for hindering the work of past governments by maintaining too close a surveillance over the socialist representatives in the cabinet and by trying to make the socialist ministers into extensions of the Soviet authority. How could ministers work fearlessly as representatives of all the Russian people if such harassing techniques continued? In the future, the Soviet would have to leave government leaders with a free hand. Nekrasov then enveloped the right flank by suggesting that the socialist tinged July 8 declaration serve as the basis of the new government. Troubled times had come to the revolution, he reminded the meeting, and a strong appeal had to be made to the masses through just such a declaration. Once the future government's independence from both the Soviet and the

Kadets was established, he struck at the heart of the so-called compromise.

Nekrasov announced that Kerensky, free from the restrictions of all groups, institutions and parties, should form a new cabinet consisting of men selected from every important political faction. Kerensky, the Minister-President of the new government, would hold wide powers that enabled him to act with dispatch in the event of emergencies. He would also enjoy the public support of both the Soviet and the Kadet party. The Soviet would not interfere with the work of the new government under any circumstances, but both the Soviet of Workers' and Soldiers' Deputies and the Kadet party would have the right to recall any of their representatives that Kerensky had selected for his cabinet.

Nekrasov's scheme was acceptable to both sides, at least temporarily. Miliukov was ready to accept Kerensky as the head of a new Provisional Government, and the Menshevik leaders in the Soviet realized that a coalition led by Kerensky was the best bargain they could strike at the time. M. M. Vinaver accepted the compromise of Nekrasov in the name of the Party of the Peoples' Freedom, promising that the Kadets would work with the new government if V. M. Chernov was excluded from the cabinet. Tsereteli agreed to the settlement on behalf of the Soviet of Workers' and Soldiers' Deputies and on behalf of the socialist parties, the Bolsheviks and Menshevik Internationalists excepted. At 6 a.m. on July 22, 1917, the conference was adjourned, and the delegates departed for home. That morning Kerensky withdrew his resignation and the Russians were well on their way to installing the fifth government that ruled in Petrograd in the year 1917.

When the cabinet was finally chosen on July 24 it held four Kadets, a majority of socialists and the liberal "progressives" Nekrasov, Tereshchenko and Efremov. Tsereteli refused to participate, preferring to remain only as the leader of the Soviet but M. I. Skobelev accepted the post of Minister of Labor. The new government did include V. M. Chernov as the Minister of Agriculture, but his presence did not please the Kadets. It was called the Government to Save the Revolution, or as Sukhanov less enthusiastically wrote, the Third Coalition. In any case, it was the instrument of Alexander Kerensky. Both the Mensheviks and the Kadets let him take the initiative. He could appoint and remove ministers at will, and he occupied the offices of Minister of War and of the Navy as well as the post of Minister-President. The longevity of the new government, however, depended on more than the skill of Kerensky. It could live only as long as the Kadets and the Mensheviks worked together.

The Mensheviks promised to support the new government, but their attitudes were as ambiguous as they had been at the formation of the first coalition. Official statements were quite encouraging. A *Rabochaia Gazeta* editorial praised the work of Kerensky and expressed hope in the future of Russia under the leadership of the July coalition. Obviously influenced by Tsereteli, the writer declared that "Neither the revolutionary democracy without the propertied classes nor the propertied classes without the revolutionary democracy are able to take power into their hands and save the country from ruin." *Rabochaia Gazeta* even reserved its strongest criticism for the extremists in Russian politics, the Bolsheviks and Black Hundreds who had "opened a campaign to undermine the Government."[39] But just below the smooth surface of official acceptance the innuendoes, accusations and bitterness told a very different story. Before the negotiations of July 21, the Mensheviks let it be known that no bourgeois government would meet with their absolute approval, especially if it included a place for the Kadet leaders. Their hostility toward Miliukov and his followers was frozen solid, making chances for future cooperation with the Kadets very slim indeed. The "bourgeoisie" could expect only criticism and opposition from the Mensheviks and the Soviet. Even Tsereteli cautioned Miliukov and told him to expect no change in the attitude of many Mensheviks. Nor were Miliukov and the Kadets the only political figures to draw the hostility of the Mensheviks. Kerensky was also suspected of unproletarian designs, and the Mensheviks were determined to remain skeptical in their dealings with him. "Was it a stroke of good fortune to have A. F. Kerensky form a new coalition ministry? We are not so sure." The Mensheviks were not prepared to extend the hand of friendship to this "Napoleonic figure."[40]

This contradictory stance toward the Kadets and the Provisional Government was certainly not a new development. It was exactly where the Mensheviks stood in late April and in early May when Lvov offered cabinet positions to the Soviet leaders, and it was precisely where the Mensheviks had stood in their traditional arguments against Russia's liberals since the early twentieth century. In April and May Tsereteli agreed with his comrades that the revolution was in danger and that something more than conditional support of the "bourgeois" government was required of the Soviet. In late July they reached the same conclusions, but their long-lived hostility toward the so-called bourgeoisie made it unlikely that the third coalition government would enjoy any more success than the first coalition; cooperation with liberals was possible, as far as the Mensheviks were concerned, but only in its abstract form. The Mensheviks accepted a coalition settlement, reminded in mid-July of Russia's "semi-asiatic" state, but accepting a new coalition government did not guarantee that a period of cooperation would now begin between the Soviet and the non-socialist ministers in the cabinet.

Unfortunately, the situation prevailing in Petrograd at the end of July was a good deal more delicate than had been the case at the end of April. In the spring of 1917 the revolution was still very much in the hands of the leaders of the Provisional Government and the confidence of the Soviet leaders was unshaken. But in late July another story had to be told. Russia was not yet in a state of upheaval, but the signs were not encouraging. The national minorities were restless; their leaders were not addicted to visions of all-Russian unity and were now ready to exploit any unstable situation that arose in Petrograd. The Russian army was beginning to disintegrate, and already a good part of it was beyond restoration. The active population in the capital city that had given its support to the revolution at the end of February was no longer reliable. Whatever hope of success still glimmered for the February revolution now depended on close harmony prevailing between the Soviet and the Provisional Government, between the Kadets and the Mensheviks. The chances that a Kerensky government could avoid a destructive civil war and beat back a *coup d'etat* by extreme groups rested in the ability of the strongest leaders in Petrograd to work together. Domestic reform was also in order, but it could not be carried out unless the Mensheviks and the Kadets worked together.

A study of July 1917 in Petrograd would not be completed without reviewing Lenin's class interpretation of the events. In *Three Crises* Lenin quickly summarized his view of the July riots. According to the Bolshevik leader, the riots were a spontaneous act on the part of the "proletariat" that had grown dissatisfied with the policies of the Provisional Government. But recognizing this sudden outburst on the part of the proletariat in July, the forces of the "bourgeois" counterrevolution rapidly counterattacked, crippling the efforts of the masses and causing Russia to be sharply divided into two great warring camps: the revolutionary and the counterrevolutionary. The middle "elements," those hapless Mensheviks, had now disappeared, at least for the time being, according to Lenin. To illustrate this phenomenon, Lenin introduced the wave theory. The July crisis "appeared in waves," Lenin wrote, "a sudden fall following a rapid rise, revolution and counterrevolution becoming acute with the middle elements being 'washed out' for a more or less prolonged period of time."

Following the riots, Lenin continued in *On the Political Situation*, Petrograd and Russia fell into the hands of the counterrevolution, organized and led by the Kadets, the army (Kerensky and Kornilov) and the Black Hundreds. The Mensheviks handed over state power to these groups "definitely betraying the cause of the revolution by placing it in the hands of the counterrevolution ..." Concluding his analysis, Lenin stated that "All hopes for a peaceful development of the Russian revolution have definitely vanished," and that the slogan of transferring power to the Soviet was "no longer correct" since the Soviet was now in the hands of the counterrevolution. He urged his followers "to struggle" against the counterrevolution (*On Slogans*) and to harbor no "peaceful illusions" about the final outcome of the revolution now that the cause had been betrayed and its followers forced to resort to illegal means.[41]

In July the differences between Lenin and the Mensheviks came out in bold relief, more clearly perhaps than at any time since 1903; this point has not been realized by many historians, although it was fully appreciated by Lenin. Early in the century, the Mensheviks made a covenant among themselves that included a stipulation to work with Russian liberals during the revolutionary period. If socialists tried to walk an independent path the democratic bourgeois revolution would be doomed. The troubles that occurred in early July shook the Mensheviks and they were tempted to abandon the Kadets, Russia's chief organized liberal political party. In control of the Petrograd Soviet, the Mensheviks tried for a short time to operate in a unilateral manner, retaining the liberals only as an abstraction. But the turbulence of mid-July drove them back toward the Kadets and a renewal of the covenant. They found themselves unable to abandon the Kadets, because traditional strategy and ideas governed their political actions: the democratic bourgeois regime in semi-asiatic Russia required the support of the liberals. It was true that an anti-liberal bias was tugging the Mensheviks to the left and preventing them from ever cooperating fully with the Provisional Government, but it was not strong enough to bring the Soviet into Lenin's camp, so the tactics of Plekhanov and Axelrod prevailed. Lenin, on the other hand, had long ago branded all cooperation with the "bourgeoisie" as treason to the revolutionary cause in Russia. He sought political isolation, and strove to secure allies only in abstract forms. Only those thinkers and revolutionary politicians who walked his path were correct, and he even criticized the demonstrators in early July for their failure to understand his plans with sufficient clarity.

After the renewal of the coalition in late July, Lenin realized that the Mensheviks would never be brought to accept his views, so he was determined to destroy them once and for all. The July announcements made his intentions very clear. He may have misunderstood or deliberately distorted the position of the Mensheviks between April and July, but not after July. After the formation of the third coalition, he knew the state would not fall to the "proletariat" unless a conspiracy of trusted revolutionaries seized command. The Mensheviks would not seize control of the government and invite Lenin to rule Russia, nor would they establish a Soviet government that excluded liberals. Lenin stood alone among Russian socialists and, in fact, the destruction of the Soviet leaders now became his first order of business. As he stated the case, the so-called peaceful period of the revolution had come to an end.

Current Soviet historians follow Lenin to the letter in their interpretations of the events of July 1917. Znamensky stated that following the July riots "It was necessary to reorganize for agitational work, to relieve the masses from the illusion of a peaceful 'constitutional' path of revolutionary development." He restated Lenin's July argument in various ways, actually quoting *Three Crises, On the Political Situation* and *On Slogans*, which embody the master's thought on the subject.[42] In a recent review of Znamensky's work a student of the Russian revolution from the west called the Znamensky hypothesis "the current Soviet concept of the peaceful development of the revolution," and throughout the review implied that the work was a change from an earlier position held by Soviet writers. But Znamensky drew Lenin's conclusions as did those dominated by "Stalinist historiography."[43] Many students in the west, so anxious to find change in Soviet historiography, often see change where there had been continuity.

Chapter VI
August

a) Kerensky and the Moscow State Conference

In the four short weeks that passed between the foundation of the third coalition and its dissolution, Kerensky did everything that could have been reasonably expected to strengthen the Provisional Government. He tried to gain the support of all political groups in Petrograd and to establish close contact with cultural and commercial institutions whose leaders showed inclinations of loyalty to the principles of the February revolution.[1] He issued orders designed to restore discipline in the army, a near impossible task, and clearly emphasized to his revolutionary comrades the dangers they faced from fiscal problems and production decline. Kerensky's political strategy at this time was not very different from the one the Mensheviks purported to use themselves. The Minister-President tried to unite all liberals and socialists who wanted to protect the revolution. Nor were Kerensky's efforts in August hopeless. There is certainly no warrent to conclude that his government would have fallen without the crushing blow it received after the intrigue involving General Kornilov.

On the other hand, Kerensky faced formidable obstacles. Beside the severe economic problems that faced his government, the stubbornness of the Kadets and the Soviet leaders stood ready to undo his efforts. Neither group was prepared to work enthusiastically with the other, and now serious signs of division were beginning to appear inside the Soviet camp. To make matters worse, Kerensky himself was not altogether above suspicion; in fact, he may have been his own greatest enemy. He was not entirely trusted by those he wished to use for the good of the new commonwealth. The Kadets cautioned the Minister-President in early August about his readiness to rely on administrative arrest and banishment without trial. These measures were used by the old regime, *Rech* reminded Kerensky, and should not be revived by the revolutionary government unless absolutely necessary for the protection of society from criminals.[2] Then, Kerensky's appointment of General Kornilov as head of the army brought fear to the hearts of the Soviet leaders who were always ready to believe that the new Minister-President secretly wished to don the mantle of a despot. But Kerensky, like Lenin, was not to be deterred by signs of unpopularity from liberal and socialist quarters, and he went forward with his plans.

The biggest step taken by Kerensky to strengthen the government and revive a spirit of confidence was to convene the Moscow State Conference, a gathering of delegates that supposedly represented all groups, institutions and committees friendly to the February revolution. His objective was to bring under one roof "all live forces," as Kerensky liked to call them, in the hope that a collective effort could be organized to grapple with some of the problems facing the revolution. The notion of holding such a meeting as a kind of preliminary Constituent Assembly had been in the air since early July and Kerensky tried to capitalize on it for his own advantage.

Oddly enough, many of those socialists and liberals who were initially in favor of a solidarity meeting greeted Kerensky's invitation with reservation. The Kadets were lukewarm. One of the biggest problems facing the revolution, according to *Rech*, was its disunity and the lack of cooperation among its leaders. Unless Kerensky's conference in Moscow could overcome these difficulties, it could easily make matters worse. The Kadets expressed a willingness to attend the conference, and some of them seemed optimistic, but skepticism dominated the non-socialist camp.[3] The Soviet leaders were no more enthusiastic than the Kadets, and the Mensheviks in particular seemed quite bored with the project. "So," sighed *Rabochaia Gazeta*, "all organized society is going to meet and discuss questions of support for the new government and safety for the country and the revolution." Well, we will attend, the Mensheviks assured their readers, but only to make certain that the Soviet opinion is correctly represented. Very little in the way of positive results was anticipated.[4]

The Moscow State Conference opened on August 12 just as one might have expected. The differences between the Kadets and the Soviet leaders were as strong as ever with Kerensky trying to minimize the significance of this savage competition by drawing attention to himself and to the practical problems that had been placing increasing pressure on the revolutionary leaders. The Minister-President sought to dominate the center of the stage in the hope that the Provisional Government might finally become a rallying point, and his ministers badgered the squabbling party leaders with economic and labor proposals that would require their mutual cooperation for effective implementation. Some Kadets and some right-wing socialists seemed friendly toward Kerensky, which might serve as evidence of the general rightward swing of the Provisional Government, but in general the conference was divided into two camps with the Minister-President and his close followers appearing to stand in between.[5] Kerensky opened the sessions with a dramatic speech describing the troubles that lay ahead and explaining the aggressive role he intended to play in the work "to save the revolution." Once he set the stage, however, he left to others in his cabinet the task of unravelling the details.[6]

Perhaps the most important issue brought before the Conference dealt with the scarcity and high prices of bread. Soon after the war began, the imperial government anticipated the shortages that were bound to occur and regulated both the domestic sale of grain and the production of flour. Through the State Duma and by imperial edict a series of committees were created and rules enacted that gave to the Ministry of Agriculture the power to establish what became known as the bread monopoly.[7] As the demands of war became increasingly burdensome, however, most government officials realized that the scope of the monopoly had to be extended. Inadequate means of determining exactly how much grain Russia produced and the growing feebleness of transportation facilities prevented a close enforcement of the regulations. Shortages became more pronounced as time passed, and peasant resistance made it clear that a more thorough system needed to be devised.

When the revolution took power in February of 1917, its leaders faced the same problem of grain shortages that had confronted the officials of the imperial government, and they attacked it in much the same manner. It was true that some members of the Kadet party were altogether opposed to the bread monopoly on the grounds that following the free flow of unrestricted trade would lead the new government out of the mess, but most of the liberals agreed that the controls used by the monopoly had to continue and in some cases be made more stringent. The law of March 25, 1917 reflected the new thinking. It created more bureaucratic machinery to administer the operation. It also extended tight regulations over the peasant producers and over some distributers by prohibiting the use of grain as a mortgage or an interest payment. At the Moscow State Conference, S. N. Prokopovich, Kerensky's Minister of Trade and Industry, who had no party affiliation, called for an acceleration of the trend set by the government earlier in the year and asked for a major increase in the scope of the bread monopoly. He rejected the recommendation that widescale requisition of grain could bring fruitful results, but urged the delegates at the Conference to cooperate with Kerensky in his efforts to strengthen further the government's control over supply and prices. Only then, according to Prokopovich, could Petrograd and the army maintain a lifeline to the great agricultural resources of Russia and keep the revolution from starving and falling into the hands of its enemies.[8]

The thinking of the Petrograd Soviet about the controls over flour and grain was generally similar to that of Kerensky, but its approach to administration was quite different. The Soviet leaders agreed that a tighter supervision of grain mill owners must be exercised both to prevent bread prices from rising and to ensure a steady flow of grain to the cities and the army; in fact the Mensheviks had been quite outspoken in demands for legislation along these lines since March.[9] The basic difference between the Soviet and Kerensky arose over the question who was to administer the government grain monopoly. The Soviet demanded that its selected representatives assist in running the control machinery. On the government State Supply Committee, where policy was made and inspectors appointed, the Soviet wanted its officials to preside or to at least share in the decision making. The Soviet had formed its own economic council in the spring of 1917, led by the Mensheviks V. G. Groman and F. A. Cherevanin, and it had been trying to gain recognition as an equal partner with the committees appointed by the Provisional Government; in the field of economic relations the Soviet was not shy about taking up the post of watchdog, and throughout 1917 it actually sought to make policy in areas where shortages and high prices were causing worry among the population.[10] Chkheidze left no doubt about Soviet feelings during his speech at the Moscow State Conference: "Only the large-scale participation of democratic organizations can assure that this control over production ... will serve the true interest of the country ..."[11]

The motives behind Chkheidze and his comrades rested in fears that the Kadets were protecting the profits collected by the "landlords" and "industrialists" who were to blame for the shortages and high prices. The Menshevik newspapers *Rabochaia Gazeta, Novaia Zhizn, Vpered,* and *Den* developed this theme in discussions about the production and distribution of grain, sugar, fuel, meat and salt. Since early spring they had tried to install Soviet officials on all the government committees charged with the task of supervising and ordering trade and commerce.

The "bourgeoisie" could not be trusted.[12] The rising price of grain had brought on a battle between the Soviet leaders and the Kadets, and it was almost as disruptive as the one waged over foreign policy.

Historians writing today in the Soviet Union have discussed the issue of bread production; western historians have almost completely ignored the economic aspects of the revolution save for a few scattered remarks of a highly speculative nature. The contemporary Soviet argument will not come as a surprise to those who are familiar with the historiography of 1917. Greater government control over both production and distribution was necessary, but even this control would be ineffective unless the government itself was transferred into the hands of "the people." In his heavily documented account of the economic politics of 1917, P. V. Volobuev used first the arguments of the Mensheviks, charging that the banks and "the propertied classes" controlled the supply of grain and used it as a political weapon against the masses and the revolution. He then blamed the Mensheviks for allowing this situation to continue. It was the leaders of the Petrograd Soviet, according to Volobuev and also B. M. Freidlin, who were responsible for the chaos because they were insufficiently aggressive in their demands on the bourgeois Provisional Government;[13] Volobuev made no mention of the abysmal failure of the grain supply policies that helped bring the young Communist government to the brink of extinction in 1921.

Next to the grain shortages on the long list of practical economic problems that faced the Provisional Government, the inadequacy of the railroad system stood out prominently, and here again the revolutionary government inherited a burden from the past. Russia's railroad network was not as mature as those constructed in western Europe, considering the enormous distances that had to be travelled. The war had put an inordinate strain on all European railroad systems, but the technically superior industry of Germany, France and England could endure losses where the Russians could not. Soon after the outbreak of the war, many overworked steam locomotives and much rolling stock were in need of repairs that were not easily made; spare parts and skilled mechanics were in short supply and often minor damages would incapacitate an otherwise good locomotive for an indefinite period of time. As a result, the flow of supplies began to dwindle and material often had to be stored in areas where it could not be used. The reduced flow of supplies, especially fuels and metals, further aggravated the railroad problem because these products were essential to power the engines and manufacture new machines.[14] The imperial government tried to alleviate the difficulty by increasing the use of water transportation and by importing machinery from its allies, but these measures only slowed the steady pace of decline.

When the Kadets took power in February they followed the same measures used by the imperial government and also tried to expand the scope of bureaucratic supervision over the private industries connected to rail transportation. But the Provisional Government was not prepared to tighten control over such a vast operation in the midst of revolutionary conditions without the close cooperation of labor and management, both of whom were reluctant to cooperate and quite unable to tap all their own resources. Independent industrialists were usually willing to accept government supervision only so long as they maintained a voice in the administration of their particular sphere of the operation, and the Petrograd Soviet refused to call on support of labor unless the socialist leaders shared in the overall supervision of the lines; there was also some question as to how closely the railroad workers would follow the Soviet lead on this issue, even though this sector of the working force seemed loyal to Soviet leadership.[15] Some leaders in the Provisional Government tried to separate the Soviet from the railroad workers, even before the rise of Kerensky, by appealing directly to the various worker organizations on the railroad lines. But the workers were badly divided among themselves and little serious attention was paid to the Nekrasov circular issued by the government on May 29. Its attempt to persuade workers to support the government brought insignificant results.[16]

By August the transportation tangle in Russia had reached menacing proportions, and Prokopovich was reduced to pleading. He asked that workers, industrialists and the Soviet leaders cooperate with the Provisional Government and give Kerensky the power to use the rails when he felt it was necessary for the protection of the government.[17]

The anarchic state of the industrial labor force pervaded all the issues that arose during the Moscow State Conference, and it was also discussed by the delegates as a separate problem. The factory workers throughout Russia were restless even before the revolution, and had played a major role in the overthrow of the Romanov family. Unfortunately, the political freedom brought in February was not accompanied by an alleviation of either economic woes or severe working conditions. Groups of strikers were quickly disappointed when their demands (openly voiced and at times willingly met by management) failed to achieve economic stability. Discontent mounted and was expressed in various ways, and by early summer incidents of criminal activity were occurring with increasing frequency. Extreme measures taken by some workers were followed by lockouts and soon the Russian industrial system was threatened by utter chaos. At the Moscow State Conference, Prokopovich appealed to the Soviet for help in the task of bringing the labor force under control, and he went so far as to ask its approval of a plan for the conscription of labor into state service. He balanced this and other proposals for strict measures with promises that Kerensky would gradually institute a series of political reforms designed to protect the health of the workers and the freedom of worker councils to engage in collective bargaining.[18]

The Soviet response to Prokopovich was not unsympathetic, but an understanding of its significance requires a further explanation of the fickle character of Russian labor in 1917. The new organizations and committees that sprung up to represent the Russian worker were not subject to Soviet authority. Most of the industrial force in Petrograd and Moscow supported the Petrograd Soviet (at least until the autumn of 1917), but this loyalty was not disciplined and not subject to discipline. At any moment the wishes of political leaders might be brushed aside by workers determined to act independently on a whim or as a result of a rumor. The Executive Committee lectured to its turbulent supporters but the Mensheviks and Social Revolutionaries were intellectuals and quite without means of coercion. Furthermore, the factory committee movement appeared for the first time in 1917, and it was even less inclined to follow Soviet leadership. It was made up of small groups that formed in each individual factory rather than among the various crafts and professions. It was usually sympathetic to Bolshevik views and became the center of the most radical worker criticism of the government.[19] By the late summer of 1917 the influence of the Petrograd Soviet was weak among the factory committees and was even showing signs of faltering among the less radical trade unions.

The Mensheviks themselves further complicated the situation by taking what many less sophisticated citizens must have interpreted as an ambiguous approach to industrial relations. When the revolution first broke out the Menshevik leaders encouraged workers to press their demands against factors owners. Improvements were needed in general working conditions and organized and conscious labor was supposed to serve as a bulwark against efforts to restore the old sys-

tem of bondage. The Mensheviks denounced factory owners and officials who tried to restrict the growth of labor unions; in some respects
Rabochaia Gazeta read like an anarchist journal during the early weeks of
the revolution.[20] At the same time, however, the Mensheviks had set
limits to proletarian ambitions and the restrictions became increasingly
clear in the weeks following the July uprising. While encouraging
working people to organize and show no fear in making demands
against employers, they reminded laborers that the ownership of the
industrial system must remain in the hands of the government and
private employers and that the production of goods must not come to
a halt. Strikes, yes, but under no circumstances were local soviets,
trade unions or factory committees to expect the cure for economic ills
to rest in the seizure of factories. This was Bolshevism and a fatal
mistake that would destroy the bourgeois revolution. As the revolution deepened in the spring and the summer of 1917, the Mensheviks
shifted the emphasis in their propaganda from energetic support for
worker demands to grim warnings of the dire consequences that
awaited the revolution if labor pushed against management too hard.
At the second Petrograd conference of Factory Committees held at
Smolny under the auspices of the Bolsheviks, the Menshevik econo-
mist Cherevanin repudiated the assertion that only worker control of
the factories could save the revolution. The worker seizure of factories
would bring the same results as a Soviet seizure of state power and he
warned against proletarian domination of the industrial system.[21]

When Chkheidze responded to Prokopovich in Moscow he was well
aware of the difficulties facing the government and equally aware of
the weakening grip the Petrograd Soviet held on the labor force. But
at the same time he knew the obligations the Mensheviks had imposed
on themselves and were now determined to carry out among the
working classes. His speech seemed to be an exercise in resolving his
own difficulties, at least at the theoretical level. He agreed that worker
demands for higher wages should be carefully limited, and that the
overall decisions about the direction of the economy should remain in
the hands of the government. He also agreed that the conscription of
workers by the state might be necessary to save the industrial system
from its present state of chaos. But he denounced employers who
might deliberately ignore worker organizations and he demanded that
both representatives of labor and the Soviet participate in the official
committees charged with the responsibility of restoring harmony in
industrial relations. Chkheidze was apparently aiming at some of the

same objects as Kerensky and seemed willing to help the government employ stricter supervision than it had been able to do since February, but he stood firm in the conviction that the organized labor movement and the Petrograd Soviet must share in the direction of reform projects.[22]

One source of the economic hardships endured by Russians in 1917 was the near bankruptcy of the government's treasury, and it was left to the unpopular N. V. Nekrasov, Kerensky's Minister of Finance, to inform the delegates at the Moscow State Conference just how grave the situation had become. Drains on the money reserve through higher wages and military expenditures plus the inability to collect tax obligations had brought the level of available cash to a dangerously low point. If the money losses continued to accelerate at this rate, the government would soon be unable to guarantee the value of a single kopek.

Serious difficulty came to the Russian treasury as a result of the high expenses directly or indirectly connected to the war effort, but the revolution made matters much worse. A great financial strain was placed on the imperial treasury as early as 1915 when Russia found itself forced to mortgage gold in western Europe in order to meet obligations.[23] But the gold store was limited and the French and English allies were also pressed financially by the war. The tsar's government had to find other sources of income in order to remain solvent. It succeeded, but only after imposing austerity measures in most sectors of the domestic economy and by securing credit abroad on expensive terms.[24] Unfortunately, the Provisional Government was unable to do as well. The tax collecting machinery in Russia became less efficient after the overthrow of the Romanovs and foreign banks became skeptical of Russia's future, making them unavailable as lucrative sources of support. At the same time, the drain of financial resources out of the treasury continued and grew to enormous proportions throughout 1917. The leaders of the Provisional Government made a valiant effort to stem the tide. They were able to borrow some money abroad. They also increased taxes and took full advantage of the fiscal benefits gleaned through the increased supervision of the food and fuel monopolies. They also floated a domestic loan. But these measures were not nearly enough to match the growing list of expenses. The monopolies soon yielded only enough revenue to keep their expanded operations intact, taxes could be gathered only haphazardly, and the Liberty Loan gained only lukewarm support once the intensive drive for supporters cooled down in the late spring. To make matters worse, foreign credit became unavailable as soon as the significance of the internal political squabble between the Kadets and the Mensheviks became widely understood in the west.[25] The darkening picture was visible all too easily during the summer of 1917 as paper money made its appearance in increasing quantity but at decreasing value.

Nekrasov said as much as he could say on the subject of finance without doing injury to the pride of any one party at the Moscow State Conference. The gravity of the problem was obvious and he promised to attack it by intensifying the government's campaign to secure foreign credit, holding down wages and increasing taxes. The implications of his plan were quite clear. The freezing of wages would place pressure on the Soviet leaders to quiet the workers, while the tax policy would supposedly extract its greatest toll from whose who owned property. Nekrasov also announced plans to strengthen even further the government's hand over the monopolies, but that procedure was part of a trend toward centralization and would meet with little resistance. Throughout his address, Nekrasov blamed the war and tsarist management for the mess facing the revolutionaries in August of 1917, despite the fact that his report showed that the bickering between the Soviet and the Kadets had been responsible for much of the trouble. He completed his address with a plea for cooperation. He asked for public order and further sacrifice from all Russians.[26]

The Soviet response to Nekrasov was not hostile, but Chkheidze did issue a qualifying note: the representatives of the "revolutionary democracy" would have to approve each new step in financial arrangements as they were taken. Speaking on behalf of the Executive Committee, the Georgian Menshevik endorsed the program designed to secure funds from abroad and certainly did not oppose measures to strengthen the hand of the government in its efforts to raise money at home. He was even willing to let Kerensky exercise tight control over workers' wages and to raise taxes on commodities used for mass consumption. But none of these steps should be taken without the consent of the Soviet and its inspection of the operations once they commenced.[27] Thus, Chkheidze's reply to Nekrasov, like his reply to Prokopovich, was far more significant for its political rather than its strictly economic overtones. Chkheidze stopped short of Lenin who now called for an end to all financial transactions taking place outside the control of the Soviet. The Executive Committee of the Soviet did expect the financial health of Russia to take a turn for the better if

Soviet officials shared in the overall direction of economic matters and once property owners paid as great a price as workers in the campaign to balance accounts in the treasury.

The old hostility between the Soviet leaders and the Kadets added a bleak aspect to the Moscow Conference, but there were some optimistic signs. Immediately after the close of the Conference, Miliukov found good reason to strike one cheery note. The Kadet leader blamed ideology for causing the Mensheviks and their socialist allies to cling to "utopian" ideas and he again warned that divisiveness was weakening the Kerensky government. But at the same time he did think a compromise was within the realm of possibility. If the Soviet leaders wished to rally around the Minister-President, Miliukov would be ready to cooperate. This same ray of light was shed a few days after the Moscow Conference in a *Rech* editorial, perhaps the work of Miliukov himself. The writer obviously realized the issues that divided the revolutionary forces and the dangers that threatened them with economic chaos. But he praised the friendly speech delivered by Tsereteli at the Moscow State Conference and expressed hope that the Soviet would widen its perspective of the revolution.[28] The official Soviet reaction to the Conference was reserved but like Miliukov the editor of *Izvestiia* left some hope that cooperation among revolutionary leaders might now be possible. *Izvestiia* was especially pleased by the appearance of a large number of speakers who praised the Soviet leadership; the waning prestige of the Soviet had been cause for concern and it was reassuring to find friends in the cooperative movement, the zemstvo councils and the peasant organizations. *Izvestiia* wrote nothing complimentary about either the Kadets or Kerensky, but at the same time its sharp anti-Kadet propaganda of mid-July was gone and its deep concern over the practical economic problems faced by the revolution was an encouraging sign.[29] The editors of *Den* glowed with satisfaction at what appeared to them as a victory over all extreme elements: "Both Leninism and Miliukovism suffered a defeat." Potresov expressed confidence in the future of the revolution for the first and the last time in 1917.[30] Even *Rabochaia Gazeta* was open minded about the future of the relations between the Soviet and the Provisional Government. Its editors were not convinced that all the Kadets were ready to compromise with either the Soviet leaders or Kerensky, nor were they pleased to see General Kornilov occupying a place on the platform next to high government officials, but they praised the conciliatory speech of Tsereteli.[31]

The Menshevik Internationalists were totally displeased with the outcome of the Conference and continued to drift closer to Lenin. Although this displeasure meant that trouble was in store for the Menshevik leaders when the party Congress convened in late August, it also indicated that efforts made to reach a mutual understanding between some liberals and socialists had not been a mirage seen only by Kerensky and the editors of *Den*. Sukhanov denounced the cooperation between the Soviet and the Provisional Government as a bankrupt policy and criticized the Moscow speech of Chkheidze as unduly friendly to the "imperialist bougeoisie;"[32] the man who had demanded the establishment of a Kadet government in February as the only correct step permitted by history had changed his mind by August without understanding why. The Menshevik Internationalist interpretation of the Moscow Conference was exactly the one used by Lenin and also the one followed in the most recent analysis of the Moscow State Conference published in the Soviet Union.[33]

The Conference closed on August 15 in the same manner in which it had opened, a long speech delivered by Kerensky. He sounded the same notes then that he did on August 12. The need for unity was stressed and the differences among the February leaders were made to appear as insignificant as possible. Speaking of the government in its relations with the various political parties, Kerensky declared that differences in opinion were healthy, but only the government, "by virtue of its position, can see the entire picture." The government had to work on a level above partisan political squabbles in order to bring about political stability in Russia, according to the Minister-President. As usual, Kerensky acused no one political party of fomenting trouble, and he blamed the tsarist regime for all the difficulties encountered by the revolutionary leadership.[34]

The fate of the February revolution was sealed after the misguided Kornilov adventure brought about the collapse of the government at the end of August, so a strong tendency has developed among historians to ignore the Moscow State Conference as wasted effort unworthy of analysis. This trend, however, should be viewed with a good deal of skepticism; among other things it diverts attention away from some of the most important causes for the collapse of the democratic movement in Russia. The meeting in Moscow brought out some instructive points. Merely the fact that the February leaders could meet with one another and discuss economic problems after the bitterness of July was an encouraging sign. And for the first time the Soviet leaders viewed economic problems on their own merits and not simply as political issues. Moreover, both the Soviet leaders and Kadets seemed willing to accept Kerensky's leadership of the Provisional Government. Sharp divisions between the socialists and liberals caused problems at Moscow, just as they had since the revolution began in February, but some kind of unity and confidence were present. It would take more than the military setback at the front and the severe economic troubles to destroy the strength of the Provisional Government.

b) The August Congress of Social Democrats

After the Moscow State Conference, Tsereteli, Chkheidze and Dan once again resisted an attack against their leadership in the Menshevik party. It was an important victory. These men stood at the helm of the Petrograd Soviet, a depository of conflicting moods and opinions, and their ability to harness its energy depended to a considerable degree on their ability to remain as representatives of a consolidated bloc of socialist opinion. If the Mensheviks broke apart, Tsereteli would fall from his perch in the Soviet as well as in the party, and the consequences would turn the course of the revolution. Neither the Social Revolutionaries nor the Popular Socialists commanded enough confidence or unity to direct the restless and naive followers who rallied around the Petrograd Soviet. If the Mensheviks broke ranks, the Soviet would quickly fall into the hands of radical leadership, bringing an end to the Provisional Government and the revolution as it was perceived by the February leadership. Lenin was working day and night to achieve precisely these ends, but as long as the Mensheviks retained a semblance of unity a strong part of the revolutionary leadership would follow the path marked out largely by them.

The situation within the Menshevik party in mid-August was extremely sensitive. The forces gradually bringing the Mensheviks together into a single unit were growing stronger, but at the same time the divisive factors were still potentially dangerous. A unifying trend had been developing since the revolution broke out in February and it had erased most of the former factional lines. The Mensheviks were lining up in conformity to the editorial policies of the principle newspapers, *Rabochaia Gazeta* in Petrograd and *Vpered* in Moscow. It was a vague and certainly unwritten political and intellectual agreement rather than a formal administrative convention and it reflected support for Tsereteli and the *poskol'ku postol'ku* tactics for and against the Kadets in the bourgeois revolution. The Menshevik May conference helped to boost this unifying trend by establishing the reputation of the Soviet leaders as the chief party figures and by drawing the Bund, the Letts and various other Social Democratic organizations into the Menshevik fold. Of course, individual party members continued to identify themselves with one of many small groups rather than with a national political party. The Committee of Petrograd Mensheviks, the Mensheviks in the Soviet delegation, the Organizational Committee of the All-Russian Menshevik party (elected at the May Conference), the group of defensists writing for *Den* and the Internationalists writing for *Novaia zhizn* were some of the most important circles.[35] Still other Mensheviks or Social Democrats loosely identified with Menshevism drifted to and from the various neighborhood Menshevik committees that first appeared and then disappeared from sight during the events of 1917; because of close collaboration with Lenin in 1917, it would be a mistake to include Trotsky and the *Mezhduraionists* Lunacharsky and Riazanov in the Menshevik orbit.[36]

As we have already seen, the Menshevik Internationalists created the most serious divisive force in the Menshevik party in 1917. Martov was their chief figure, although he was in no way the leader of one cohesive faction (the Internationalists were as badly organized as the party majority); even after the Kornilov affair, Lindov, Sukhanov, Avilov, Bazarov and Stroev avoided formal affiliation with Martov. The Menshevik Internationalists made life difficult for Tsereteli and Chkheidze. They delivered embarrassing speeches in the Soviet and published polemical articles in both *Novaia zhizn* and *Letuchii listok*, criticizing socialist policies on coalition government and international affairs. They even formed a faction of the June All-Russian Congress of Soviets and made an attempt to wrench the initiative from the hands of Tsereteli. At first these efforts were not particularly dangerous. The Internationalists were weak in numbers, and despite all their fiery rhetoric they supported the party policy on the occasion of the June offensive, during the spring campaign to raise money through the liberty loan and in all the local and neighborhood elections where Menshevik candidates competed against Bolsheviks and Social Revolutionaries. After the July days, however, matters changed. In mid-July the Internationalist-influenced Committee of Petrograd Mensheviks came very close to endorsing Martov's suggestion that the Soviet leaders take over temporary control of the government, and on August 5 they

convinced the 3rd Petrograd City Conference of Mensheviks to adopt
the Internationalist program of A. S. Martynov, overcoming the authority of the party majority by a vote of 59 to 49.[37] At that meeting
the Petrograd Committee also elected a representative body composed
largely of Internationalists. Neither the Petrograd Committee nor the
City Conference represented the official voice of Menshevism nor did
either body accurately reflect the opinion of the Menshevik party in
Petrograd, let alone all of Russia, but their success came at a time
when the Menshevik party could ill afford a nasty internal quarrel.

Recognizing the precarious balance of forces that kept the party
from being upset and afraid of the consequences if it was upset, the
Mensheviks approached their August Congress with caution. The
leaders elected at the May conference did not fear a loss of control
over the party (nobody controlled the Menshevik party), but they did
fear that a public battle between the majority leaders and the Internationalists might lead to a general breakup of the socialist camp. For this
reason, Potresov, Tsereteli and even Martov urged that unity serve as
the major theme of the party congress. On the 3rd of August, *Den*
called on all Mensheviks to use the Congress to seek agreement of
action. Applying some of the terms that were popular in 1917, Potresov encouraged the Menshevik leaders to look beyond their differences: "Defensists and Internationalists neutralize one another, and
the political results are not worth a penny." He implored the Internationalists not to carry their defiance of the elected party leadership to
the point where it created a block against unity; his cries for unity
became even more shrill after the August 5 city conference voted to
adopt the resolution of A. S. Martynov, calling for reforms that were
identified with the style of the Internationalists.[38] *Rabochaia Gazeta*
joined *Den* in pleading for harmony. When the Congress formally
opened, the official Menshevik journal registered a final call, hoping
that "this old psychological factionalism could be ended and from its
death would rise the unity of the proletarian struggle."[39] Fear of divisiveness even touched the Internationalists who called for unity on
the eve of the Congress and it extended to Moscow where the Menshevik editors of *Vpered* warned of dire consequences if a battle began
among Mensheviks.[40]

The Congress opened at the Petrograd Polytechnic Institute on
August 18 and extended through August 26. More than 220 delegates
were supposed to represent 195 organizations and the 200,000 members who were part of the Menshevik movement throughout Russia.

In fact, the Congress bore quite an auspicious title: The Unification Congress of the Russian Social-Democratic Workers' Party. Like the May Conference, however, it was dominated by the Menshevik leaders in Petrograd and by provincials who had become part of the Menshevik complex in Petrograd. *Rabochaia Gazeta* listed rural organizations and committees, especially in the Donets region and the Caucases that were included as part of the Congress, but a cursory glance at the statistics indicates that representation outside the capital city area and Moscow was minimal. Of the nine men elected to the Presidium and the Secretariat of the Congress only one man resided outside Petrograd. The new Central Committee elected to replace the old Organization Committee and to represent all factions within the Menshevik party was dominated by men from Petrograd. In addition, the sound of most of the names mentioned during the Congress had a familiar ring. They belonged to those intellectuals and journalists who had been identified with Menshevism for some time and had participated in the events in Petrograd; the Bolsheviks and Plekhanov's group refused to attend the Congress. Close contact between Petrograd and other areas of Russia was minimal throughout most of 1917 and the Mensheviks were effected by that limitation.[41] Of course, it would probably be a mistake to accept the conclusions of some contemporary Soviet historians who have described the Menshevik party in August of 1917 as little more than a "paper party." On the other hand, Menshevik sympathizers who accept the party statistics at face value are relying on questionable evidence.

Despite the early advice, the Congress quickly developed into a debate between the Internationalists, led by Martov and Astrov, and the majority leaders by Tsereteli. Martov drew the first blood. His long speech on the 19th of August and his remarks made throughout the Congress revealed a determination to chart a new course for the party. Following Martov's plan, the Petrograd Soviet of Workers' and Soldiers' Deputies would extend its control over most political affairs in Russia, at least temporarily. According to Martov, much of the bourgeois liberal force with which the Mensheviks had been working was now aggressively anti-democratic and needed to be curtailed in order to prevent a counterrevolutionary assault from gathering steam. Martov did not wish to establish a socialist dictatorship and destroy the political base of the non-socialist parties in Russia, on that point he made known his own Menshevik character and his separation from Lenin. But he did advise the Mensheviks to desert the coalition and

withdraw Soviet support from Kerensky. He called for the organization of "worker blocs" to defend the revolution from its anti-Soviet
enemies, and advised that the Provisional Government be forced to
play a minor role for the time being; Martov also thought the time was
ripe to enlist the support of the peasants in behalf of the revolutionary
effort. Once this moment of crisis had passed, the Mensheviks and the
Soviet could return to the traditional forms of struggle and allow a
chastened bourgeoisie to exercise more authority in Russia.[42]

Two factors caused Martov to speak out strongly in favor of this
radical interpretation and departure from traditional Menshevik thinking about revolutionary tactics. First, the faltering prestige of the
Soviet frightened Martov. It was his conviction that the retreating
Soviet represented the only hope of survival for the democratic revolution. He had warned about the waning power of this institution since
the July uprising, and this fear, more than any other factor, gained him
a goodly share of interest among Mensheviks at the party Congress.[43]
Martov was convinced that the Soviet was losing its fight for life, and
he had no faith in Kerensky's promises to maintain it as a force in
Russian politics. If the Soviet was destroyed, what course would the
revolution take? A second factor in Martov's motivation derived from
the importance he placed on the theory of imperialism. The uniqueness
of Russia's struggle against the tsar in a semi-asiatic society (a factor
that was an important part of Plekhanov's thinking about the revolution) had now to compete in Martov's mind against his belief in the
destructive power of international banking. The internal politics of
Russia may have been unique but they could no longer be isolated from
world events, as had been the case in 1905. He pointed to the Kadets
with whom the Soviet leaders had cooperated and branded them as
dangerous enemies of the revolution. His revulsion against the Kadets
went much further than the guarded skepticism harbored by most
Mensheviks. Miliukov, Rodzianko and Riabushinsky were no longer
timid yet essential collaborators in the fight for democracy in *krepostnichestvo* Russia, according to Martov. They were now anti-democratic
agents of the west European imperialist conquerors. These agents of
imperialism had successfully helped their English and French masters
weaken the Petrograd Soviet, Martov explained, and now they planned
to apply the *coup de gras* to the revolution. They must be stopped before
the revolutionary forces were beaten to death. Since Martov was convinced that Kerensky served as a tool of Russian liberals, he called for
the Soviet to sever its connections with the Provisional Government.[44]

Martov was supported at the August Congress in speeches delivered by his friend Astrov and also by Boris Avilov, the Internationalist from the *Novaia Zhizn* editorial office, but these men were unable to remove the serious flaw that weakened Martov's argument. Martov's theoretical analysis had some appeal; his party comrades were certainly worried about the waning prestige of the Petrograd Soviet. But Martov's practical political program looked to them too much like the one presented by Lenin. Martov tried to separate himself from the Bolshevik leader by denying that his plan would culminate in a permanent socialist dictatorship, but at the time his call on socialists to play a strong role in government politics sounded like Leninism. Those who supported the Menshevik majority leaders made their criticism of Martov focus on this point, and they met with success. Both Potresov and Tsereteli rejected Martov's views of imperialism, but the bulk of their polemics were devoted to undermining Martov's "non-program," or his "confusing program" or his "Leninist program." The majority leaders acknowledged that Soviet prestige had weakened since early July, but they defended the policy of cooperation between the Soviet and the Provisional Government as the only way to preserve the gains made by the revolution. They remained anchored to the old Menshevik tactic of cooperation with the Russian liberals in the task of changing the face of non-European Russia. In his resolution of August 20, Tsereteli recognized the weakened state of the Soviet and the decline of Menshevik influence among soldiers and workers, but he refused to abandon faith in the tactics that kept the socialists and the liberals in a common league against the enemies of the revolution.[45] Martov could not overcome this opposition. He tried to pull the Mensheviks to the left, but failed. He was unable to parry the charge from his own comrades that branded his program as a Leninist one.

Soon after the Congress opened, it became clear that the majority leaders would again regain their leadership and a serious rupture within the party would be avoided. Martov's resolutions were rejected. First, his attempt to tie the Russian revolution to a Franco-English finance system was unconvincing. When the foreign policy issue was raised for a vote the party accepted the majority report of Mark Liber who called for a continuation of the alliance between the Provisional Government and the Allies; the margin was 99 against 44. When the question of coalition government, or Soviet support for Kerensky, was considered, the Mensheviks again agreed to continue the policy of Tsereteli; the margin was 117 voices against 79. At no time during or immediately after the Congress did Martov take steps to leave the party, or the Congress, or to induce a rupture that might destroy what unity the Mensheviks enjoyed.[46] Regardless of his deviation from the traditional path he did not rebel. When the new party leadership was elected, the victorious majority showed deference to Martov by including eight Menshevik Internationalists on the Central Committee of Twenty-five; the fact that the eight accepted was evidence of comradeship. It was true, of course, that a serious ideological deviation had appeared within the party and that the Menshevik Internationalists had gained considerable strength since the May Conference. In this respect, Potresov's assessment of the Congress as a meeting of a Social Democratic party of the European variety, and one that had solved its organizational problems, was misleading.[47] The division was serious and it did limit the Soviet's efforts to retain the loyalty of the masses in Petrograd. In addition to these troublesome factors the rapid decline of Tsereteli's health, followed quickly by news of his imminent departure for the Caucausus, did not bode well for the cause of unity in the party. His skill as a political leader had done much for both the Mensheviks and the Soviet and it was doubtful that Chkheidze could carry on in Tsereteli's place; obviously, Dan could not. On the other hand, the party did survive the Congress with its cohesiveness still intact. Despite Martov's challenge, the various splinter groups that constituted Menshevism in Petrograd did not break ranks, and as long as the Mensheviks held some semblence of unity, Lenin would find his road to power blocked. It was not until after the Kornilov affair that all cohesiveness fell away and Lenin's small band of socialists became the largest one in Petrograd.[48]

c) The Kornilov Revolt

The extended discussions that normally followed a congress of Russian Social Democrats were omitted after the August meeting because the attention of the Mensheviks, like that of everybody else in Petrograd, was focused on the events connected with the famous Kornilov affair. The city had been on pins and needles for several weeks due to the wide circulation of rumors that the Bolsheviks would soon "again" attempt a *coup d'etat*, and tension was further increased when the German army, taking advantage of the Russian defeat in July, launched an offensive of its own; Riga fell into German hands on August 25. When it appeared that a Russian general with a reputation for boldness and patriotism was preparing to place the city of Petrograd under martial law, excitement reached a fever pitch.

Kornilov first gained notoriety as a figure unfriendly to the Soviet during the April Crisis. At that time he was the commander of the Petrograd garrison and a politically unsophisticated man who aligned himself with no faction or party. During the riots he ordered troops from their barracks into the streets to protect the government. His orders were countermanded by Tsereteli, and after the incident was closed Kornilov was promptly given the command of the 8th Army on the Southwestern front. Everybody expected the April confrontation to bring an end to Kornilov's career, at least in Petrograd, but he was involuntarily drawn back toward the center of the political arena at a time when the delicate relationship among the liberals, the socialists, and the Russian army generals was coming under severe strain.

Earlier in the year, the top Russian officers were able to avoid conflice with the contending political groups, although their sympathies usually rested with the liberals rather than with the socialists. Generals Alexeev and Brusilov who were appointed alternately as supreme commanders-in-chief held out some hope that the turmoil would subside and that the Provisional Government would sooner or later guide Russians toward a stable political order. They tried to keep the deteriorating state of the army off the list of items that were causing the greatest friction within the revolutionary leadership. Whatever success they enjoyed in this regard can be attributed less to their own cunning than to the fact that the Russian front remained quiet in the early spring of 1917. The period of calm made the foreign policy illusions of both the socialists and the liberals seem more real than fanciful and it permitted experiments with lax military discipline to be carried out under relatively peaceful conditions. This happy situation changed after the Russian military defeat in early July when both the army commanders and the liberal politicians began to make loud calls for the introduction of strict measures to reshape Russia's fighting forces.

On July 19, Alexander Kerensky became the Minister-President of the fourth and hastily reconstructed Provisional Government, and he appointed General Kornilov as the supreme commander of all Russian armies. Kornilov accepted the post on the condition that the general staff be given a free hand to restore tight discipline in the ranks. Kerensky had very little respect for Kornilov, but he hoped to use the General as part of a plan that would resolve all the serious trouble in the army, strengthen the government and at the same time quiet the fears of the Soviet leaders who were worried about a right-wing counterrevolution. His tactics were deceptive and complicated. He pretended to accede to Kornilov's demands with an eye toward boosting the morale of the officers and calming the anxiety of the liberals who were upset by the country's flimsy defenses, while at the same time he assured the socialists in Petrograd that he would prevent both the military leaders and the liberal politicians from using the army to make government policy. Unfortunately, Kerensky was unable to control the events that he had set in motion.

On August 7 Kornilov ordered a cavalry regiment under General Krymov to move from the Southwestern front to the Petrograd area, ostensibly to protect the city against threats posed by the Bolsheviks and the advancing German army. At first the transfer of troops enjoyed the approval of Kerensky and the order may well have initiated in his office, but it became embarrassing after it was strongly denounced by the socialists. At this point the Minister-President began to back away from his first commitment, such as it was, and on August 14 and again on August 19 angered Kornilov by criticizing the Krymov troop movement and by threatening to renege on the conditions that had been set down in the agreement of July 19. Kornilov in the meantime continually pressed his demands for the authority to increase the scope of military control over the army.[49] It was also about this time that political groups on the right became very active. Several liberal politicians who had conspiracy on their minds tried to take advantage of the growing friction between Kornilov and Kerensky by urging the Commander-in-chief to establish a military dictatorship.[50] The extent to which these suggestions swayed Kornilov is not known, which is unfortunate because the question as to whether there was really a Kornilov revolt may go unanswered due to lack of clarity at this point.

By August 24, the issue between Kornilov and Kerensky was quickly coming to a head. Tension built to the breaking poin which released the inevitable efforts to postpone a dangerous confrontation. Both B. V. Savinkov and V. N. Lvov visited Kornilov at this time. Both men enjoyed some official status as Kerensky's representatives, as far as Kornilov was concerned, and both men were familiar with the groups and circumstances involved in the difficulty. After holding separate discussions with Kornilov they returned to Kerensky convinced that the political and military questions that had created confusion between military headquarters and Petrograd were on the way to being solved. On August 26, however, the political crisis occurred. Kerensky communicated with Kornilov through an electrical apparatus that connected the capital city with Mogilev 500 miles away. He asked if Kornilov expected his arrival at military headquarters and the reply was positive. Mention was also made of the earlier exchange between Lvov and Kornilov. Perhaps neither the Minister-President nor the General fully understood one another during this exchange, or it may be that one or the other man was deliberately trying to leave certain aspects of the situation unclear, but the break in communications was shortly followed by Kerensky's order for Lvov's arrest. Kornilov was then declared to be a traitor. The cabinet resigned, and the last stable government formed by the democratic forces in 1917 collapsed. Kornilov was arrested and retained for a short time at military headquarters.

The Soviet leaders had no trouble deciding how to treat the Kerensky-Kornilov disagreement once some of the details became public knowledge. Kornilov was now made the number one enemy of all socialists in Russia, and the announcement of his rebellion released all their fears of counterrevolution. The Soviet committee for the Peoples' Struggle Against the Counterrevolution was formed. Its leaders urged all workers to take up arms and even released from jail several political prisoners who had been arrested after the July uprising; Leon Trotsky, the man who eventually did overthrow the Provisional Government, was in this group. All the socialist newspapers issued calls to arms. The convulsive rhetoric of *Rabochaia Gazeta* and *Novaia Zhizn* reached a new high pitch of intensity. People were urged to assemble at certain key locations in order to receive arms and money.[51] The Mensheviks and other socialists held different views about finances, government organization, and whether or not to fight against the German army, but against General Kornilov there stood only a solid wall of resistance without any signs of dissent or sounds of disagreement.

Once the moment of greatest hysteria had passed and whatever danger lurking in the dark corners of military headquarters had vanished, the significance of the Kornilov affair for the February revolution became clear: the period of socialist-liberal cooperation was at an end. The political agreement that had served as the cornerstone of Provisional Government tactics was not going to survive the shock. The Mensheviks accused the Kadets of duplicity and vowed to place very tight restrictions on any future business undertaken with them. After the dust had settled in late August, there were no defenders of the Kadets to be found among the Mensheviks or in the Soviet. It had been a revolt in the army, according to the Mensheviks, and the Kadets were considered to have been part of the conspiracy. If any lingering doubt existed in their minds, it was removed on August 27 when *Rech* appeared on the streets of the city with a blank space in place of an editorial; it correctly implied that the editors of *Rech* had their own ambiguous feeling on that particular occasion. "The Kadets clearly have some binding ties with the counterrevolution," and must be dismissed as untrustworthy; anybody not prepared to wage instant warfare against General Kornilov was not a friend of the revolution.[52] *Novaia Zhizn* lost all of its small store of patience and even printed the absurd story that a new plot against the revolution was being hatched by the Kadet leaders being supported on this occasion by the German general staff.[53] One may have been inclined to dismiss the tirades of *Rabochaia Gazeta* and *Novaia Zhizn* as typical and to be expected on this occasion, but even the editors of *Den* were exasperated with the Kadets and could find nothing favorable to redeem the liberal leaders.[54] The Kornilov affair brought the Soviet leaders and especially the Mensheviks to that point where they could no longer cooperate with the Kadets, so a new and very short chapter began in the history of the Petrograd Soviet. In this respect, Sukhanov's analysis of the situation was typically inaccurate. He observed that the early weeks of September brought the revolution "back to the old post-July, pre-Kornilov situation."[55] He did not realize how deeply the Kornilov events damaged the relationship between socialists and liberals.

Was there really a Kornilov revolt? Kerensky and the socialist leaders in the Petrograd Soviet would certainly have us believe so, and this line has been vigorously promoted by historians presently writing in the U.S.S.R.[56] They point to Kornilov's anti-revolutionary sympathies, his own army record of insubordination, and the important fact that he was prepared to use force, in Petrograd if necessary, as part of his plan to restore the army's fighting capacity. They also bring to our attention the fact that some Kadets who were talking about conspiracy had started to collect in the General's entourage in mid-August; Lvov may have been one of their number. Most important, they presume that the troop movement commanded by General Krymov was sent north for the purpose of bringing about a military *coup d'etat*. The evidence is impressive, but there is another side to the story. Kornilov himself was certainly not a conspirator, and the demands he made on Kerensky were always of a military character or designed to strengthen the army, not to overthrow the government; even the order to move Krymov's troops was executed to protect the government from the Germans or the Bolsheviks as far as Kornilov was concerned.[57] Nor does the fact that Kornilov leaned toward dictatorship as a political solution to the problems faced by Russia mean a great deal in this context, because strict government control had been mentioned by Kerensky, Miliukov and even Tsereteli all summer long as a likely possibility to replace the freedom that had prevailed since February; at the Moscow State Conference, the socialist (Menshevik) program certainly resembled a form of dictatorship and the only condition preventing its implementation seemed to be the demand that socialists be included in the ruling circles. Finally, the tie between the leaders of the Kadet party and an organized conspiracy against the Provisional Government is not strong enough to settle the issue.[58] A government inquiry held after the event took place was supposed to shed light into all the dark corners. It produced a welter of contradictory testimony, indicating that some of those involved had either lied or withheld information from their colleagues, particularly Kerensky and Lvov, but no solid evidence that a conspiracy had been organized and certainly nothing that resembled the counterrevolutionary movement marching forward in the collective imagination of the socialist leaders. To add the last note of confusion, on August 30 General Alexeev, acting on Kerensky' behalf, asked Kornilov to continue to administer the army, which he did until September 1.[59]

Nevertheless, Kerensky's public accusation against the commander-in-chief of the army did serve the purpose of destroying the Provisional Government. By branding Kornilov a traitor, the Minister-President heightened the socialists' dread of counterrevolution and caused them to withdraw permanently from the coalition upon which Kerensky's authority depended for support. After the statesman-like guidance given at the Moscow State Conference had brought the Soviet and the Kadets to recognize some of their common problems, and after Tsereteli had beaten away the radical challenge at the Menshevik Congress, Kerensky lost control at the top. He was unable to solve the problem of army deterioration by playing one side against the other. He used demagoguery to attack Kornilov which encouraged the socialists to draw the only conclusion they could from such an explanation of the events. After the Kornilov affair, his government drifted about without protection. It was found and destroyed by Lenin and Trotsky on October 26, 1917.

Chapter VII
The Final Collapse

a) The Provisional Government Becomes a Shadow

The desire for cooperation that bound the Soviet Executive Committee to the Kadet leaders was the single most important factor bringing political stability to Petrograd in 1917. It took institutional form in the establishment of the Provisional Government, a body that could administer the affairs of state only as long as a fair degree of harmony was maintained between the Executive Committee of the Petrograd Soviet and the Central Committee of the Kadet party. The vitality of the Provisional Government did not depend on the personality of the men who occupied its official posts, but on the spirit of compromise (however weak) prevailing between the socialist and the liberal camps. The fact that the revolutionary government was powerless to keep order if abandoned by either the socialists or the liberals is amply demonstrated by the evidence. The Provisional Government collapsed and Petrograd became an open city in April when the socialists withdrew support, again in June when the Kadets quit and finally in late August when both the Kadets and the Soviet officials forgot all about cooperation during the Kornilov affair.

Following the Kornilov affair, the Provisional Government was revived in name only to lead a short and melancholy existence. It was no more powerful than many of the other political clubs active throughout the city. The reconciliations between the socialists and the liberals that had restored life and faith in Russia's revolutionary power in May and again in July did not come forth in September. The events of September began with an intense anti-Kadet campaign carried on by most Mensheviks and Social Revolutionaries and concluded at the Democratic Conference where the socialists refused to endorse any government in which Kadets held cabinet positions.

The first significant sign that the late August rupture had damaged the February compromise beyond repair was the public attack by Victor Chernov on Alexander Kerensky. The popular Soviet leader charged the Minister-President with duplicity in the Kornilov affair and then went on to denounce the policy of compromise between the

Kadets and the Petrograd Soviet. It had outlived its usefulness. The appearance of Chernov's early September editorials in *Delo Naroda*, the official Social Revolutionary newspaper in Petrograd, was a serious matter. They were written at a time when the anti-Kadet and the anti-Provisional Government sentiment was at a high point among both the Soviet delegates and the soldiers in the Petrograd regiments. Moreover, Victor Chernov was not just another radical socialist orator. He had bound himself to Tsereteli's coalitionist policy and had been a cabinet member in the second coalition. His attack against Kerensky signified that an important Soviet official was deserting the Menshevik-inspired policy that had prevailed in high socialist circles during the first six months of the revolution.

Even more serious than Victor Chernov's attacks on both Kerensky and the coalition policy was the leftward shift now noticeable among a majority of Mensheviks. The Internationalists were of course the most obvious. Riding high on the wave of popular suspicion, they declared that the Kornilov affair represented an act of betrayal by the liberals against the democratic revolution in Russia. The hasty resignation of the Kadet ministers from the Provisional Government during the last week in August and the appearance of a blank space in the place of an editorial in *Rech* on August 27 exposed the link binding the Kadets and the mutineers. The Menshevik Internationalists were certain that now even the right-wing Mensheviks would realize the connection between Russian liberalism and the counterrevolution. Boris Avilov wagged his finger at Potresov: "During the Kornilov revolt you should have recognized that all of propertied Russia showed itself to be in the camp of the counterrevolution."[1] This theme was repeated over and over again. According to the Menshevik Internationalists, a striking example had now been given to validate Martov's theory of imperialism: the imperialist bourgeoisie in Russia, bound to the world imperialist bourgeois centers in London and Paris, held the strings on which General Kornilov danced. "How can we now have a coalition," the editors of *Novaia Zhizn* demanded, "when one side is in open opposition against the other?"[2]

The Internationalists were joined by Mensheviks at the party center, the once strong supporters of Tsereteli who rallied around the journals *Rabochaia Gazeta* and *Vpered!* The center now rejected the Kadets who had "compromised themselves during the Kornilov affair," and anti-Kadet sentiments could even be found among some Mensheviks identified with the right wing of the party. Ivan Kubikov accused the

Kadets of turning against the democracy. Some isolated efforts were made to stem the rising tide, but they were not strong. The leftward swing that took place after the July riots was being repeated, but in September the Mensheviks were not going to return to their old stance and renew the line of compromise with the Kadets.

A certain disorientation accompanied this leftward shift in early September. It was emotional and spontaneous and completely without design, and the Mensheviks had no certain thought about replacing the old ways. Against the Kadets, yes! But no agreement as to how to move beyond that point. A Menshevik writing in *Novaia Zhizn* suggested that the forthcoming Democratic Conference be converted into a Russian parliament, and that it be controlled exclusively by socialists and charged with the responsibility of governing Russia until the meeting of the Constituent Assembly. Another recommended a more radical step by urging that the Soviet itself serve as a temporary parliament until the meeting of the Constituent Assembly. Avilov called for a democratic dictatorship, but did not elaborate on how such an instrument might be used. Martov repeated his demand for a government made up of socialists ranging along the political spectrum from Bolsheviks to Popular Socialists; several well-known Bolsheviks arrived at the same conclusion; added to this confusing scene were the outnumbered handful of Mensheviks who still hoped to revive the coalition in its traditional forms. By mid-September there were almost as many political plans as there were Mensheviks. The cohesiveness that had kept the party together since February was quickly falling away.

The danger grew even greater because the hostility toward liberals and the internal confusion among Mensheviks spread to other moderate socialist groups. Fractional quarrels began to rend the Social Revolutionaries creating an atmosphere of bitterness and suspicion.[3] In fact early and mid-September saw the rapid dissolution of the bonds that formally tied the Soviet parties to the Provisional Government and the progressive fragmentation of each Soviet party. The moderate socialist camp seemed to be disintegrating, and its breakup helped to encourage chaos among the masses. It contributed heavily to the increased radicalization of the workers and soldiers who were now without proven leaders. Lenin was in the best position to take advantage of this disorder, and the Soviet rank and file did elect Bolshevik leadership on September 25. Those few socialists who recognized the dangers generated by this distress hoped to salvage something at the Democratic Conference.

The Democratic Conference was a new body to appear in Petrograd. It was called together on September 14[4] by the Mensheviks who sent out invitations through the Soviet Central Executive Committee and through the Executive Committee of the Peasant Soviet, a group of Social Revolutionary supporters of Tsereteli. Only the socialist camp was asked to attend. The Bolsheviks were included, but since Tsereteli hoped to use the Conference to discourage his most radical comrades from seizing power, organizations shaped by moderate opinion were also asked to participate. These non-Soviet, so-called petty bourgeoisie groups, came from the Central Committee of the All-Russian Cooperatives, the Peasant Soviet, the labor unions, the town dumas, and the professional organizations that had been sympathetic to the moderate socialist cause. Most of these groups were first formed in the spring of 1917. For the most part, their short histories are hidden in obscurity, but they made a forceful appearance at the Moscow State Conference and seemed to be good prospects for Tsereteli who was now searching Petrograd and Moscow for any socialist inclined to shy away from the radical policies being propagated by Lenin and Trotsky.

In view of the controversy that now raged among socialists, and between socialists and liberals, it is a wonder that so much was expected to emerge from the deliberations of the Democratic Conference. In fact, its opening sessions on September 14 were marked by even further factionalism, intense bickering and anti-Kadet demonstrations. One of the few bright rays of hope appeared from the much maligned figure of Alexander Kerensky who had a vested interest in the revival of coalition government. His opening speech at the Conference was well received by the 1500 delegates. The Minister-President still commanded respect, and still remained the only acceptable candidate for the highest office in the unlikely possibility that another grand compromise could be reached.

Once the Conference was opened for debate, it was the anti-coalitionists who first gained access to the podium. B. O. Bogdanov, who had formally supported Tsereteli, spoke out firmly against the policy of coalition government. He held the Kadets responsible for the political weaknesses of the past Provisional Governments and called upon the delegates to take power into their own hands and form a socialist government immediately.[5] He was followed by Skobelev, another defector from the coalition camp, a Menshevik and a former Minister of Labor in the Provisional Government. Skobelev advocated a continuation of the coalition policy, but without the Kadets. He urged the Conference to seek out more suitable liberals who might be inclined to accept direction from the socialist leaders. Skobelev wanted "to crack the bourgeois nut," as he stated the case, "and create a coalition with truly revolutionary bourgeois elements;"[6] at the time, few people considered Skobelev's suggestion very helpful. Victor Chernov also spoke at the Democratic Conference. This popular figure whose acquiescence did much to keep the Social Revolutionaries in line with the Menshevik leadership now denounced the liberal alliance policy. He blamed the Kadets for all the trubles that had plagued the Russian government since February, and in place of a coalition Chernov advised the delegates to form a new socialist program. Announcing a plan that seemed to enjoy considerable popularity among the delegates, the prominent agrarian reformer asked the Conference to endorse a series of reform measures, generally comparable to the Soviet program unfolded at the Moscow State Conference, and then find political figures who would agree to carry out the program. Martov also spoke out at the Conference. He condemned the coalition policy, of course, as did the Bolsheviks Kamenev, Riazanov and Shliapnikov. By the end of the second day the applause and shouts of praise that accompanied the anti-coalitionist speakers made it clear that a return to the political strategy of the previous six months was out of the question.

On the other hand, nobody at the Democratic Conference advocated Lenin's plan. It is difficult to imagine how Avilov and Martov could have avoided the type of dictatorship Lenin was working to establish in Russia, but these delegates took pains to point out that sharp distinctions existed between their socialist state and that of the Bolshevik leader. They wanted to exclude the Kadets from the government, but not from all Russian political life, and they wanted to encourage a free exchange of views among all socialist parties represented at the Conference. They also agreed that strict anti-Kadet measures were to be temporary, lasting only until the Constituent Assembly could meet to establish a formal government structure. The distinctions between the left-wing socialists and Lenin were perhaps unimportant and unlikely to prove substantial once exposed to political reality, but they were made with the best intentions. Even the Bolsheviks who spoke at the Democratic Conference disassociated themselves from Lenin, and the continuing isolation of Lenin from the main stream of Russian socialism was an encouraging sign for those who hoped to revive the coalition. Moreover, the anti-coalitionists readily admitted to their one grave weakness. They simply could not unite around one alternative plan. They leaned toward no one tactic or leader that could replace those who had been directing the Soviet strategic operation since February.

All these factors were well known to those few Mensheviks and Social Revolutionaries who still gathered around the person of Tsereteli and who hoped that the Democratic Conference would eventually lead socialists back to a new agreement with the Kadets. Using subtle methods at first, the old guard tried to bolster the sagging confidence of their own supporters by readily agreeing to exclude from the new government all those Kadets who had been implicated with Kornilov. But the next step was to suggest that many Kadet leaders were above suspicion and that the revolution would be well served if some Kadets were selected to remain in the government.[7] They also promised that "propertied elements" acceptable to the Democratic Conference would be required to make a statement denouncing their own "sick and reactionary elements."[8] Throughout the argument, Tsereteli continually reminded the socialists of the dangers posed by Lenin and how closely moderate socialist opinion was coming to resemble Leninism. All this maneuver brought Tsereteli as close as he could come to presenting the old program in a respectable fashion and to appeasing the anti-Kadet spirit that prevailed among most of his comrades. It was a phony scheme in many respects because it had little likelihood of being accepted by the Kadets even if it was accepted by the Democratic Conference, but in mid-September Tsereteli's first purpose was to overcome the opposition in his own camp. Miliukov could wait.

Tsereteli's plan for a new coalition was presented at the Conference and supported by the traditional arguments. The socialists and the liberals must work together if democracy was to survive in Russia, and this cooperation included working within the formal structure of government: neither a socialist government without liberals nor a liberal government without socialists could survive to bring about the good ends so many people hoped to achieve from the revolution. Tsereteli and his colleagues hoped the spirit of compromise could be revived, and most right-wing Mensheviks soon came to his support. Falling back to the old strategy, Ivanovich and Potresov both spoke about the poverty of Russian culture, which they linked to the lack of capitalist development. They still saw the need for both socialists and liberals in a government that worked for the salvation of the democratic revolution.[9]

Despite his poor health, Tsereteli spoke with eloquence during the meetings of the Democratic Conference. He repeated warnings about Leninism and anarchy. His opinion was echoed by Chkheidze, the most popular leader in the Menshevik party, and by Dan. Liber spoke in favor of reviving the coalition on behalf of the Jewish Bund. The coalition policy was also defended by Berkengeim, Merkulov and Oder, representing the Central Cooperative Congress. Berkergeim, although a Social Revolutionary, left little doubt about the roots of his political philosophy: "Without coalition, without a general harmony of forces, it will not be possible to save our country."[10] The compassionate and devoted P. N. Kolokolnikov, a Menshevik leader from the labor groups in Petrograd, also spoke in favor of the renewal of the coalition government.[11]

On September 19, once all the speakers had been heard, the issue of government power was submitted to the delegates. The results threw the Democratic Conference and the Petrograd socialists into a state of chaos even greater than the one that had prevailed since the Kornilov affair. The delegates first chose to continue the policy of coalition by a margin of 766 votes against 688 votes with 38 abstentions, but then promptly voted to exclude the Kadets from the coalition cabinet: 595 votes against 493 votes with 72 abstentions. Beyond that expression of their collective will the delegates had nothing to offer — coalition, but no Kadets. Tsereteli's attempts to revive the spirit of compromise with the liberals had failed, but the desire to retain the facade of that compromise still survived. Most of the delegates were obviously unwilling to trust the Kadets with portfolios, but at the same time they rejected the various conclusions drawn by Martov and other anti-coalitionists. The Democratic Conferenece had listened to two different alternatives and responded by rejecting them both. The path to compromise with the Kadets would lead the revolution to defeat at the hands of another Kornilov, yet the door still remained closed to anything that resembled a socialist government: Neither Tsereteli nor Martov, neither Kerensky nor Lenin. The editors of *Den* had been absolutely correct in their early September prophecy that the Democratic Conference would wisely turn down the opportunity to establish a socialist government, but they were incorrect when they predicted that the Conference would restore life to the old coalition.

One interpretation of the voting at the Conference suggests that the delegates wished to establish a coalition government in Petrograd without Kadets in the cabinet, but there was very little support for that particular plan. A coalition with the bourgeoisie but without the Kadets was absurd, on that point almost everybody agreed. The Menshevik leaders were in a state of shock, and the editors of *Rabochaia Gazeta* shifted what little hope remained to future meetings of the Democratic Conference.[12] The editors of *Den* threw up their hands in disgust: "Something much worse than expected has occurred. This is a collapse."[13] Even the Menshevik Internationalists were in a fog.[14] Only the Social Revolutionary editors of *Delo Naroda* found some fragments worth salvaging from the shipwrecked Conference, but even they seemed less than enthusiastic about the future of the revolution. On the closing day of the Democratic Conference the dejected state of the socialist soul was well expressed by Woytinsky: "The Conference ended on September 24. The concluding session was gloomy. Chkheidze sat at a long table on the stage, a picture of melancholy and despair. Many chairs at the table were empty. I wanted to leave also, but Chkheidze implored me to deliver the concluding speech. There was not much to say about the results of the Conference. Then Chkheidze got up and left the stage, forgetting to declare the meeting adjourned."[15] Lenin greeted the results of the Conference with ridicule.

After the failure of the Democratic Conference, it was Tsereteli who again began to set the stage for renewing contact between the socialists and the remnants of Kerensky's government; it was his last important act prior to leaving Petrograd. Taking advantage of the exhaustion and pessimism in the Alexander Hall, the cunning Georgian Menshevik quickly moved against the majority will of the Conference. He invited the delegates to leave political matters temporarily in the hands of the Conference leaders, largely the friends of Tsereteli. He gained their confidence by making a series of changes and promises. The former Soviet leader expanded the size of the Conference leadership body to include many popular figures from the main body of delegates, and he promised that once a new government was formed it would give allegiance to the Democratic Conference. He received a mandate from the tired delegates and immediately made contact with Kerensky.

Kerensky was ready to discuss political matters with Tsereteli, but he had not been idle during the month of September, nor did his intentions coincide with the confusing wishes of the Democratic Conference. Kerensky spent the month of September trying to bolster his prestige, and he sought support quite independently of socialist assistance.[16] His aim was simply to maintain the Provisional Government as a vital political force in Petrograd and to maintain his supervision over it. The makeshift five man Directory he created on September 1 was inadequate for this task and his dramatic announcement of the same day that Russia had officially become a Republic did little to secure Kerensky's political future. As the great depth of the political crisis became obvious to Kerensky, he made contact with the liberals in the Trade-Industry Union in Moscow and made no secret of the fact that he expected to include Kadets in the next cabinet;[17] just because the socialists were in the midst of an anti-Kadet tirade did not mean that the Kadets were unpopular in many influential quarters. The Minister-President even retained A. V. Kartashev on his list of potential cabinet ministers. Kerensky expected socialists to be a part of the reconstituted Provisional Government, but this thoughtfulness on his part was due less to the influence of Tsereteli than to Kerensky's desire to make use of any group that would give him support. In fact, two socialist ministers were finally included in the cabinet that was assembled on September 25, 1917, but the new government was little more than the tool of Alexander Kerensky.

Tsereteli had promised the Democratic Conference that the next government would be made responsible to its wishes, but Kerensky evaded that trap. He spoke to the Conference in late September, now expanded to include the Kadets (at Kerensky's insistence), and renamed the Provisional Council of the Russian Republic or simply the Preparliament: "The Preparliament will have the right to put questions to the government," Kerensky assured his audience, "and the government will be obligated to reply to them. The government will not bear formal legal responsibility to the Preparliament, but it stands to reason that no Provisional Government will, in fact, be able to exist without receiving a vote of confidence from the Preparliament."

It would be a mistake to conclude that Kerensky's clever words and Tsereteli's cunning maneuver were sufficient to put the old coalition back together again. Despite the fanfare that accompanied the distribution of cabinet offices, the Provisional Government destroyed during the Kornilov revolt was not revived. The coalition of September 25, 1917, had no more support than most other political clubs to the right of the Bolsheviks. It was a government only in name and never came close to serving as a center where liberals and socialists could work together which former Provisional Governments had done at least in some small measure. The September "government" was simply Kerensky's entourage, although it did contain some honest and intelligent men. Throughout October, the socialists continued to show the strong anti-Kadet strain that had dominated the Democratic Conference. They did issue a statement formally recognizing the Kerensky government, despite the appearance of Kadets in the cabinet, but spent most of their time attacking the Minister-President. At the end of October they refused to defend the government against Lenin's assault. Even the Kadets scoffed at the September government and refused to take it seriously. The hope that the new government would find the support it needed in the Preparliament was dashed almost immediately. When that body began to deliberate in early October, it quickly became a battleground between socialists and liberals in addition to being a strong center of anti-Kerensky criticism.

b) Disintegration of the February Leadership

The late August and September storms that broke the weak ties holding the Mensheviks and the Kadets together continued with even greater intensity into the month of October. Every public issue that arose seemed to inspire hatred rather than a spirit of cooperation. The Menshevik majority had definitely abandoned the tactics that accompanied the party into the dramatic events of 1917, and this change was reflected in the bitter rhetoric that passed as criticism in the Preparliament. Nor did the party gain internal strength as a result of its drift away from the old moorings. It fell into complete fragmentation and decline.

One might have though that questions about foreign policy and army reform could no longer prove the painful bones of contention that had prevented close working relations between the Soviet and the Provisional Government earlier in the year. The collapse of the June offensive and the disintegration of the army left socialists and liberals alike without a viable plan. The Kadet hope of continuing the war with the energetic participation of Russia was now obviously extinguished as were prospects for a Soviet inspired general peace. But Russia's now feeble posture in international relations made little difference to the antagonists facing up to each other in Petrograd. The intensity of the debates on foreign policy increased during October with Kerensky and most Kadets arguing in favor of one set of proposals while the Mensheviks and their socialist comrades argued in favor of another.

The Kerensky government clung to the Allied powers in the hope of restoring some of Russia's international prestige. The Minister-President tried to enlist allied support in order to prevent the total collapse of Russian arms before the unfolding German attack. Kerensky's task was not an easy one. In addition to explaining his motives to the hostile socialists in the Preparliament, he also had to deal with the skepticism of the Allies; the English and French had concluded that Russia could render little assistance to the work of defeating the Central Powers and were not prepared to be lavish with military aid unless tangible steps were taken by the Provisional Government to introduce order at home and in the Russian army. In most of this action Kerensky had the support of the Kadets.

In total opposition, the Mensheviks still hoped to lead Europe away from military victory and toward a general peace. They refused to accept Kerensky's invitation to bargain with the Allies. They filled the Preparliament sessions with demands for a general peace in Europe and with polemics against the imperialist character of Kerensky's diplomacy. Only the united working classes could peacefully settle the European struggle and maintain an adequate defense for Russia. Attempts to end the war without their leadership would bring disaster. Charges of treachery were made by socialists after the circulation of rumors that the Allied governments were preparing to conclude an armistice with Germany at the expense of Russia. These sordid tales probably arose out of the Vatican's unsuccessful attempts to secure a general peace in Europe, but they were interpreted by the Mensheviks as a devious maneuver to crush the revolution and shift conditions in Europe from an imperialist war to an imperialist peace. Most socialists in the Preparliament held Kerensky responsible for the unpleasant situation. When would Kerensky understand that peace and national self-determination would be gained only through the victory of labor in its struggle within each belligerent coalition?[18] Mark Liber asked government officials: "When will the propertied classes realize that victory to the end is out of the question?"[19] Participating with the Allies in an effort to end the war on exclusively military terms, the Provisional Government worked for neither peace nor the safety of the revolution. The Mensheviks wanted no part of such a policy. The debate became even more detrimental to the hopeless cause of internal unity when Kerensky tried to cultivate the friendship of some Mensheviks in the Preparliament. Most Mensheviks responded by using even more vile terms of abuse against the Minister-President, and to make matters worse the Kadets responded to Kerensky's leftist twitches by demanding that the Provisional Government insure the territorial integrity of Russia. It soon became a three-cornered battle.

One particularly lively exchange took place just prior to the meeting of the Inter-Allied conference on war aims scheduled for sometime in the fall of 1917. The conference was to be another in a series of efforts designed to improve the Allied military effort, and this particular meeting was expected to result in the formation of an inter-Allied military staff to coordinate strategy in the field. It was first scheduled to meet in early October by the redoubtable David Lloyd George both to sharpen the Allied military posture and to undermine the political influence of his home opposition; the conference was postponed several times, and it finally began only after the Bolshevik *coup d'etat*. The Mensheviks were suspicious that the dark hand of imperialist diplomacy would be at work during the conference throttling cries for a truly just peace, so they introduced an amazing innovation. They announced in the Preparliament that socialists throughout the world would send their own representative to the Inter-Allied conference. A representative of "democracy throughout the world" would be sent to preach the message of a general peace without annexations and indemnities to the high war council. The narcissistic Menshevik Michael Skobelev was selected to undertake this task of changing the character of international diplomacy.[20] The socialists in the Preparliament became disgusted and further annoyed with Kerensky when the Allied leaders announced their refusal to permit Skobelev to join the sessions of the conference.

The lack of unity in Petrograd hurt Russia's chances of holding even a weak position among the Allied powers, and it did nothing to slow down the advancing German armies. The fall of the island of Osel to the Germans, giving them an important tactical advantage in the Baltic region, frightened many socialists, but when Kerensky suggested that the government undertake a military reform and remove Russia's capital from Petrograd to Moscow, the socialists immediately suspected treason and counterrevolution; it was to Moscow that the Bolsheviks moved after the *coup d'etat* precisely to increase the distance between themselves and the German army. As the Germans drew closer and the military situation passed from serious to grave, the Mensheviks and their friends became quite disconcerted, but apart from the right-wing Mensheviks of *Den* they made no effort to prepare an adequate defense. As the end approached, the chief socialist spokesmen in the Preparliament only persisted in making demands for a general peace and continued to insist that only the abolition of the death penalty in the army could restore military discipline in the ranks.[21]

The battle that raged in the Preparliament between the socialists and the liberals in late September and October spread to include technical issues that had already been drawn into the political arena. Among the most important of these were the government monopolies on bread, meat and fuel. The seriousness of these problems had been acknowledged but not fully understood until Kerensky brought them to the attention of the Moscow State Conference. Unfortunately, the socialists and liberals who had reluctantly agreed to work together in August were poles apart in October. Whatever progress had been made in Moscow was wiped out during the Kornilov affair, and the mere mention of the word monopoly brought on a barrage of abuse from both groups. This reaction was obviously detrimental to reform, and it gave the whole matter an ironic twist because the remedies suggested by both the Mensheviks and the Kadets were alike in many respects. Unlike the disagreement in foreign policy where differences often seemed irreconcilable, the polemics over the monopolies came down to a question of who would carry out the reform and not how to change the direction of government policy.

In the Preparliament and throughout the socialist newspapers the government food and fuel monopolies were now viciously condemned as devices used by "property" to force the "socialist camp" into meeting the ruthless demands of its domestic foes. Avilov considered the shortages of bread and other products and the rapidly rising prices of food as evidence of a plot executed by "the knights of greed ... to strangle the country." He demanded that the entire administration of the monopolies be taken away from the government and turned over to representatives of the people.[22] Other Mensheviks and Social Revolutionaries were not as radical as Avilov in their assessment of the facts, but they too saw a conspiracy at the heart of the problem. They were not prepared to make the conciliatory gestures that were made in August. In some cases the Mensheviks prescribed the requisition of grain as a measure for relieving the crisis, but they most often recommended that Kerensky rely exclusively on the advice of socialists in all matters pertaining to the production and distribution of food and fuel.[23] On October 14 a committee dominated by Mensheviks was established in the Preparliament to formulate a plan of action, but aside from calling for price regulation nothing was accomplished by the committee.

Kerensky was supported in this exchange by the Kadets and a few Menshevik economists, and he refused to surrender leadership. He held the opinion that food and fuel shortages could not be relieved simply by changing the personnel who managed the monopolies or by using requisition gangs to collect supplies. The official position of the government remained what it had been at the Moscow State Conference. Shortages were blamed on the lack of transportation facilities and the devaluation of the currency. Moreover, they were made worse by the hoarding practices employed by the peasants in rural Russia. Kerensky intended to maintain government control over grain and fuel production in areas where control could be exercised and he asked for the assistance of the Preparliament. But his efforts to persuade socialists to cooperate with Kadets and to respond favorably to action by the Provisional Government brought him up against a stone wall.

Despite the one-sided interpretations of historians writing today in the Soviet Union, they are absolutely right in concluding that the argument over the monopolies reached a dead end by the fall of 1917.[24] The intense politicization of the supply and production issues at a time when resolute and united action was needed eliminated the chances for effective reform and encouraged further breakdown. By October, the first question that required an answer was how could a united management group be formed to administer the government monopolies on food and fuel. An impasse had been met. The Provisional Government, the Kadets and the socialists in the Preparliament could no longer work together. The technical problems that might have been unraveled in the spring or even in the summer of 1917 were a mess by October because friction among the February leaders prevented movement in almost every phase of public life.

The darkening political outlook was not brightened by a rapid increase in the number of peasant disturbances that broke out in late September and early October of 1917, although there is a question as to whether these disturbances ever came near reaching the magnitude of the rural civil war described in Lenin's writings. As usual, the socialists and the government were at odds as to how to cope with both the peasants and the dilemma of land ownership in Russia, and matters were complicated even further by the wide division that existed between the Mensheviks and the Social Revolutionaries on questions of land reform.[25] Friction between the Petrograd Soviet and the Provisional Government first appeared when the Major Land Committee was established by the government on April 21 and placed under the direction of both Social Revolutionaries and Kadets (the Committee did not convene until after the May coalition was formed). The task of the Major Committee was to prepare reports on the subject of land reform and to deal provisionally with those rural problems that just could not wait until the meeting of the Constituent Assembly. Unfortunately, the Major Committee became a major battleground because the Social Revolutionaries possessed one mentality and the Kadets another, and because local land committees appeared throughout rural Russia to make demands on the government.[26] When the local committees found themselves in disagreement with the Major Land Committee, they could usually count on sympathy and support from Social Revolutionaries sitting on the Major Land Committee. In the summer of 1917 some local committees began to exercise more power than the government could allow, but the Soviet leaders proved reluctant to help curb this activity. In fact, Tsereteli moved against the expressed wishes of most Kadets in the Major Land Committee by creating the July 12 law that forbade the buying and selling of land prior to the Constituent Assembly.[27] The law was supposed to protect the peasantry from land speculators until the meeting of the Constituent Assembly, but the Kadets interpreted the law as an illegal move designed to restrict the rights of the landowning peasantry and the gentry; its enactment was also a rare act of leadership undertaken by a Menshevik in 1917 against the agrarian problem.

In October, Kerensky put forth a makeshift land program that was the work of S. M. Maslov (Social Revolutionary and Minister of Agriculture) in hopes of attracting support from most socialists and of salvaging for the government as much of the fall grain crop as possible. The quickly deteriorating Social Revolutionary party could muster little support for the Kerensky-Maslov plan and the Mensheviks reacted in the Preparliament by criticizing both the government plan and the Social Revolutionaries who rejected it.[28] No agreement was reached on the Maslov plan, or on any other plan, which seems ridiculous in retrospect because all the February leaders from right-wing Kadets to Menshevik Internationalists opposed random peasant seizure of land and agreed that all final land reform measures be left to the Constituent Assembly; Lenin was the only important political leader in favor of the direct seizure of land.

The failure of the Petrograd Soviet and the Provisional Government to devote a great deal of energy to the land tenure question has been criticized by many historians, although much of the criticism has been based on dubious assumptions. The peasant role in the revolution has not yet been carefully investigated, perhaps because the evidence is not readily available and even the rare Soviet publications on the subject are only pioneering efforts. Obviously, the Mensheviks paid little attention to the peasants in 1917, except for a brief discussion of the question during the August Congress by Maslov, Rozhkov and Cherevanin, and it was equally obvious that the Kadets were willing to let the whole matter rest until the political stability of the new regime was assured. The Social Revolutionaries showed a deeper interest in peasant affairs, but just how closely their plans met the real needs and demands of the peasant is difficult to tell; the Social Revolutionaries themselves could not reach unanimity on this issue.

In the final battle for control of the state the peasantry played no direct role. The Provisional Government did not fall as the result of a peasant upheaval. As one contemporary writer concluded, Lenin even planned to divert peasant energy that might have been directed toward Petrograd in order to deal with his political adversaries without interference.[29] On the other hand, the question of land tenure in rural Russia became an important political factor because it helped to increase the friction that already existed within the February leadership.

The breakup of the Menshevik party added yet another ominous dimension to the dreary picture depicting relations between the liberals and socialists in October. Cohesion within the movement first appeared as a significant factor in March of 1917 and it carried the party leaders above the petty factionalism that had devoured so much energy up to that point. It was a tenuous unity, but it enabled the Mensheviks to give direction to Soviet politics and to exercise an influence in government affairs far beyond their small numbers. It was one chief reason why the Soviet remained bound to the Provisional Government for six months and why the February regime enjoyed stability. Unsuccessful attempts were made by Martov and the Internationalists to dissolve this unity, but not until after the Kornilov affair did the movement lose its internal cohesion and return to the pre-revolutionary state described so well by Lenin: Mensheviks, groups in the minority. In the fall of 1917 the Menshevik party began to resemble little more than a collection of squabbling political cells without a leader or a tactic to draw it together.[30]

The party's first big step toward disintegration was the rejection of the leadership of Tsereteli and Chkheidze. These former Soviet leaders could not persuade enough Social Democrats in Petrograd to sign a petition placing their names among those candidates competing as Mensheviks in the forthcoming election to the Constituent Assembly. The two Georgians were also prevented by the Menshevik Internationalist-dominated Petrograd city organization from entering the lists as Menshevik candidates from the Petrograd *guberniia* organization or from one of the *raion* committees in Petrograd. They were rejected as acceptable candidates by Menshevik party members from the Vyborg *raion* and by the representatives of the general *raion* meeting held in Petrograd on October 9; only the Narvsky *raion* committee stood against the majority and requested that Tsereteli's name be included on the ballot.[31] Nor could Tsereteli and Chkheidze secure a position on the lists as Menshevik representatives from Georgia, their native land. Both men were finally listed as party candidates in some rural *guberniia* and in some army units (established as election districts), but this weak response only emphasized the rejection that took place after the close of the Democratic Conference.

The rejection of Tsereteli and Chkheidze was only the beginning of the disintegration of the Menshevik party after the Kornilov revolt. A quarrel arose after Tsereteli was removed from the election lists. An exasperated Potresov soon persuaded the self-defensists of *Den* to reject the Menshevik Central Committee's new list of candidates and present their own Menshevik self-defensist candidates. The move attracted some followers in the party, but it was declared illegal by the Central Committee.[32] Adding to the growing factionalism, the Menshevik Internationalists decided to retain their independence as a distinct Menshevik group and presented their own list of Constituent Assembly candidates, but even they lost strength during the autumn collapse. Internationalists left Martov's *Iskra* and drifted about in small groups, calling for the adoption of various reform measures or, as in the case of Iuri Larin, joining the Bolshevik party. Still others like Sukhanov and Avilov continued to write for *Novaia Zhizn*; these Mensheviks did not join Martov, although they usually found themselves in agreement with his political tactics. Needless to say, none of this divisive activity could lure Plekhanov's small group into the Menshevik party fold.[33]

A good illustration of the troubles that beset the party in the fall of 1917 was the sorry state of the new Central Committee, elected at the August Congress but truncated during September. The higher administrative committees of the Menshevik party never wielded much political strength, being unable to coerce party members, and Tsereteli's ability to unite the Mensheviks at the May Conference was an exceptional moment in party history; the confidence and strength of the party between late March and late August was clearly reflected in the straightforward and courageous writing that appeared in *Rabochaia*

Gazeta. After the Kornilov revolt and the weakening of Tsereteli's position as leader, old habits quickly reappeared. As the party separated
into many pieces, the Central Committee lost most of its prestige and
all of its verve. Part of the reason rested in the loss of many of the best
Committee members. Ivan Kubikov, F. Iuden, and G. Broido deserted
their posts on the Committee and went in their own directions, some
joining the editorial staff of *Rabochaia Mysl*.[34] The columns of *Rabochaia
Gazeta* soon began to reflect the shabby state of affairs. Hesitancy and
vacillation replaced confidence and leadership in the articles written in
September and especially in October. Nor did the Central Committee
make a substantial effort to reverse the trend toward party disintegration. It announced its intention to remain neutral and stand above the
fighting factions. Nothing better illustrated the wretched condition of
the Central Committee in October than the meagre qualities of its
new leading figure, Feodor Dan, a man capable of neither creative and
clear thinking nor decisive leadership.[35]

One historian concluded from his study of this period that Martov's
influence in the movement increased considerably after the Kornilov
affair and that he finally gained control over the Menshevik party in
December of 1917.[36] It was true that Martov's ideas became increasingly important among the Mensheviks between May and August and
that his Internationalist faction helped to force Tsereteli and Chkheidze
into isolation in September and October; it was also true that Martov
gained the title of party head late in 1917. By December, however,
there was no longer a Menshevik party to control. It had disappeared
for all practical purposes in September and October. Martov had
simply become the head of a faction that made the exaggerated claim
to represent Menshevism.

c) Lenin Takes Command

On only one point did the Mensheviks remain unified, and then only
for a short period of time. They were in complete opposition to Lenin's
plans to seize state power. All the Menshevik newspapers in Petrograd
and Moscow, whose editors were now arguing among themselves,
implored Lenin to cease his preparations to execute a *coup d'etat*. In this
respect the weakened condition of the Menshevik party and the dissolution of the moderate socialist bloc had no effect on these outspoken
critics of Lenin's adventure. According to the Mensheviks, the few

months that passed between February and September had not given the revolution enough time to transform bondage Russia into a society that could tolerate political dominance by socialists.[37] An attempt made now to place socialists in control of all political life would quickly isolate the proletariat, to use the jargon of the day, and invite the destruction of the revolution. In fact, the political situation in Petrograd and throughout Russia was even more dangerous now than it had been during the July days when Lenin's first attempt to meddle with the "correct form of revolutionary government" brought out signs of "philistine power." Had not Lenin learned his lesson?[38]

Even the Menshevik Internationalists opposed Lenin in October. Martov exclaimed in an often quoted passage recorded by Sukhanov: "Now the revolution is endangered not by the Right, but by the Left."[39] Martov continued to oppose Kerensky and Miliukov, but Lenin's propsed dictatorship of the proletariat and poor peasantry drew most of his fire in the three weeks prior to the seizure of power. The left-wing Menshevik and former Bolshevik V. Bazarov joined the anti-Lenin parade and added his own finesse to the criticism. Unlike most Mensheviks, who dismissed Lenin's arguments as unworthy of serious analysis, Bazarov accepted at face value Lenin's expressed desire to dismantle the bondage system by using a popular dictatorship in order to drive all adversaries into exile. But his willingness to examine Lenin's motives did not make Bazarov a sympathizer. In his opinion the Soviet was technically unprepared to function as a substitute for government power in Russia. It would be incapable of completing the lofty and arduous mission assigned to it by Lenin. Moreover, he cautioned Lenin not to be deceived by the radical mood prevailing among the workers and soldiers in Petrograd. It was only a temporary expression of contempt for the Provisional Government, and efforts to found the revolutionary order on such fleeting moods would soon result in chaos and ultimate victory for the enemies of the revolution.[40]

The Menshevik criticism intensified into a barrage as Lenin's arguments in support of a *coup d'etat* continued to unfurl. In response to his declaration that a socialist dictatorship was needed to save the Russian revolution, as the Jacobin Committee of Public Safety was needed to save the French revolution in 1793, a Menshevik editorial quickly reminded Lenin that the Jacobins of 1793 represented much of French society while the Bolsheviks of 1917 represented only themselves; the Bolsheviks were in Petrograd, not in Paris.[41] Nor were the Mensheviks convinced that Lenin's group would long enjoy the support of the poor peasantry if it seized government power. In spite of the appearance of that anomalous abstraction among the Bolshevik battle slogans, the Mensheviks had long taught that remnants of the bondage system could be found in abundance and firmly entrenched among the peasantry. Rural Russia would ultimately turn against true socialists of all convictions. When Lenin then tried to emphasize the peasant character of his venture by including some radical Left Social Revolutionaries among his followers, his efforts were met with ridicule by the Mensheviks. True peasant representatives would come only from liberal or bourgeois radical groups, perhaps from the center and right wing of the Social Revolutionary party. Since politicians of this stamp were not to be found in Lenin's entourage, the Mensheviks urged him to call off his attack lest he introduce a regime ominously foreign to Russia's real needs.

In spite of their unity on this matter, the Mensheviks faced an awesome challenge in dealing with Lenin in October. The Bolshevik leader was well aware that differences stood between himself and the Mensheviks and for exactly that reason he had no intention of establishing a government in which the fullness of his authority depended on judgments made by the Mensheviks or by any other group. He ignored all pleas and demands to compromise, and brushed aside the "scare stories" told by the Mensheviks. He also rejected the advice of several well-known Bolsheviks, "strike-breakers," who refused to follow him up the steps to the vacant throne of the Romanov emperors. According to Lenin, one supported either his venture or counterrevolutionary plans to continue the bondage system. "There is no middle course," was one of his favorite expressions as the moment of insurrection approached. If the Mensheviks and their friends wanted to prevent Lenin from using the political confusion that reigned in Petrograd, it was clear they would have to use armed force.

Attempts made by the Mensheviks to organize active resistance against Lenin revealed once again all the confusion and fragmentation that had plagued the party since the Kornilov affair. They were united in their disapproval of Lenin's plans and methods, but once they tried to move beyond rhetoric and prevent the Bolsheviks from seizing power, no acceptable plan could be found. Furthermore, a great many Mensheviks made the situation even more difficult by objecting to the use of force under any circumstances. A few Mensheviks and Social Revolutionaries urged that armed force be employed against the Bolsheviks and pleaded with the socialists in the Preparliament to cooperate with the Kadets, at least on this particular occasion. But only persuasion was used, apparently in the hope that Lenin could be moved by verbal arguments or discouraged if a sufficient number of radical politicians could be prevailed upon to desert his following. During the final week before the seizure of power, *Rabochaia Gazeta* implored citizens to ignore Bolshevik demogoguery, answering the usual Bolshevik charges against the government and the Preparliament in a daily column pessimistically entitled "The Coming Bolshevik Uprising." The October 19 publication of the letter of the Bolsheviks Zinoviev and Kamenev, advising Lenin against seizure of power, and the general feeling among politicians in Petrograd that Lenin was making a serious error, kept alive the faint hope that the Bolshevik leader would withdraw at the last minute on his own initiative. On the eve of the opening of the Second All-Russian Congress of Soviets, *Rabochaia Gazeta* expressed a last feeble hope that the delegates might reexamine the political dangers pointed out by the Mensheviks and refuse to endorse Lenin's scheme.[42]

The last public attempt made by the Mensheviks and their socialist allies to prevent the seizure of power came at the October 24th meeting of the Preparliament, the institution Lenin had energetically denounced exactly because it stood in his way. The assembly was brought together at the request of Minister-President Kerensky, and the atmosphere was thick with anxiety. Kerensky delivered a long and dramatic speech. It began with a detailed examination of Lenin's plans for insurrection and ended with the plea: "I ask for the sake of the country — and let the Preparliament forgive me — I *demand* that this very day, at this afternoon's session, the Provisional Government receive your answer as to whether or not it can fulfill its duty with the assurance of support from this exalted gathering." Kerensky wanted to use force but his request was rejected. The reply came from Dan who stated that the proletariat was not interested in joining the Bolsheviks' "truly criminal" act that was bound to fail and induce a counterrevolution. "If the Bolshevik uprising is drowned in blood," Dan told the delegates, "then whoever wins — be it the Provisional Government or the Bolsheviks — it would mean a triumph for a third force, which would sweep away both the Bolsheviks and the Provisional Government and the whole democracy." Martov then delivered a speech in which he made his disapproval of the coming Bolshevik action quite clear, but the speech culminated in a thorough denunciation of Kerensky and the Provisional Government. He concluded his remarks by calling for the establishment of a government "guided by the interests of the democracy." During a brief recess in the sessions Dan prepared a resolution for the inspection of the assembly. The resolution stated that the pending Bolshevik revolution would not bring the Russian people peace, land and bread (as Lenin promised), but "civil war, pogroms and counterrevolution." In order to prevent this danger, Dan urged the organization of a "Committee of Public Safety consisting of representatives of municipal governments and of organs of the revolutionary democracy, acting in contact with the Provisional Government."[43] The Committee was not to use force. The resolution received 123 votes against 102 and 26 abstentions. A last minute Kadet-sponsored resolution that criticized Dan and called for the use of armed force to repel the pending insurrection was defeated. Stankevich attended the last session of the Preparliament, leaving us with a record of the pathetic finale:

> Then the voting on the resolution began, a blind voting, without preliminary agreements. A resolution worked out by Dan, stating that the Preparliament held both the Government and the Bolsheviks responsible for the Bolshevik uprising and proposing to transfer the matter of defending the country and the revolution to some kind of committee of safety composed of representatives of the Municipal Duma and to the parties, turned out to be adopted. I immediately came to the conclusion that such a resolution was nothing but a refusal to support the Government, and I expressed the supposition that the Government would resign.[44]

The right-wing Mensheviks uttered a final gasp of disgust. Writing in *Den*, Potresov concluded: "I do not know how Lenin and Trotsky will be engraved on the pages of history .... But I know one thing, the leaders of the Russian Preparliament are guaranteed the immortality of comic characters .... And on its part history will give them a kick and will say: you were contemptible."[45] Several years following the Bolshevik revolution, Dan wrote an article in which he described yet additional steps taken by the Mensheviks to prevent an uprising. On the fateful night of October 24, he and several socialists burst into Kerensky's chambers and urged him to flood Petrograd immediately with posters. They would announce a new program for the Provisional Government. It would now demand that negotiations begin for a general peace. It would also transfer land to the local land committees and convene the Constituent Assembly, "setting it for some date which I do not remember exactly." Understandably exasperated, Kerensky dismissed Dan and his companions.[46]

Lenin and his followers did not disappoint the Preparliament. They struck on October 24, having been organized in the Military Revolutionary Committee which was established by the Bolshevik-dominated Soviet on October 10, ostensibly for the defense of Petrograd; Trotsky, released from jail during the Kornilov affair, served as the tactical commander of the operation.[47] Detachments made up of sailors, soldiers, industrial workers and some hoodlums seized several important positions in Petrograd, including the State Bank, the Telephone Exchange, and the Mariinsky Palace where they "dissolved" the Preparliament. The Bolsheviks sailed the cruiser *Aurora* from its dry dock into the Neva River where it fired a few blanks salvos. The insurrectionists met little resistance. For most practical purposes the city was in Bolshevik hands by noon; as early as 10:00 a.m., the Bolsheviks announced that the Provisional Government had been deposed. Lenin's object was to seize control of the important centers of politics and communications, to depose the Provisional Government and scatter the delegates in the Preparliament (the only institutions that held the legal authority to condemn his *coup d'etat*). He then expected the Petrograd Soviet, the sole remaining institution with political authority, to transfer power from an already deposed Provisional Government to the Bolshevik leaders. Some strategic areas resisted capture, notably the Winter Palace, seat and symbol of legal government in Russia. Thus, Lenin was unable to present a *fait accompli* to the Soviet delegates at Smolny; the failure of his plans to mature at this point made Lenin extremely impatient and he threatened to shoot members of the Military Revolutionary Committee who failed to deliver the final blow.[48] In fact, Lenin had to wait until October 26 before resistance at the Winter Palace collapsed and the Soviet could stand officially as the only governing authority in the capital city. Moscow fell to the Bolsheviks several days after Petrograd, and by the end of the week it could have been said that the initial stage of the bolshevization of Russia had met with unqualified success.

The editors of *Rabochaia Gazeta* devoted almost the entire October 26 issue to a thorough castigation of Lenin and his followers. The Mensheviks were furious. Lenin had not led a mass uprising, the Menshevik newspaper insisted when explanations about the mass character of the *coup d'etat* appeared in *Pravda*. The act perpetrated by the Bolsheviks was a conspiracy carried out by a few radicals against the legitimate government: "This was not a revolution, not even an uprising. This was a military plot ... as one recollects from his reading of the history of the South American republics."[49] The editors of *Rabochaia Gazeta* compared Lenin to Napoleon III. Writing in *Izvestiia*, Dan emphasized the same point:

> Yesterday we called the Bolshevik uprising an insane venture. Today, when the attempt was crowned with success in Petrograd, we have not changed our mind. We repeat, there has been no transfer of power to the Soviets, but a seizure of power by one party — the Bolsheviks .... They can call themselves whatever they please, but this will not alter the fact that the Bolsheviks alone participated in the uprising.[50]

The Bolsheviks could now redeem themselves only by returning state authority to the hands of the Provisional Government or to a group representing all "democratic forces." The Mensheviks also argued their case amid the hostile jeers of the jubilant revolutionaries who met at the Smolny Institute on October 25th. The Menshevik Khinchuk announced that Lenin's action had not saved the country, but frustrated the true nature of the Soviet organization. "The only possible path away from the present situation is to begin negotiations with the Provisional Government."[51] Martov spoke to the crowd in the name of the Menshevik Internationalists, denouncing the conspiracy that now threatened "to drown in blood the whole proletarian movement." He tried to raise his weak voice and compete against the din created by excited revolutionaries. The only hope of escape from the danger brought on by the Bolshevik insurrection, according to Martov, was to open negotiations at once between the insurrectionary part of "the democracy" and the rest of the democratic organizations for the establishment of a popular government.[51] Neither Khinchuk nor Martov were certain what forms the future would take, but both were certain the Bolsheviks had incited a counterrevolution that would sweep away the victories they had fought so hard to achieve.

The Mensheviks remained only a few hours among the victors, and then departed in anger, accompanied out of the Smolny by the vulgarities of the soldiers and the cliches of Trotsky. They continued to harangue the Bolsheviks after leaving the Second Congress either directly or through the intermediary of the *Vikzhel* group (the All Russian Executive Committee of Railwaymen), but their pleas fell or deaf ears.[53] The harmless cries of indignation against the seizure o power actually helped Lenin more than hindered him, because the Bol shevik leader could consolidate his victory without having to fac armed resistance from the moderate socialists.

It is with considerable confidence that contemporary Soviet historians conclude that the Mensheviks and their allies, "the petty bourgeois bloc," stood no chance of preventing Lenin's *coup d'etat*, and this assertion seems especially sound to other historians who have studied the self-destruction of the Menshevik party following the Kornilov affair. But mystery still surrounds the subject, because the Mensheviks held back in their efforts to break up the Bolshevik conspiracy. True, they did not remain silent in the face of the threat. They spoke out against Lenin's plans weeks before the revolt, and courageously continued their rhetorical efforts at Smolny and through Vikzhel and other groups even after the fall of the Provisional Government. These final efforts were absolutely useless, having taken place after the fact, but they were undertaken in dangerous circumstances showing that the Mensheviks expected to gain nothing for themselves as a result of Lenin's coup. On the other hand, the Mensheviks knew fully well that only force could serve as an adequate deterrent to the Bolshevik leader. Yet force was the one method the Mensheviks refused to use and tried to prevent others from using. Perhaps it is unfair to hold them culpable for Lenin's victory, because using force implied working with some Kadets whom they suspected of forming a conspiracy all their own. But it cannot be denied that a stronger Menshevik effort in October might have forced the Bolsheviks into accepting a compromise, modifying the character of the new regime that took power.

A few days after Lenin gained control of Petrograd, the Menshevik party deteriorated even further and reduced to zero whatever chances remained for the moderate socialists to force the Bolsheviks into accepting a compromise. The party divided over its opposition to Lenin, the one issue that had the approval of all Mensheviks during the October turmoil. It was not the successful insurrection that further divided the Mensheviks, but the character of the opposition as it began to appear within a week after the *coup d'etat*. On October 30 the cadets or junkers from the Petrograd military academies tried to carry out a counter insurrection against the Bolsheviks. It was loosely connected to an anti-Bolshevik military force positioned near Tsarskoe Selo and led by General Krasnov. The junker counter insurrection ended in failure, but the appearance of non-socialist military opposition to Lenin's regime caused many Mensheviks to review their own attitudes. The action of October 30 certainly did not bring the Mensheviks back from political insignificance, but it forced them to choose sides in the coming civil war. If the civil war had begun, would the

Mensheviks support the Bolshevik government or enter the field against Lenin?[54]

The Mensheviks gave two answers to this question that quickly separated their little groups into two contending camps and established a division within the movement that was to endure for years to come. The two factions came to be known as left and right wing Menshevism. The left Mensheviks were associated with Julius Martov who decided to support the new Bolshevik government against its military opposition. The left continued to express its disapproval of Lenin and remained outspoken in its demands that the Bolshevik government stop using terror, but Martov and his friends took no steps that could "further divide the ranks of the proletariat." The new right wing Mensheviks, on the other hand, announced their determination to assist in the effort to bring an abrupt end to Lenin's government, even if they felt queasy about the use of military action. In general, the right Mensheviks were the men and women who had been loyal to Tsereteli during the events earlier in 1917. The division, however, was a new one and it should be traced to the origins of the civil war in Russia not to a disagreement about the legality of Lenin's seizure of power.

In the first week of November the left Mensheviks dissolved their relations with the *Vikzhel* resistance and made known to the Bolsheviks their desire for a reconciliation. "Social Democracy was forced to decide an urgent question," Dan wrote. Under what banner was it to fight in the civil war? He concluded that the party must not take up the sword against the Bolsheviks nor engage in illegal action against the new regime. On the contrary, in the "new Bolshevik" phase of the revolution "the party should work for harmony among the proletariat and establish unity inside the democracy and the working class by walking the path of conciliation ...."[55] The former supporter of Tsereteli retained his strong Menshevik character, demanding that the Bolsheviks reject terror as a political weapon, but essentially he called upon his comrades to capitulate to Lenin. Once the civil war developed into a major military confrontation the left Mensheviks took an even more firm stand within the Leninist camp. They denounced white military forces, "Kadets, cossacks and tsarist generals," that had taken up arms against the new government and refused to hinder Lenin's progress in any way. Martov's Mensheviks did not become Bolsheviks. They continued to urge Lenin to seek a compromise solution to the problem of state power and criticized his officials for perpetrating unprecedented acts of savagery.

The right Mensheviks took the opposite stand. They rejected their left wing comrades and refused to acquiesce in the Bolshevik insurrection. "In these days of folly, when the imposter rattles his saber in the name of the working class," the Moscow Mensheviks declared, "the working class is silent. Only an insignificant part of it, organized in the Red Guard ... is drawn toward the Bolsheviks."[56] During a brief return visit to Petrograd in November, Tsereteli tried unsuccessfully to rally his forces. He criticized the new regime, using arguments that kept within the bounds of traditional Menshevik theory. According to the former leader of the revolution, the Bolshevik plot was an adventurist enterprise that would quickly bring victory to the counterrevolution. He encouraged the use of illegal means to dislodge Lenin and Trotsky.[57] Liber, the eloquent Bundist politician joined the criticism. "The Bolsheviks are playing a major role in the counterrevolution and paving the way for a full restoration." Liber encouraged the masses to rebel against the Bolsheviks and urged the Mensheviks to give every assistance.[58]

The victory of Lenin and the outbreak of civil war presented the Menshevik right with a predicament no less frustrating than the dilemma faced by the Menshevik left. The right opposed Lenin's government and was ready to resist the new regime, but it could not coordinate its strategy nor enlist in the ranks of the White armies. Deep suspicion of the Kadets and outright hostility toward the various other groups that entered the lists against the Bolsheviks made most right wing Mensheviks reluctant to join forces with "the Kaledins and Kornilovs." The right Mensheviks opposed the Bolshevik regime and some even participated in the fighting against the Red Army, but they made an insignificant contribution. Despite the bellicose talk, the right Mensheviks were as impotent as the left Mensheviks who tried to reconcile their views with the new Soviet government. The banners that unfurled on both sides of the battlefield had little appeal to the Mensheviks. In fact, it soon became obvious that the heaviest fighting carried on by Mensheviks would be among themselves.

The left and right began to squabble against one another for titular control of what remained of the party. Aided by the prestige of Dan, the left Mensheviks were able to win a majority of seats in the Central Committee on November 1 by a vote of 12 against 11. This important capture by the left was balanced, however, by a feeling of doubt. The vote was very close and several well-known Menshevik Internationalists refused to support the left conciliation policy. On November 2 the right minority counterattacked and announced it would leave the Central Committee if the "Martov Dan Line" became the official statement of party objectives. The right opposition statement was signed by M. Goldman (Liber), B. S. Tseitlin (Batursky), K. Gvozdev, K. Dmitriev (Kolokolnikov), and S. Zaretskaia.[59] The self-defensist Potresov joined with the Mensheviks opposing Dan and Martov. The new left majority refused to compromise, although it is difficult to imagine how a compromise could have been reached, and it retained control of the Committee until November 30 when the two quarreling factions met once again. By the end of November, however, Dan and Martov had strengthened their grip in the Central Committee and further widened their numerical majority as indicated by the party's 50 against 31 vote in favor of conciliation with Lenin. The right had no choice but to withdraw and carry on the campaign through other means: convening a party congress was out of the question.

The November 30 conference of the Menshevik Central Committee had no effect on the events that were taking place in Soviet Russia. It was merely an epilogue to the democratic period and the opening chapter of the history of Menshevism in exile. Meanwhile, the Bolsheviks were launching the first campaigns to cleanse Petrograd and Moscow of all opposition parties. The Mensheviks felt the effect. On October 26 Potresov's *Den* was closed, according to the Bolshevik chroniclers, for counterrevolutionary activity. Plekhanov's *Edinstvo* was closed a few days later. *Rabochaia Gazeta* followed *Den* and *Edinstvo* into the archives, being closed in November of 1917; it opened again under different names, *Fakel* (Torch), *Luch* (Ray), *Klich* (Call), and *Novyi Luch* (New Ray), playing cat and mouse with Lenin until he closed it permanently in 1918. *Vpered*, the Menshevik newspaper in Moscow, was closed on April 2, 1918 for "counterrevolutionary activity." *Novaia Zhizn* appeared until June of 1918. The last issue of the Menshevik Internationalist *Iskra* appeared in December 1917.

The Menshevik party members shared a like fate. Many fled Petrograd for southern Russia and the Caucasus where protective family ties were strong. Here they played an outstanding role in the foundation of the Georgian Republic. Some others wandered about until the advancing Red Army forced them into exile. Those who remained in Petrograd and Moscow continued to criticize the Bolsheviks and to work in the few areas of institutional life open to them. They were arrested, released, and arrested again, harassed and persecuted until some were permitted to emigrate to Western Europe in 1920 and again in 1922, Martov and Dan, for example. Those who remained in the Soviet Union under Lenin and Stalin were eventually rounded up and executed after the Menshevik trials of 1930 and 1931, or immediately after the German invasion of the Soviet Union in 1941. A few men enjoyed active careers serving Russia's new masters. We will probably never come to know the fate of most of the thousands of men and women throughout Russia who fought under the banner of Menshevism during 1917. Some probably accepted the new Soviet government quietly, once the handwriting became clearly visible on the wall, but many probably perished during the civil war they predicted would commence if the Bolshevik leader seized control of state power.

Conclusions

The year 1917 ended with the Bolsheviks in power in Petrograd and Moscow. The Mensheviks, the Provisional Government, the Constituent Assembly and the *Vikzhel* committee were either swept aside or soon to be swept aside by men who promised to bring all people to freedom from political tyranny and economic poverty. According to Lenin, the old Russian bondage system would not surrender peacefully or even compromise with the forces of progress, nor could Russian liberals and petty bourgeois "socialists" establish a regime strong enough to complete the work started by the revolution. The cause of progress required a seizure of political power by the proletarian class and its dutiful allies. The instruments of authority had to be forcefully wrenched from the hands of those who would never use power for worthwhile purposes. Without Lenin's control over all political institutions, the revolution would not mature.

The Mensheviks rejected this political philosophy. They criticized its basic premises very early in the twentieth century, and expressed fear of its practical implications in the debates with Lenin that raged from 1905 to October 1917. When the Bolshevik plans to seize power became generally known in Petrograd and Moscow, one Menshevik writer even criticized the Bolshevik program as "asiatic socialism."[1] The Mensheviks were cautious because studies of Russian institutional history had convinced their best strategists that a regime in the hands of socialists alone would induce a counterrevolutionary uprising and lead perhaps to the restoration of the old order. Russia was not a western country, according to the Mensheviks (a conclusion they shared with Marx), and its semi-asiatic institutions could not be obliterated by socialists who excluded liberals and other groups from positions of political influence. Old Russia, the bondage system, needed to be enfeebled gradually by the efforts of several classes and even in conjunction with the work of those who could not easily be described in class terms; in fact, according to the original Menshevik revolutionary strategy, the class struggle was to play only an auxiliary role in Russia during the revolution against the tsar. If the socialists seized government power before the revolution destroyed the bondage system, they would fall as one of its victims.

This notion introduced a moderating factor into Menshevism because it encouraged socialist parties to share the political stage with other anti-tsarist groups, especially with liberals whose desires to introduce many features of capitalism in Russia were being frustrated by the restraining influences of the old system. In the eyes of the Mensheviks, a Russian revolution without liberals and socialists working toward a common goal (although for different reasons) would end in failure. The alliance between socialists and liberals could take several forms, as long as the socialists maintained political independence and as long as the liberals remained enemies of old Russia. Throughout the year 1917 the Mensheviks clung to these tactics, even if the asiatic character of Russia's political institutions was not usually made a general topic of their conversations. As leaders of the Petrograd Soviet, they shied away from political power in February and helped to pave the way for the establishment of a provisional government made up of Kadets. In May, when they reluctantly joined a coalition government, it was done only to avoid a situation in which power would fall unexpectedly into socialist hands. They took some power in order to avoid taking all power. In the summer of 1917, the Menshevik leaders in and outside the Petrograd Soviet supported the candidacy of Alexander Kerensky as Minister-President of the Provisional Government and accepted the presence of liberals in his cabinet largely to prevent a socialist force (Lenin) or the Anarchists from becoming the focus of state power. Even after the Kornilov revolt when the Mensheviks lost all confidence in the revolutionary fervor of the Kadet leadership, they still could not bring themselves to rally behind a plan that aimed at placing socialists in exclusive control of the state apparatus.

Unfortunately, the scheme that looked so reasonable possessed a fatal flaw because the Mensheviks could not develop cordial relations with the revolutionary allies they called Russian liberals. Despite Tsereteli's determination to work harmoniously with Miliukov, the hostility between the two men grew to great proportions. Despite the readiness of the Mensheviks to assist in the establishment of a liberal government in Russia, no liberal minister was free from their debilitating criticism. In fact, it might be said that the determination of the Mensheviks to work with the liberals against bondage Russia was cancelled by their determination to oppose liberal leadership in the cause of socialist purity. A few bright moments appeared in May and again in August when the signs of cooperation were evident, but these smooth moments were few and far between during a long period of hostility.

Nor were the Mensheviks prepared to cope with this contradiction in their strategy. Most party members followed Tsereteli, Chkheidze and Dan, fully expecting the policy of *poskol'ku postol'ku* to lead the revolution toward a satisfactory consummation. Only the right wing Mensheviks associated with A. N. Potresov recognized the danger and urged their comrades to compromise to a greater degree with the Kadets. Action on the Menshevik right, however, strengthened the anti-liberal sentiments among the left wing Menshevik Internationalists who then began to call for the establishment of a socialist Provisional Government in which liberals were present only as abstract figures. The poorly understood problem of how to deal with the liberals (needed but not wanted) remained with the party even after its defeat. In his memoirs, Martynov asked his Menshevik comrades why they had not obtained prior to 1917 a promise from the liberals to defend only those interests that would serve "the people," a clear indication that he still saw Russian liberals only as the tools of Social Democrats. Martynov and the Mensheviks were prepared to deal with an independent liberal party only if it obeyed their instructions.

At the root of the Menshevik dilemma was the incompatability of their liberal-socialist alliance scheme and their radical mentality encouraged by doctrinaire Marxism. Their suspicion and even hatred of class enemies hampered the plans to carry on the Russian revolution in two distinct phases and left the Mensheviks with an ambiguous attitude toward liberals. The notion that modern history was dominated by an international proletariat struggling to free itself from capitalism made sharing power with the Kadets in 1917 a painful concession that could not be made with the devotion required to bring about a stable government. It was true that Russian liberals were not the most pliable of politicians, as the Mensheviks and many contemporary historians have taken great pains to point out, but it was not the lordly behavior of the Kadets that made them enemies of the Mensheviks.

Lenin's attempt to diagnose this predicament as a typical example of petty bourgeois behavior sheds very little light on the subject, nor does it help to confine the Menshevik issue to the mystical realms of group psychology.[2] The Mensheviks were torn by an intellectual dilemma. Two complicated interpretations of Russian history came together in their tradition. One stressed Russian institutions and the other stressed international class antagonism, and when the revolution broke out each one pointed toward contradictory tactics. The more the Mensheviks tried to follow both ideas and both tactics the closer their schemes came to chaos.

With a problem of this magnitude nagging the revolutionary leadership at every step it was no wonder that the Provisional Government soon began to founder and the volatile population of Petrograd quickly lost its small store of patience. Squabbling first began between the Mensheviks and the Kadets over the relatively harmless issue of how to defuse the monarchy, but it soon carried over into the more dangerous areas of foreign policy and army reform. It was the divisions over these issues that brought riots and an early end to the first Provisional Government with the Mensheviks in the Soviet denouncing the liberals in the cabinet as propertied Russia, imperialist Russia, or, in the words of Sukhanov, the plutocracy. The imperialist plutocrats of March and April quickly reverted to the revolutionary allies in May, however, once the Mensheviks decided it was necessary to reestablish a stable government in order to dismantle bondage Russia. In the time between the riots of April 21-22 and the foundation of the coalition on May 5 the Mensheviks switched their political emphasis from class antagonism (the imperialist war) back to institutional cooperation (the alliance of revolutionary forces against bondage Russia). Unfortunately, the problem of instability was not solved in May because the tendency to attack liberals for creating the evils of society did not go away when the Mensheviks entered the first coalition. The second Provisional Government fell in July when the Marxist consciousness of the Soviet leaders again got out of hand, and at this time it was assisted by the Kadets themselves who were now irritated at being assigned the role of bourgeois exploiter.

After the collapse of the May coalition, the Mensheviks made an attempt to free themselves from the traditions of institutional history and almost succeeded in altogether rejecting the liberal alliance. They toyed with the idea of abandoning the liberals or keeping them in the government only as ornaments; in mid-July Martov even called for a temporary Soviet seizure of power, although somewhat timidly. But the second wave of rioting in mid-July revived the Menshevik fear of asiatic Russia. The images of class struggle receded from the center of the stage for the second time in 1917 and the Soviet leaders drifted once again back toward the Kadets.

Lenin recognized the Menshevik problem and tried to use it to his own advantage. When he returned to Russia in April, he urged the Mensheviks to junk the alliance strategy. He presented his argument more forcefully at the June All-Russian Congress of Soviets and again in the Soviet-sponsored parade on June 14. In July he ran a considerable risk by placing his name at the leadership of an unruly mob that was urging the Mensheviks to "depose the ten capitalist ministers" and take power themselves. But Lenin was rebuffed in late July when the Mensheviks decided to renew the old lines with Russian liberalism and allowed a new coalition government to be formed. At this point Lenin changed his own tactics. He abandoned all hope that the Soviet would seize state power under Menshevik leadership and resolved to destroy the leaders of both the Provisional Government and the Executive Committee of the Petrograd Soviet.

It fell to Alexander Kerensky to organize the last unsuccessful effort to keep the democratic regime alive. One strong point in his favor was an ability to see that the rivalry between the Soviet and the Kadets was destroying the democracy, although his understanding of what caused the rivalry was shallow. He opened a campaign to unite the February leadership around his standard at the Moscow State Conference, a meeting that has not yet received the serious scholarly attention it deserves. The conference unfolded as a discussion of the problems faced by the revolution, which Kerensky's spokesmen were careful to blame on the fallen regime and the deprivation caused by the war. The crux of all the speeches delivered by the government, however, pointed to the need for the Soviet parties and the Kadets to work together if they hoped to survive. The blame placed on the tsarist government was only a distracting gimmick used by Kerensky to avoid antagonizing men who had already antagonized themselves to the breaking point. The heart of his argument was to plead that the dismal military and diplomatic pictures, the shortages in the supply of fuel and bread, and the growing intensity of labor disturbances could be alleviated only through a cooperative effort.

Unfortunately, Kerensky's effort failed. The Mensheviks were unable to accept the intrigue surrounding the Kornilov affair without thrusting the blame on the Kadets, and when they met at the Democratic Conference in September they closed their ears to the explanation that only a few unimportant Kadet party members had been involved in a plot to overthrow the Provisional Government. Cooperation ended once and for all. The Kadet party now became and remained counterrevolutionary in the eyes of the Mensheviks and as a result both the strategy and the regime that depended on mutual cooperation fell to a final collapse. Back to the forefront came the class struggle.

Of course, the Mensheviks remained bound to some degree to their traditions and remained as opposed as they had been in the past to

Lenin's plan. They were fearful that the installation of a socialist government without any political competition or diversity would invite a restoration of the political system they were trying to destroy, and in this respect they showed good judgment. When the Bolsheviks began to prepare for the seizure of power, the Mensheviks led the attack against them in the Preparliament. They again used the strategy of Plekhanov, and the entire party from Potresov on the right to Martov on the left spoke out against Lenin. It was in fact the last act of Menshevik unity, but it stood little chance of success. The party was broken by internal feuding. Its leading figures had lost control over the Petrograd Soviet and their pervasive influence over the Social Revolutionaries. Worst of all, the Menshevik hatred of the Kadets had reached its highest point, precluding any chance for united action against the real enemies of the February revolution.

The Bolshevik revolutionaries brought to an end the significant place held by the Mensheviks in Russian history. Not only because they gradually removed Mensheviks from politics but because they also forcefully removed liberals from the scene. The presence of Russian liberals was essential for the full operation and understanding of Menshevism. The Mensheviks were part of that group in the Russian socialist intelligentsia that saw the revolution against tsarist Russia as a cooperative effort, even when their anti-liberal strain was playing an influential role in the day-to-day political combat. Menshevism as a viable revolutionary program ceased to exist once the Kadets were driven from Russian politics and Tsereteli, Martov and Dan were left without their foil. The Mensheviks would not seize power in Russia on their own initiative and they refused to attach themselves to a Bolshevik party that was ready to operate in isolation from other groups. After the October *coup d'etat* they became a splinter socialist group that criticized Lenin's new government, but in that role the Mensheviks had no significance. The Bolsheviks did not permit criticism that threatened to upset their political monopoly, and the Mensheviks were arrested or driven out of the Soviet Union.

NOTES

Introduction

1. N. V. Ruban, *Oktiabr'skaia revoliutsiia i krakh men'shevizma (mart 1917-1918 g.)* (Moscow, 1968).

2. I. G. Tsereteli, *Vospominaniia o fevral'skoi revoliutsii,* 2 vols. (Paris, 1963); N. N. Sukhanov, *Zapiski o revoliutsii,* 7 vols. (Berlin, 1922).

3. The Inter-University Project on the History of the Menshevik Movement was organized in New York in 1959. One of its functions was to record the memoirs of those Menshevik emigrés who were still alive. Among those who did publish under the auspices of the Project, however, only one author dealt exclusively with the events of 1917, a collection of documents carefully edited by the late B. I. Nikolaevsky, *Men'sheviki v dni oktiabr'skogo perevorota.* Inter-University Project on the History of the Menshevik Movement, #8 (New York, 1962). The other authors dealt with periods before or after the revolution of 1917, leaving out all recollections of the most crucial year in the history of Menshevism or treating the events of 1917 in a few brief observations. The case of the authors writing for the Inter-University Project, however, was typical of Menshevik memoirists who had little to say on the subject of 1917. *Sotsialisticheskii vestnik: organ zagranichnoi delegatsii RSDRP* (Berlin, Paris, New York, 1921-1963). The best bibliography for Menshevik publications was compiled by Anna Bourguina, *Russian Social Democracy, the Menshevik Movement: a Bibliography* (Stanford, 1968). The entries are in Russian.

4. Some remarks by Leo Lande and Boris Sapir touch on aspects of 1917. Leopold H. Haimson, ed. *The Mensheviks from the Revolution of 1917 to the Second World War,* trans., Gertrude Vakar (Chicago, 1974).

5. Anatoly Vasilievich Lunacharsky, *Revolutionary Silouettes,* trans., Michael Glenny (New York, 1967), pp. 134-135. The same theme was developed by Ruban, *op. cit.,* pp. 26-27. In most cases Soviet historians rely on a quotation from Lenin to support their argument, since he was the source of the thesis that left the Mensheviks dangling between the two struggling classes. Mints quoted from Lenin's *April Theses.* Akademik I. I. Minst, *Istoriia velikogo oktiabria* (Moscow, 1968), II, 143. Andreev used an article published by Lenin in *Pravda* in 1917. A. M. Andreev, *Sovety rabochikh i soldatskikh deputatov nakanune oktiabria: mart — oktiabr' 1917 g.* (Moscow, 1967), pp. 93-97.

6. The best known biographies of Menshevik leaders are written in English or have been translated into English. Samuel H. Baron, *Plekhanov, the Father of Russian Marxism* (Stanford, 1963). Israel Getzler, *Martov: a Political Biography of a Russian Social Democrat* (Cambridge, 1967). Abraham Ascher, *Pavel Axelrod and the Development of Menshevism* (Cambridge, Massachusetts, 1972). W. H. Roobol, *Tsereteli — a Democrat in the Russian Revolution: a Political Biography,* trans., Philip Hyams and Lynne Richards (The Hague, 1976).

Chapter I

1. A. Martynov, *Istoricheskii ocherk nashikh poriadkov: doreformennye poriadki i ikh krushenie* (Berlin, n.d.), p. 7. Plekhanov was more cautious than Martynov in setting the exact time that the bondage system took root in Russia. He stressed the importance of the changes introduced during and soon after the Mongol conquest. He also drew attention to the innovations brought about in the 16th century by Ivan IV, and he mentioned evidence of a bondage system in Russia before the great conquest. G. V. Plekhanov, *Sochineniia*, ed., D. Riazanov, 2nd ed. (Moscow, 1925), XX, 84-88. (This selection from Plekhanov was first published under the title *Istoriia russkoi obshchestvennoi mysli*.) A contemporary analysis of some of Plekhanov's thoughts on the subject of oriental societies can be found in Samuel H. Baron, "Plekhanov's Russia: the Impact of the West on an 'Oriental' Society," *Journal of the History of Ideas* (XIX), 1958, 388-404.

2. Martynov, *Istoricheskii*, pp. 8-9, 16.

3. Plekhanov, *op. cit.*, XV, 31-34, 67-70.

4. *Ibid.*, XXI, 97-98.

5. P. Aksel'rod, *K voprosu o sovremennykh zadachakh i taktike russkikh sotsial'-demokratov* (Geneva, 1898), p. 15.

6. P. P. Maslov, "Razvitie zemledeliia i polozhenie krest'ian do nachala XX veka," *Obshchestvennoe dvizhenie v Rossii v nachale XXgo veka*, ed., L. Martov, P. Maslov, and A. Potresov (St. Petersburg, 1909), I, 1-8.

7. P. Aksel'rod, *Istoricheskoe polozhenie i vzaimnoe otnoshenie liberal'noi i sotsialisticheskoi demokratii v Rossii* (Geneva, 1898), pp. 2-3.

8. V. Mech, "Sily reaktsii," *Bor'ba obshchestvennykh sil v russkoi revoliutsii*, ed., Vl Gorn, V. Mech, and Cherevanin (Moscow, 1907).

9. Recent scholarship in the Soviet Union has come close to discussing the views held by Russian Marxists on the subject of early Russian history, but has avoided a collision course with the subject, perhaps because the present Soviet state structure bears too many embarrassing similarities to the old tsarist administration. G. F. Kim, ed., *Obshchee i osobennoe v istoricheskom razvitii stran vostoka: materialy diskussii ob obshchestvennykh formatsiikh na vostoke aziatskii sposob proizvodstva* (Moscow, 1966). Some European scholars have touched on this subject. F. Tokei, a Hungarian who wrote in western Europe, summarized in a straightforward manner discussions about the Asiatic society as it is to be found in some of Marx's writings, but he did not carry his treatment into a discussion of Russia and the so-called asiatic mode of production. F. Tokei, "Le mode de production asiatique dans l'oeuvre de K. Marx et F. Engels," *La Pensee* (114), 1964, 7-32. The best general introduction to the subject of Marx and asiatic societies and how oriental studies influenced some Russian revolutionary thinkers can be found in Karl A. Wittfogel, *Oriental Despotism* (New Haven, 1957).

10. Aksel'rod, *K voprosu*, p. 15.

11. Vera Figner, *Zapechatlennyi trud* (Moscow, 1921), pp. 132-134. The notion that a collective effort would be required to change old Russia was not unknown among Russian revolutionaries, having been discussed years before

the Mensheviks appeared on the scene. The practical advantages of striking a temporary alliance between socialists and the less radical enemies of the old order were considered in the 1870's and brought into the debate between A. I. Zheliabov and his opposition at the Voronezh meeting of the Land and Freedom party in 1879.

12. A. S. Martynov, *Dve diktaturi* (Geneva, 1905), pp. 58-59. On rare occasions, a Menshevik orator or writer would state that a seizure of power in Russia by socialists may be acceptable political tactics, but only if a successful socialist revolution in western Europe occurred before the revolution broke out in Russia. The unlikely unfolding of this event would, of course, change the balance of economic forces throughout the world, as far as the Mensheviks were concerned.

13. Plekhanov, *op. cit.*, XV, 72-74.

14. V. I. Lenin, *Polnoe sobranie sochinenii,* 5th ed. (Moscow, 1967), IX, 45.

15. Plekhanov, *op. cit.*, XIII, 220-221.

16. P. P. Maslov, "Narodnicheskikh partii," *Obshchestvennoe dvizhenie v Rossii v nachale XX-go veka,* ed., L. Martov, P. Maslov, and A. Potresov (St. Petersburg, 1914), III, 96.

17. P. Marev, "Politicheskaia bor'ba krest'ianstva," *Bor'ba*, ed., Gorn et al, p. 71.

18. Aksel'rod, *K voprosu,* p. 3.

19. L. Martov, "Na ocheredi," *Iskra*, #93 (March 17, 1905).

20. V. Mech, "Liberal'naia i demokraticheskaia burzhuaziia," *Bor'ba*, p. 3. The first Russian Marxist to discuss the changes that capitalism would bring to Russia was G. V. Plekhanov in his essay *Nashe raznoglasnie*. According to Menshevik writers, it was in the nineteenth century that capitalism began to appear in Russia, intruding or penetrating into the empire from outside. Like Martynov, Plekhanov and Axelrod, Dan also believed that the birth and early growth of capitalism was a west European phenomenon and that capitalism had inroaded into Russia. It did not spring naturally from Russian conditions, but imposed itself on Russia after having been developed to an advanced stage in western Europe. Like the others, Dan believed Russian society incapable of evolving into a capitalist form from its bondage (*krepostnichestvo*) form. The bondage system had to be destroyed by pressure exerted on the Russian empire from the capitalist countries of the west. Theodore Dan, *The Origins of Bolshevism*, trans., Joel Carmichael (London, 1964), pp. 14-15. These same conclusions were implied by P. P. Maslov, *Imperializm i voina* (Petrograd, 1917).

21. Dan, *Origins,* pp. 343-344. Leon Trotsky initiated an action that would have ended with the abandonment of all cooperation with Russian liberals. The Mensheviks were tempted, but resisted. Trotsky remained a figure outside the main stream of Menshevism on this and on other matters.

22. [Martov], "Rabochii klass i burzhuaziia," *Iskra*, #79 (December 1, 1904). Solomon M. Schwarz attributed authorship of this unsigned article to Martov in *The Russian Revolution of 1905: the Workers' Movement and the Formation of Bolshevism and Menshevism*, trans., Gertrude Vakar (Chicago, 1967), p. 7.

23. Dan, *Origins,* pp. 361-363.

24. Abraham Ascher, *Pavel Axelrod and the Development of Menshevism* (Cambridge, Massachusetts, 1972), pp. 217-219.

25. Plekhanov, *op. cit.*, XIII, 215.

26. G. D. H. Cole, *The History of Socialist Thought: The Second International, 1889-1914*, vol. III, pt. I (London, 1956), p. 394.

27. Sukhanov, *op. cit.*, I, 261. *poskol'ku-postol'ku* was the term Sukhanov used to describe the conditional support rendered by the Petrograd Soviet to the Provisional Government.

28. The Second Congress of the Russian Social Democratic Workers' Party was discussed in Leopold H. Haimson's *The Russian Marxists and the Origins of Bolshevism* (Boston, 1968), pp. 165-181. Haimson's discussion of this episode deals with Martov's objections to both the elimination of worker influence and the attempt made by Lenin to control debate within the party. The minutes of the Second Congress were published in the Soviet Union. *Vtoroi s"ezd, iiul'-avgust 1903 goda: protokoly* (Moscow, 1959).

At the Fourth Congress of the Russian Social Democratic Workers' Party the various factions met at Stockholm and agreed to work together, but by 1907 it was clear that unification would not be achieved. The minutes of the Fourth Congress were also published in the Soviet Union. *Chetvertyi (Ob"edinitel'-nyi) s"ezd RSDRP, aprel' (aprel'-mai) 1906 goda: protokoly* (Moscow, 1959).

29. Dan, *Origins*, pp. 385-386.

30. *Vladimir Akimov on the Dilemmas of Russian Marxism, 1895-1903: The Second Congress of the Russian Social Democratic Labour Party a Short History of the Social Democratic Movement in Russia*, trans., Jonathan Frankel (Cambridge, 1969), p. 340. Axelrod's change of mind was examined with more sympathy by Schwarz, *op. cit.*, p. 204, than by Akimov.

31. Cherevanin, *Organizatsionnyi vopros: s predisloviem L. Martova* (Geneva, 1904), p. 6. Israel Getzler discussed Martov's views on centralization prior to the break with Lenin in 1903. Israel Getzler, *Martov: a Political Biography of a Russian Social Democrat* (Cambridge, 1967), p. 85.

32. E. A. Anan'in, *Iz vospominanii revoliutsionera, 1905-1923 g.g.* (New York, 1961). pp. 25-28. Ananin discussed the relationship between Plekhanov and Potresov.

33. "Voenno-promyshlennye komitety i dumskaia fraktsiia," *Izvestiia zagranichnago sekretariata organizatsionnago komiteta rossiskoi sotsialdemokraticheskoi rabochei partii*, #9 (February 10, 1917).

34. "Svobodnaia tribuna," *Nashe slovo*, #44(431) (February 23, 1916).

35. The Self-defensists published a collection of articles in 1916 that explained their support for a policy of defense. *Samozashchita: marksistsky sbornik* (Petrograd, 1916). Among the articles was A. N. Potresov's "O patriotizma i mezhdunarodnosti." Potresov drew the attention of Marxists to the signs of patriotism that appeared among the Russian workers during the war, but instead of rejecting these phenomenon as the effects of "bourgeois" propaganda, he saw them as manifestations of citizenship. They were good signs, because a sense of citizenship would help Russians "to shake off the deadly embrace of *aziatchina* and help to sweep Russia clean of its centuries' old evil." *op. cit.*, pp. 10-11. Other contributors to the collection included Ivan Kubikov, P. Maslov, K. Dmitriev, Vladimir Volsky, Evg. Maevski, N. Cherevanin, and V. Livitsky. A helpful discussion of the aims of the Self-defensists appeared in

the memoir of Boris Dvinov, *Pervaia mirovaia voina i rossiiskaia sotsialdemokratiia* (New York, 1962), pp. 146-152, 166-175.

36. "Korennoe raskhozhdenie," *Nashe slovo*, #165 (July 19, 1916), "Moskovskaia gruppa S.-D. men'shevikov," and "Deklaratsiia initsiativnoi gruppy," *Izvestiia zagranichnago*, #5 (June 10, 1916).

37. "Protest protiv samozashchity," *Izvestiia zagranichnago*, #5 (June 10, 1916). The protest was inspired by those Mensheviks who later rejected all arguments in favor of working in the War Industry Committees, but the document was also signed by those who later approved of the War Industry Committees yet refused to join the self-defensists.

38. The distance that Martov's anti-liberalism carried him away from the original Menshevik strategy did not become clear, even to him, until July of 1917. An understanding of his political position during the war can be gained by reading a selection of his writings that were collected and published in one volume in 1917. L. Martov, *Protiv voiny! sbornik statei 1914-1916* (Moscow, 1917), especially pp. III, 42-49 and 53-71.

39. Lenin, *op. cit.*, XXVI, 292-297, and XXX, 230-237. Much of Lenin's maneuver during the war was described in the monograph of Alfred Erich Senn, *The Russian Revolution in Switzerland 1914-1917* (Madison, 1971).

40. Dvinov, *Pervaia*, p. 7.

Chapter II

1. Pitirim A. Sorokin, *Leaves from a Russian Diary — and Thirty Years After* (Boston, 1950), p. 8.

2. "Vse—li za svobodu?" *Rabochaia gazeta,* #2 (March 8, 1917).

3. "Rossiiskaia revoliutsiia i mezhdunarodnoi proletariat," *Ibid.,* #2 (March 8, 1917).

4. Vlad Rozanov, *Organizatsiia verkhovnoi vlasti* (Petrograd, 1917), p. 3.

5. "Zhenshchina rabotnitsa," *Rabochaia gazeta,* #1 (March 7, 1917).

6. Arkadii Volgin, *Analiz russkoi revoliutsiii* (Petrograd, 1917), p. 2.

7. Andreev, *op. cit.,* pp. 43-50.

8. The maneuver between Duma leaders and Nicholas II prior to and during the February uprising was discussed by George Katkov, *Russia 1917: the February Revolution* (New York, 1967), pp. 219-223.

9. On the Kadets as a bourgeois party, see William G. Rosenberg, *Liberals in the Russian Revolution: the Constitutional Democratic Party, 1917-1921* (Princeton, 1974), pp. 20-32.

10. Sukhanov, *op. cit.,* I, pp. 274-277.

11. "Sovet rabochikh i soldatskikh deputatov," *Rabochaia gazeta,* #1 (March 7, 1917).

12. "Vremennoe pravitel'stvo," *Ibid.,* #1 (March 7, 1917).

13. "Pribytie vtorodumtsev S.-D.," *Izvestiia petrogradskogo soveta rabochikh i soldatskikh deputatov,* #20 (March 21, 1917). Hereafter cited as *Izvestiia.*

14. Sukhanov, *op. cit.,* I, pp. 21-23, and O. A. Ermansky, *Iz perezhitogo: 1887—1921 gg.* (Moscow, 1927), pp. 150-151.

15. Oskar Anweiler, *Die Rätebewegung in Russland 1905—1921* (Leiden, 1958), p. 176.

16. The appearance of two centers of power and the strong position of the Petrograd Soviet at one of the two centers was discussed by Tsuyoshi Hasegawa, "The Formation of the Militia in the February Revolution: An Aspect of the Origins of Dual Power," *Slavic Review,* XXXII, #2, June 1973, pp. 303-322. Hasegawa's conclusion, however, that the workers in Petrograd established "the essential nature of dual power" in 1917 (p. 321), was left far from proven by his analysis.

17. Boris Dvinov, *Moskovskii sovet rabochikh deputatov 1917—1922: vospominaniia* (New York, 1961), p. 16.

18. G. Aronson, *Revoliutsionnia iunost': vospominaniia 1903—1917* (New York, 1961), pp. 139-144.

19. "Bor'ba ne konchena — organizuites!" *Rabochaia gazeta,* #1 (March 7, 1917).

20. "Vse—li za svobodu?" *Ibid.,* #2 (March 8, 1917).

21. "Bor'ba ne konchena — organizuites!" *Ibid.,* #1 (March 7, 1917).

22. "Vremennoe pravitel'stvo," *Ibid.,* #1 (March 7, 1917).

23. "Pribytie vtorodumtsev S.-D.," *Izvestiia,* #20 (March 21, 1917).

24. Oskar Anweiler, "The Political Ideology of the Leaders of the Petrograd Soviet in the Spring of 1917," in Richard Pipes, ed., *Revolutionary Russia* (New York, 1969), pp. 148-149. Anweiler concluded that an "ideological" consistency

did appear in the Soviet leadership, but not until late March. He did not discover this consistency in early March, nor did he trace its source to the Bolshevik—Menshevik debates of the early twentieth century.

25. Oliver H. Radkey, *The Agrarian Foes of Bolshevism: Promise and Default of the Russian Socialist Revolutionaries: February to October 1917* (New York, 1958), p. 133.

26. Andreev, *op. cit.*, pp. 38-40, 43-46, 94-97. The same explanation of the events was advanced by G. I. Zlokazov, *Petrogradskii sovet rabochikh i soldatskikh deputatov v period mirnogo razvitiia: fevral'—iiun' 1917 g.* (Moscow, 1969).

27. Marc Ferro, *La revolution de 1917: La chute du tsarisme et les origins d'Octobre* (Paris, 1967), pp. 95-99. Ferro attributed the Menshevik refusal to seize power in February to a critical strain in their character which rendered them "comfortable only in opposition [to the government]."

28. Ortodoks, "Revoliutsiia dogmatizm," *Delo,* #3-6 (Spring 1917), pp. 17, 24-25.

29. Ermansky, *op. cit.*, pp. 156-157.

30. "K narodam vsego mira," *Izvestiia,* #15 (March 15, 1917).

31. "Nakonets — to,"*Rabochaia gazeta,* #9 (March 16, 1917).

32. "Voina i revoliutsiia," *Ibid.,* #10 (March 17, 1917).

33. Sukhanov, *op. cit.*, II, p. 201.

34. Tsereteli, *op. cit.*, I, p. 46.

35. Robert Paul Browder, and Alexander F. Kerensky, eds., *The Russian Provisional Government 1917: Documents* (Stanford, 1961), II, p. 1042.

36. Paul N. Miliukov, *Political Memoirs 1905—1917* ed., Arthus Mendel, trans., Carl Goldberg (Michigan, 1967), p. 434.

37. "My i oni voine," *Rabochaia gazeta,* #7 (March 14, 1917).

38. "Pervaia lastochka," *Ibid.,* #12 (March 19, 1917).

39. Sukhanov, *op. cit.*, II, pp. 321-322.

40. *Ibid.,* II, pp. 336-337.

41. Tsereteli, *op. cit.*, I, pp. 46-47.

42. "Vserossiiskoe soveshchanie delegatov ot Sovetov Rabochikh i Soldatskikh Deputatov: zasedanie 3 aprelia," *Izvestiia,* #35 (April 8, 1917).

43. Sukhanov, *op. cit.*, II, pp. 339-340. Sukhanov's reinterpretation of these events (March 21-22) has influenced many authors. A recent example appeared in Rex A. Wade, *The Russian Search for Peace, February—October 1917* (Stanford, 1969), p. 20.

44. Sukhanov, *op. cit.*, II, pp. 344-345. Roobol, *op. cit.*, pp. 92-94, saw both foreign and domestic political considerations as having influenced Tsereteli during the confrontation of March 21. Roobol seemed unaware, however, of the March 3 meeting of the Mensheviks when defensists and internationalits first set the stage for compromise. The meeting was held and the party established before Tsereteli arrived in Petrograd from Siberia.

45. Ermansky, *op. cit.*, p. 157.

46. A. N. Potresov, "Rokovyia protivorechiia russkoi revoliutsii," *Delo,* #3-6 (Spring 1917), pp. 112-116.

47. "Sozdanie organizatsii R.S—D.R.P.," *Rabochaia gazeta,* #2 (March 8, 1917).

48. Ruban, *op. cit.*, p. 85.

49. K. V. Gusev, and Kh. A. Eritsian, *Ot soglashatel'stva konterrevoliutsii: ocherki*

istorii politicheskogo bankrotstva i gibeli partii sotsialistov-revoliutsionerov (Moscow, 1968),
pp. 67-72.

50. Tsereteli's tactical plans can be traced back to Paul Axelrod, an important participant in the discussion on Russia's asian political heritage. Roobol, *op. cit.,* pp. 36, 37, 89.

51. "Vserossiiskoe soveshchanie delegatov ot Sovetov Rabochikh i Soldatskikh Deputatov: zasedanie 3 aprelia," *Izvestiia,* #35 (April 8, 1917), pp. 3-4.

52. "Vremennoe Pravitel'stvo o zadachakh voiny," *Rech',* #75 (March 28, 1917).

53. "Pobeda demokratii," *Rabochaia gazeta,* #19 (March 29, 1917).

54. P. N. Miliukov, *Istoriia vtoroi russkoi revoliutsii* (Sofia, 1921), I, p. 87. Miliukov did not claim the Declaration to be a victory for the Provisional Government, but he called the Soviet victory "empty and imaginary."

Chapter III

1. Sukhanov, *op. cit.*, III, pp. 93-94.
2. Tsereteli, *op. cit.*, I, pp. 82-83.
3. A translation of Lenin's April Theses can be found in Browder and Kerensky, *op. cit.*, III, pp. 1205-1207.
4. "Opasnost' s levago flanga," *Rabochaia gazeta*, #24 (April 6, 1917).
5. Current Soviet historians overlook no shred of evidence in their attempts to prove that Lenin enjoyed a strong influence among the Bolsheviks when he appeared in Petrograd in April.
6. Tsereteli, *op. cit.*, I, p. 85.
7. "Posledniia izvestiia," *Rech'*, #91 (April 20, 1917).
8. Tsereteli, *op. cit.*, I, p. 88.
9. *Ibid.*, I, p. 90.
10. Miliukov, *Istoriia*, I, p. 92.
11. "Bezumnyi shag,' *Rabochaia gazeta*, #36 (April 21, 1917).
12. N. Sukhanov, "Demokratiia i Vremennoe Pravitel'stvo," *Novaia zhizn'*, #3 (April 24, 1917).
13. "Uroki dvukh dnei," *Rabochaia gazeta*, #38 (April 23, 1917).
14. Dvinov, *Moskovskii*, p. 21. Dvinov, a Menshevik member of the Moscow Soviet during 1917, had to refresh his memory in this matter by referring to *Velikaia Oktiabr'skaia sotsialisticheskaia revoliutsiia: revoliutsionnoe dvizhenie v Rossii v aprele 1917 g.* (Moscow, 1958), pp. 781-782. This book is only one in a multivolume edition of documents on the revolution of 1917 published in the Soviet Union. It is the largest collection of material yet to appear on the revolution, or ever likely to appear.
15. Mints, *Istoriia*, II, p. 309, and Akademik I. I. Mints, "Pervyi krizis vlasti v aprele 1917 g. v Rossii," *Voprosy Istorii*, #1 (1967), p. 7.
16. Tsereteli, *op. cit.*, I, p. 105.
17. "K sobytiiam' dnia," *Rabochaia gazeta*, #37 (April 22, 1917).
18. "Krizis," *Ibid.*, #37 (April 22, 1917).
19. *Idem*.
20. Rosenberg, *op. cit.*, p. 110.
21. Alexander Kerensky, *The Catastrophe* (New York, 1927), p. 138.
22. V. B. Stankevich, *Vospominaniia: 1914—1919* (Berlin, 1920), p. 118.
23. St. Ivanovich, "Koalitsionnoe ministerstvo," *Den'*, #28 (April 8, 1917).
24. V. Kantorovich, "V zashchitu koalitsionnago ministerstva," *Ibid.*, #45 (April 28, 1917).
25. "Ministerstvo obshchestvennago spaseniia," *Ibid.*, #42 (April 25, 1917).
26. "O koalitsionnom ministerstve," *Izvestiia*, #52 (April 28, 1917).
27. Tsereteli, *op. cit.*, I, p. 130.
28. "Koalitsionnoe ministerstvo," *Rabochaia gazeta*, #39 (April 25, 1917).
29. Tsereteli, *op. cit.*, I, p. 120.
30. W. Woytinsky, *Stormy Passage: A Personal History Through Two Russian Revolutions to Democracy and Freedom 1905—1960* (New York, 1961), p. 252.
31. Stankevich, *op. cit.*, p. 92.

32. Nik Sukhanov, "Koalitsionnoe ministerstvo," *Novaia zhizn'*, #8 (April 27, 1917).

33. Tsereteli, *op. cit.*, I, p. 130.

34. "Iz zhizni R.S—D.R.P.," *Rabochaia gazeta*, #43 (April 29, 1917).

35. Both Sukhanov and Miliukov (Miliukov rather implicitly) stressed the importance of the letter of Kerensky in helping to lead the Mensheviks into a coalition government: Miliukov, *Istoriia*, I, p. 108, and Sukhanov, *op. cit.*, III, pp. 388-389. It was true that the letter of Kerensky served to increase public sympathy in Petrograd for a coalition government, and in that respect may have helped to draw the Mensheviks (Tsereteli, Chkheidze and Dan) toward a coalition. But the letter of Kerensky was not the determining factor. After all, the Kerensky note was published on April 26, two days before the Mensheviks refused to accept Lvov's first invitation to join the cabinet. If the publication of the letter had exercised strong influence on the Executive Committee, Tsereteli may have accepted Lvov's invitation. Miliukov and Sukhanov probably thought that Kerensky enjoyed as much influence among the Menshevik leaders as he enjoyed among the masses of the population in Petrograd, and based their remarks on that incorrect assumption.

36. A. N. Potresov, "Gosudarstvennye zadachi proletariata," *Vlast' naroda*, #1 (April 28, 1917).

37. N. Cherevanin, "Krizis vlasti," *Rabochaia gazeta*, #40 (April 30, 1917).

38. Tsereteli, *op. cit.*, I, p. 136.

39. "Iz zhizni partii," *Rabochaia gazeta*, #47 (May 4, 1917).

40. A. N. Potresov, "Gosudarstvennye zadachi proletariata," *Vlast' naroda*, #1 (April 28, 1917).

41. B. Gorev, "Posle krizisa," *Rabochaia gazeta*, #48 (May 5, 1917).

42. Woytinsky, *op. cit.*,

43. N. Cherevanin, "Vopros trebuiushchii neotlozhnogo resheniia," *Rabochaia gazeta*, #47 (May 4, 1917).

44. Several Social Revolutionaries also entered the cabinet, including Victor Chernov as the Minister of Agriculture and the omnipresent Alexander Kerensky as Minister of War; both men exercised more influence in their stations than the Menshevik apologists claimed they would. But the beleaguered ideologists writing for *Rabochaia gazeta* extended no effort to construct a theoretical argument in support of Social Revolutionary activity in the cabinet.

45. B. Gorev, "Posle krizisa," *Ibid.*, #48 (May 5, 1917).

46. M. Panin, "Vybor sdelan," *Ibid.*, #46 (May 3, 1917).

47. "Doverie novomu pravitel'stva," *Ibid.*, #49 (May 6, 1917).

48. M. Gol'dman-Liber, *Zadachi rabochago klassa v russkoi revoliutsii* (Moscow, 1917).

49. "Iz zhizni R.S.—D.R.P.: Obshcherossiiskaia konferentsiia Ross. S.D.—R.P.," *Rabochaia gazeta*, #51 (May 9, 1917).

50. "Deklaratsiia men'shevikov-internatsionalistov," and "Proletariat i koalitsionnoe ministerstvo," *Letuchii listok*, #1 (May 1917).

51. "I. G. Tsereteli i klassovaia bor'ba," *Pravda*, #44 (April 29, 1917).

52. Mints, *Istoriia*, II, pp. 336-337.

53. Stankevich, *op. cit.*, pp. 131-132.

54. Browder and Kerensky, *op. cit.*, III, pp. 1276-1278.
55. V. Kantorovich, "Novaia vlast'," *Den'*, #51 (May 5, 1917).

Chapter IV

1. George Buchanan, *My Mission to Russia* (Boston, 1923), I, pp. 142-143.
2. Maurice Paleologue, *An Ambassador's Memoirs,* trans., F. A. Holt (New York, 1925), III, pp. 312-313. Hildamarie Meynell, "The Stockholm Conference of 1917," *International Review of Social History* (V) (1960), pp. 1-7.
3. Tsereteli, *op. cit.,* I, p. 170.
4. *Ibid.,* I, pp. 172-173.
5. *Ibid.,* I, pp. 175-176.
6. "Postanovlenie ispolnitel'nogo komiteta Soveta Rabochikh i Soldatskikh Deputatov o konferenstii," *Izvestiia,* #51 (April 27, 1917).
7. Tsereteli, *op. cit.,* I, pp. 185, 189.
8. *Ibid.,* I, pp. 187-189.
9. *Ibid.,* I, p. 194.
10. *Ibid.,* I, p 195.
11. *Ibid.,* I, pp. 200-202.
12. Emile Vandervelde, *Souvenirs d'un militant socialiste* (Paris, 1939), pp. 237-238.
13. Henderson's private thoughts on the manner in which the Soviet leaders conducted bsuiness and political affairs were written in letters sent from Petrograd to his son in England. Excerpts were printed in Mary Agnes Hamilton's biography, *Arthur Henderson* (London, 1938), pp. 132-133.
14. Emile Vandervelde, *Trois aspects de la revolution russe: 7 mai—25 juin 1917* (Paris, 1918), p. 185.
15. "Na puti k miru," *Rabochaia gazeta,* #39 (April 25, 1917).
16. The Mensheviks finally did alter some of their restrictions, but only in the summer of 1917 after the Stockholm venture had become a moot issue as far as serious peace proposals were concerned.
17. "K sozyvu mezhdunarodnago kongressa," *Izvestiia,* #72 (May 21, 1917).
18. The failure of the Stockholm Conference is discussed from the point of view of the west European source material by Meynell, *loc. cit.,* pp. 11-23.
19. In many respects, the Menshevik peace proposals were similar to those made by Pope Benedict XV in August of 1917, although the Soviet leaders may have been reluctant to admit that fact. Like the Mensheviks, the Pope asked Europeans to seek an agreement that rejected annexations and indemnities. The Pope also feared that if a humiliating peace was imposed on the losing side after the war, another great conflict would soon follow. Humphrey Johnson, *Vatican Diplomacy in the World War* (Oxford, 1933), pp. 43-46.
20. Kh. M. Astrakhan, *Bol'sheviki i ikh politicheskie protivniki v 1917 godu* (Leningrad, 1973), pp. 225-226. Astrakhan had access to fund #275 in the Central Party Archive, which contains many documents on Menshevism in 1917. It is available only to Soviet historians, but to date has revealed no information that is new to the west.
21. "Iz zhizni partii," *Rabochaia gazeta,* #24 (April 6, 1917).
22. "Ob"edinenie men'shevikov v Sovete Rab. i Sold. Dep.," *Ibid.,* #31 (April 14, 1917). The kindred ties between the Mensheviks and the Jewish Bund were mentioned by Ruban, *op. cit.,* p. 9, who also implied that the nationalist

sentiments of the Bund were present among the Mensheviks and acted as a restraining force against internationalist aspirations.

23. Reaching the same conclusions about the dominance of the Petrograd Mensheviks at the May Conference, the Soviet historians Mints and Ruban published statistics on the Menshevik organizations in 1917. Both cited as a source the Central Party Archive—Institute for World Literature (TsPA—IML) fund #275, but neither listed the exact titles of the documents used for this statistical study. The greatest concentration of membership, according to Mints and Ruban, gave the Petrograd organizations 7,200 members, Moscow, 3,300, Kiev, 2,500, Kharkov, 2,000 and the Saratov groups 1,300 members; other cities with even fewer members included Samara, Vitebsk, Smolensk and Ekaterinoslav. Mints admitted that these statistics were based on an incomplete sample of data, but the study confirms the general impression made by *Rabochaia gazeta*, which may well have served as Mints' primary source. Outside Petrograd the party was weak and outside Petrograd, Moscow, Kiev and Kharkov it was insignificant. An exception was the Menshevik organization in Georgia. It was quite extensive, but most of its chief leaders were part of the Petrograd organizations in 1917 and the party in Georgia played no role in the capital city in 1917. Mints, *Istoriia*, II, pp. 121-122, and Noi Zhordaniia, *Moia zhizn'*, trans. (from the Georgian), Ina Zhordaniia (Stanford, 1968), pp. 73-87.

24. Tsereteli's speech to the Conference and all other speeches delivered during the Conference were published in *Rabochaia gazeta, Novaia zhizn', Edinstov* and *Den'*. These notes were later collected into one publication: *Vserossiiskaia konferentsiia men'shevistskikh i ob"edinennykh organizatsii RSDRP* (Petrograd, 1917).

25. "Iz zhizni partii," *Rabochaia gazeta*, #47 (May 4, 1917).

26. "Iz zhizni R.S.—D.R.P.," *Ibid.*, #52 (May 10, 1917).

27. G. Batursky, "Vopros o voine i mire," *Ibid.*, #53 (May 11, 1917).

28. A. Ermansky, "Kak borot'sia za mir," *Ibid.*, #56 (May 14, 1917).

29. Astrov, "Druz'ia russkoi svobody," *Ibid.*, #54 (May 12, 1917).

30. "Iz zhizni partii," *Ibid.*, #50 (May 7, 1917).

31. Iv. Kubikov, "Bez vykhoda," *Ibid.*, #58 (May 17, 1917).

32. N. Cherevanin, "Bor'ba za mir i oboron," *Ibid.*, #57 (May 16, 1917).

33. A. N. Mashkov, "Oboronitel'naia voina i nastupatel'nyia voennia deistviia," *Den'*, #47 (April 30, 1917).

34. V. Kantorovich, "Men'shevizm," *Ibid.*, #54 (May 9, 1917).

35. "Iz zhizni R.S.—D.R.P.," *Rabochaia gazeta*, #51 (May 9, 1917).

36. G. Plekhanov, "Chto zhe eto? — kak zhe eto?" *Edinstvo*, #38 (May 13, 1917).

37. Sukhanov, *op. cit.*, IV, pp. 54-55.

38. "Ob"editinitel'nyi s"ezd R.S.—D.R.P.: doklad Potresova," *Rabochaia gazeta*, #139 (August 22, 1917).

39. Lenin, *op. cit.*, XXVII, pp. 299-426. L. Martov, *Protiv*, p. III. A short discussion on imperialism and how it influenced Lenin in 1917 can be found in: Bertram D. Wolfe, "Backwardness and Industrialization in Russian History and Thought," *Slavic Review*, XXVI, #2 (June 1967), pp. 187-188. Both Martov and Lenin were attracted at the same time to the theory of imperialism, so it would probably be inaccurate to say that Martov's thought and actions were swayed by Lenin on this point. Also see P. P. Maslov, *Imperializm i voina (Moscow, 1917)*.

40. "Deklaratsiia men'shevikov—internatsionalistov," *Letuchii listok,* #1 (May 1917).

41. It is difficult to describe the personalities of most Russian Social Democrats for the simple reason that personality traits are not easily detected in their polemical writings. Some important information has been revealed through stories told by comrades, but even these accounts must be used with great caution. In some cases police records have given helpful descriptions, but these are of limited value and the individual often remains hidden behind laundry receipts, passport photographs and the reports of special agents. In some extraordinary cases the writer has revealed much of himself, for example, Sukhanov, Tsereteli or Bakunin. My own conclusions about Martov are sketchy and rely heavily on the notes made by other Social Democrats, especially Nikolay Valentinov (N. V. Volsky), *Encounters with Lenin,* trans., Paul Rosta and Brian Pearce (London, 1968), pp. 224-229, and G. Ia. Aronson, "Kak zhil rabotal Iu. O. Martov," *Martov i ego blizkie: sbornik* (New York, 1959), pp. 86-102.

42. This same conclusion was reached by Gerhard Wetting, "Die Rolle der Russischen Armee im Revolutionären Macht Kampf 1917," *Forschungen Zur Osteuropäischen Geschichte* (XII) (1967), p. 316.

43. L. S. Gaponenko, ed., *Revoliutsionnoe dvizhenie v russkoi armii: 27 fevralia—24 oktiabria 1917 goda* (Moscow, 1968), pp. 20-21.

44. Historians writing today in the Soviet Union generally concede that the soldier committees were loyal to the leaders of the Petrograd Soviet, at least until the summer of 1917. P. Golub, *Partiia, armiia i revoliutsiia otvoevanie partiei bol'shevikov armii na storonu revoliutsii: mart 1917—fevral' 1918* (Moscow, 1967), pp. 41-42. Woytinsky, *op. cit.,* p. 281, and Tsereteli, *op. cit.,* I, p. 398, II, p. 26.

45. "Kto vinovat v porazhenii na Stokhode?" *Rabochaia gazeta,* #32 (April 15, 1917).

46. "Soldat—grazhdanin," *Vpered!* #58 (May /17/, 1917), "Chto dezorganizuet' armiu," *Rabochaia gazeta,* #55 (May 13, 1917).

47. The incident was given brief treatment by Paul Avrich, *The Russian Anarchists* (Princeton, 1967), pp. 130-131.

48. "Nastuplenie ili gotovnost' k nastupleniiu?" *Izvestiia,* #68 (May 17, 1917). Contemporary Soviet historians interpret this article as evidence of a deliberate ploy on the part of the Mensheviks and the Social Revolutionaries to mislead the masses. A. V. Ignat'ev, *Vneshniaia politika Vremennogo Pravitel'stva* (Moscow, 1974), pp. 272-273.

49. I. Kushkin, "O nastuplenii," *Rabochaia gazeta,* #67 (May 17, 1917).

50. Lenin, *op. cit.,* XXXII, pp. 297-299, 365-367, and A. Shliapnikov, "Iiun'skoe nastuplenie," *Proletarskaia revoliutsiia,* III, /L/ (1926), p. 13.

51. V. S. Vasiukov, *Vneshiaia politika vremennogo pravitel'stva* (Moscow, 1966), pp. 182-188, and A. V. Ignat'ev, *Russko-angliiskie otnosheniia nakanune oktiabr'skoi revoliutsii: fevral'—oktiabr' 1917 g.* (Moscow, 1966), p. 250.

52. If the "authorities" expected to rely on anti-semitic activity, nationalist sentiments and the Church to work against the "revolution," then one needs to explain several disquieting factors. For example, neither the leaders of the Provisional Government nor of the Petrograd Soviet encouraged these "forces" to work in their behalf at any time during 1917. In fact on the eve of the

military offensive the Provisional Government passed legislation that transferred Church schools from clerical supervision to the jurisdiction of the state,
an act that drew criticism from all parties in the Church. With respect to the
nationalities question, the Soviet and the Provisional Government stalled, and
for that reason incurred the anger of most organized nationalist groups.
Finally, to conclude that the Mensheviks would allow themselves to be part of
any venture that included anti-semitism is simply absurd. Marc Ferro, "The
Russian Soldier in 1917: Undisciplined, Patriotic, and Revolutionary," *The Slavic
Review*, XXX, #3 (September 1971), pp. 496-497.

53. Wade, *op. cit.*, pp. 72-73, and George F. Kennan, *Russia and the West under
Lenin and Stalin* (Boston, 1960), pp. 29-31.

Chapter V

1. "Iz zhizni R.S.—D.R.P.; natsional'nyi vopros," *Rabochaia gazeta*, #57 (May 16, 1917). The Kadet statement on the nationality question was based largely on the report of F. F. Kokoshkin, delivered at the Eighth Congress of the Party of Peoples' Freedom in early May. "VIII s"ezd partii narodnoi svobody; mestnoe samoupravlenie i avtonomiia," *Rech'*, #110 (May 12, 1917).

2. The opinions of the Mensheviks on Finnish autonomy can be found in "Finliandskaia s.-d. i russkaia revoliutsiia," *Rabochaia gazeta*, #77 (June 10, 1917), on the Ukrainians in "Otlozhenie ukrainy," *Ibid.*, #81 (June 15, 1917) and on the Muslim delegation in Serge A. Zenkovsky, *Pan-Turkism and Islam in Russia* (Cambridge, 1967), p. 155. The Kadet opinions appeared in "Rezoliutsiia finliandskikh S.—D.," *Rech'*, #134 (June 10, 1917), and on the Ukrainians in *Rech'*, #137 (June 14, 1917), p. 1.

3. Browder and Kerensky, *op. cit.*, I, pp. 383-384. A full discussion of the issue from the perspective of the Rada can be found in Oleh Semenovych Pidhainy, *The Formation of the Ukrainian Republic* (Toronto, 1966), pp. 102-105, 111-117.

4. Tsereteli, *op. cit.*, II, p. 157.

5. "Vykhod ministrov chlenov partii narodnoi svobody iz sostava Vremennago Pravitel'stva," *Rech'*, #154 (July 14, 1917).

6. Leon Trotsky, *The History of the Russian Revolution*, trans., Max Eastman (Ann Arbor, 1957), II, p. 12. Trotsky's interpretation of the Ukrainian episode was also used by the contemporary Soviet historian O. N. Znamensky, *Iiul'skii krizis 1917 goda* (Moscow, 1964), p. 48.

7. L. Martov, "Nastuplenie v galitsii, *Novaia zhizn'*, #64 (July 2, 1917).

8. Lenin, *op. cit.*, XXXII, p. 407.

9. "Ukrainskii vopros," *Den'*, #84 (June 14, 1917), and "Vserossiiskii s"ezd sovetov Rab. i Sol. Deputatov; natsional'nyi vopros," *Den'*, #90 (June 21, 1917).

10. The Soviet historian Ruban holds the thesis that the Mensheviks dodged the nationality issue in their theoretical discussions, but joined with the "bourgeoisie" in practical politics, *op. cit.*, p. 198. The evidence, however, supports the opposite conclusion. The Mensheviks and the Kadets were very close in their theoretical discussions of the nationality issue, but differed in practice.

11. A. Tyrkova-Williams, *From Liberty to Brest-Litovsk* (London, 1919), p. 141. The strained relations between those few Kadets who supported the Kiev delegation and the majority in the Kadet party was discussed by Rosenberg, *op. cit.*, pp. 150-151.

12. Sukhanov, *op. cit.*, IV, pp. 389-396.

13. Alexander Rabinowitch, *Prelude to Revolution: The Petrograd Bolsheviks and the July 1917 Uprising* (Indiana, 1968), pp. 117, 135.

14. Sukhanov, *op. cit.*, IV, p. 409.

15. Dvinov, *Moskovskii*, p. 24.

16. "Gde vykhod?" *Rabochaia gazeta*, #98 (July 5, 1917).

17. "Pered resheniem," *Ibid.*, #100 (July 7, 1917). The same sentiments were expressed by St. Ivanovich, "Organizatsiia vlasti," *Den'*, #102 (July 6, 1917).

18. G. Plekhanov, "Kak zhe byt'?" *Edinstvo*, #81 (July 5, 1917).
19. "Mutnaia volna," *Rabochaia gazeta*, #100 (July 7, 1917).
20. B. I. Gorev, *Kto takie lenintsy i chego oni khotiat?* (Petrograd, 1917), pp. 3, 12.
21. St. Ivanovich, *Anarkhiia i anarkhisty* (Petrograd, 1917), pp. 15, 18.
22. Sukhanov, *op. cit.*, IV, p. 440.
23. A. Potresov, "Ukreplenie vlasti," *Den'*, #103 (July 7, 1917).
24. Tsereteli, *op. cit.*, II, pp. 152, 154.
25. Alexander Kerensky, "Iz vospominanii," *Sovremennyia zapiski*, XXXVIII (1929), p. 251.
26. Tsereteli, *op. cit.*, II, p. 350.
27. The resignation of Lvov was thoroughly discussed by Radkey (*op. cit.*, pp. 287-289) who finally accepted the Miliukov—Sukhanov interpretation; the program of July 6 and 8 was designed to eliminate Lvov from the cabinet. Miliukov, *Istoriia*, part I, II, p. 20, and Sukhanov, *op. cit.*, IV, 484-492. A recent Soviet account, however, concluded that peasant pressure applied to the February leaders brought the need for such a program, especially the sections on land tenure. N. A. Kravchuk, *Massovoe krest'ianskoe dvizhenie v Rossii nakanune oktiabria (mart—oktiabria 1917 g. po materialam gubernii evropeiskoi Rossii)* (Moscow, 1971), p. 30.
28. P. Iushkevich, "Vsiakomu—po zaslugam," *Den'*, #108 (July 13, 1917).
29. "Konter-revoliutsii ne dremlet," *Rabochaia gazeta*, #101 (July 8, 1917).
30. A. Potresov, "Puti k soglasheniiu," *Den'*, (July 14, 1917).
31. *Rech'*, #164 (July 15, 1917), p. 1.
32. Tsereteli, *op. cit.*, II, pp. 372-373.
33. "Zaiavlenie I. G. Tsereteli," *Izvestiia*, #119 (July 16, 1917).
34. "Kak spasat stranu?" *Rabochaia gazeta*, #105 (July 13, 1917).
35. "Novoe pravitel'stvo i burzhuaziia," *Ibid.*, #104 (July 12, 1917).
36. Martov wrote two articles that revealed his views at this time. "Chto zhe teper'?" and "Revoliutsionnaia diktatura," *Novaia zhizn'*, #76 (July 16, 1917) and #77 (July 18, 1917).
37. Potresov's views were expressed in two articles. "Iskusstvo generala Rennenkampfa," and "Leninizm na iznaky," *Den'*, #116 (July 18, 1917) and #117 (July 20, 1917).
38. Iv. Kubikov, "Neprimirimoe protivorechie," *Rabochaia gazeta*, #109 (July 18, 1917).
39. "Novoe pravitel'stvo," *Ibid.*, #116 (July 26, 1917).
40. "Krizis pravitel'stva," *Ibid.*, #115 (July 25, 1917).
41. Lenin, *op. cit.*, XXXII, pp. 428-432, XXXIV, 1-5, 10-17. *Three Crises* was published on July 7, 1917. *On the Political Situation* appeared on July 10, 1917. *On Slogans* was published in mid-July 1917.
42. Znamensky, *op. cit.*, p. 288.
43. *Kritika: a Review of Current Soviet Books on Russian History*, #1, II (1965), pp. 50-57.

Chapter VI

1. Kerensky was the only leading politician in the Provisional Government who tried to make a compromise with the Russian Orthodox Church. He rcognized its pervasive influence among the Russian people and was devoid of the anti-clerical moods that restricted many liberals and socialists.

2. *Rech'*, #185 (August 9, 1917), p. 1.

3. *Ibid.*, #184 (August 8, 1917), p. 1.

4. "Moskovskoe soveshchanie," *Rabochaia gazeta*, #125 (August 5, 1917).

5. "Moskovskoe soveshchanie," *Den'*, #127 (August 4, 1917), and G. Plekhanov, "Nakanune moskovskago soveshchaniia," *Edinstvo*, #100 (August 8, 1917).

6. "Gosudarstvennoe Soveshchanie v Moskve: rech' A. F. Kerenskago," *Rech'*, #189 (August 13, 1917), p. 3.

7. K. I. Zaitsev, N. V. Dolinsky, and S. S. Demosthenov, *Food Supply in Russia during the World War* (New Haven, 1930), pp. 82-111.

8. "Gosudarstvennoe soveshchanie v Moskve: rech' S. N. Prokopovicha," *Rech'*, #189 (August 13, 1917), p. 4.

9. "Ekonomicheskaia programma isp. komiteta Soveta Rabochikh i Sold. Deputatov," *Novaia zhizn'*, #31 (May 25, 1917).

10. D. Dalin, "Finansovye eksperimenty," *Novaia zhizn'*, #58 (June 25, 1917). J. L. H. Keep, *The Russian Revolution: a Study in Mass Mobilization* (New York, 1976), p. 176.

11. "Zasedanie 14-go avgusta: rech' N. S. Chkheidze," *Den'*, #136 (August 16, 1917), p. 2.

12. N. Cherevanin, "Bor'ba s Sovetami," *Rabochaia gazeta*, #127 (August 8, 1917).

13. P. V. Volobuev, *Ekonomicheskaia politika Vremennogo Pravitel'stva* (Moscow, 1962), pp. 388-389, and B. M. Freidlin, *Ocherki istorii rabochego dvizheniia v Rossii v 1917 g.* (Moscow, 1967), pp. 94-96.

14. S. O. Zagorsky, *State Control of Industry during the War* (New Haven, 1928), pp. 46-51.

15. N. G. "Kak khotiat promyshlenniki borot'sia s razrukhoi?" *Rabochaia gazeta*, #126 (August 6, 1917), and "Zheleznodorozhnaia strada," *Ibid.*, #45 (May 2, 1917).

16. Volobuev, *op. cit.*, p. 204.

17. "Gosudarstvennoe Soveshchanie v Moskve: rech' S. N. Prokopovicha," *Rech'*, #189 (August 13, 1917), p. 4.

18. *Idem.*

19. Paul Avrich, "Russian Factory Committees in 1917," *Jahrbücher für Geschichte Osteuropas*, XI (1963), pp. 161-182, and Anweiler, *Die Rätebewegung*, pp. 155-156. Contemporary Soviet historians emphasize the importance of the Factory Committees, but they reject the views of most western historians who argue that the influence of the Bolshevik party among these groups was insignificant. Avrich's views on the subject are criticized by L. S. Gaponenko, *Rabochii klass Rossii v 1917 godu* (Moscow, 1970), p. 302. A strong account of the

development of the factory committee movement in 1917 and the place of the
Bolshevik party in it can be found in Keep, *op. cit.*, pp. 78-89.

20. N. Garvi (Iu. Chatsky), *Kapital protiv truda* (Petrograd, 1917), pp. 5-6.

21. "Vtoraia konferentsiia fabr—zavod. komitetov," *Rabochaia gazeta*, #130
(August 11, 1917).

22. "Zasedanie 14-go avgusta: rech' N. S. Chkheidze," *Den'*, #136 (August 15,
1917), p. 3.

23. Alexander M. Michelson, Paul N. Apostol, and Michael W. Bernatzky,
Russian Public Finance during the War (New Haven, 1928), p. 305.

24. *Ibid.*, pp. 190-191.

25. Volobuev, *op. cit.*, p. 366-367.

26. "Gosudarstvennoe soveshchanie v Moskve: rech' N. V. Nekrasov," *Rech'*,
#189 (August 13, 1917), p. 4.

27. "Zasedanie 14-go avgusta: rech' N. S. Chkheidze," *Den'*, #136 (August
15, 1917), p. 3.

28. *Rech'*, #192 (August 17, 1917), p. 1. These same sentiments were also
expressed by V. Maklakov in the speech he delivered at the Moscow State
Conference.

29. "Gosudarstvennoe Soveshchanie v Moskve," *Izvestiia*, #145 (August 16,
1917).

30. "Chestnaia koalitisiia," *Den'*, #139 (August 18, 1917).

31. "Itogi soveshchaniia," *Rabochaia gazeta*, #135 (August 17, 1917).

32. Nik Sukhanov, "Pirrovy pobedy na moskovskom front," *Novaia zhizn'*,
#104 (August 18, 1917).

33. Astrakhan, *op. cit.*, pp. 288-289.

34. "Gosudarstvennoe Soveshchanie v Moskve: zakliuchitel'naia rech' A. F.
Kerenskogo," *Rech'*, #191 (August 16, 1917), p. 4.

35. The divisions among the Petrograd Mensheviks prevailed even within
the small party groupings. For example, Martov's Menshevik Internationalists
were not the sole configuration on the Menshevik left. Many of the men writing for *Novaia zhizn'*, like Avilov and Sukhanov, considered themselves to be
Menshevik Internationalists but did not join forces with Martov. Other groups
and individuals also existed on this left fringe, some of whom joined the Bolsheviks, like Trotsky and Lunacharsky, while others, like Zinoviev and Kamenev, remained Bolsheviks but were unable to support the seizure of power
in October; both Zinoviev and Kamenev stood on theoretical ground similar to
Martov when they rejected Lenin in October. On the right of Tsereteli the
situation was much the same. Plekhanov, the chief founding father of Russian
Menshevism, remained aloof from all party maneuver in 1917 and tried to
form his own Social Democratic party. But even Potresov, a strong proponent
of Tsereteli's leadership, kept his distance from the Menshevik leaders in the
Soviet. His group included Ivanovich and other Mensheviks who wrote for the
Petrograd journal *Den'*.

36. Isaac Deutscher, *The Prophet Armed: Trotsky, 1879—1921* (New York, 1954),
pp. 255-282.

37. "3-ia obshchegorodsk konferentsiia, R.S.—D.R.P.," *Rabochaia gazeta*, #128
(August 9, 1917).

38. A. N. Potresov, "K voprosu ob ob"edineii partii," *Den'*, #126 (August 3, 1917).

39. "K ob"edinitel'nomu s"ezdu," *Rabochaia gazeta*, #136 (August 18, 1917).

40. G. Lindov, "K ob"edinitel'nomu s"ezdu," *Novaia zhizn'*, #104 (August 18, 1917), and A. G. Kipen, "K edinstvu," *Vpered!* #117 (July 28, 1917).

41. "Ob"edinitel'nyi s"ezd R.S.—D.R.P.," *Rabochaia gazeta*, #143 (August 26, 1917), and "Ob"edinitel'nyi s"ezd R.S.—D.R.P.: Iz materialov s"ezda," *Ibid.*, #144 (August 27, 1917).

42. "Ob"edinitel'nyi s"ezd R.S.—D.R.P.," *Ibid.*, #139 (August 22, 1917).

43. L. Martov, "Chto zhe teper'?" *Novaia zhizn'*, #76 (July 16, 1917).

44. L. Martov, "Sryv mezhdunarodnoi konferentsii," *Ibid.*, #90 (August 2, 1917).

45. "Ob"edinitel'nyi s"ezd R.S.—D.R.P.," *Rabochaia gazeta*, #139 (August 22, 1917), and #140 (August 23, 1917).

46. *Novaia zhizn'*, (August 30, 1917), as cited by Astrakhan, *op. cit.*, p. 301.

47. A. N. Potresov, "K itogam ob"edinitel'nyi s"ezda," *Den'*, (August 27, 1917).

48. P. A. Garvi, *Professional'nye soiuzy v Rossii v pervye gody revoliutsii 1917—1921* (New York, 1958), p. 23, and Aronson, *Revoliutsionnia*, p. 288.

49. B. Savinkov, *K delu kornilova* (Paris, 1919), pp. 20, 23. According to Savinkov, Kornilov was especially irritated at Kerensky's unwillingness to approve orders designed to restore discipline in the army by increasing the severity of the punishment meted out to soldiers.

50. Abraham Ascher, "The Kornilov Affair," *The Russian Review*, XII (October 1953), pp. 244-245, and Rosenberg, *op. cit.*, pp. 222-224.

51. *Rabochaia gazeta*, #144 (August 27, 1917), p. 1.

52. "Vdokhnoviteli kornilova," *Rabochaia gazeta*, #146 (August 29, 1917), and N. Ch. "Sabatazh kadetov," *Ibid.*, #144 (August 27, 1917).

53. B. Avilov, "Neodorazumenie," and "Novye soiuzniki," *Novaia zhizn'*, #144 (August 29, 1917).

54. "V otkrytuiu," *Den'*, #150 (August 30, 1917).

55. Sukhanov, *op. cit.*, VI, p. 183.

56. N. Ia. Ivanov, *Kornilovshchina i ee razgrom* (Leningrad, 1965). Kerensky's account of the incident can be found in *The Prelude to Bolshevism* (London, 1919).

57. James D. White, "The Kornilov Affair; a Study in Counterrevolution," *Soviet Studies*, XX (July 1968), p. 190, and Savinkov, *K delu*, p. 24.

58. Rosenberg, *op. cit.*, p. 288 fn.

59. George Katkov, *Russia 1917: The Kornilov Affair; Kerensky and the Break-up of the Russian Army* (London, 1980), p. 107. Katkov's study of the Kornilov affair is the most thorough and precise to be found. In treating the episode of Kornilov's retention as Commander-in-Chief, he commented: "We thus have the ludicrous situation of a government ordering the troops to obey a general whom it had charged with rebelling against it."

Chapter VII

1. B. Avilov, "Ispugannye obyvateli," *Novaia zhizn'*, #123 (September 9, 1917).
2. "Novyi zagovor," *Ibid.*, #124 (September 10, 1917).
3. Radkey, *op. cit.*, pp. 393-413.
4. Andreev, *op. cit.*, p. 346.
5. "Vserossiiskoe soveshchanie demokr. organizatsii," *Rabochaia gazeta*, #161 (September 15, 1917).
6. "Vserossiiskoe soveshchanie demokr. organizatsii," *Ibid.*, #163 (September 17, 1917).
7. V. Ezhov, "V chem delo?" *Ibid.*, #153 (September 6, 1917).
8. "Nakanune demokraticheskago soveshchaniia," *Ibid.*, #157 (September 10, 1917).
9. St. Ivanovich, "Predosterzhenie," and A. Potresov, "Rubikon," *Den'* #156 (September 6, 1917) and #163 (September 14, 1917).
10. V. V. Kabanov, *Oktiabr'skaia revoliutsiia i kooperatsiia (1917g.—mart 1919g.)* Moscow, 1973), p. 114.
11. "Vserossiiskoe soveshchanie demokr. organizatsii," *Rabochaia gazeta*, #164 (September 19, 1917).
12. "Itogi demokraticheskago soveshchaniia," *Ibid.*, #168 (September 23, 1917).
13. "Krakh," *Den'*, #168 (September 20, 1917).
14. Nik Sukhanov, "Pora konchat'!" *Novaia zhizn'*, #133 (September 21, 1917).
15. Woytinsky, *op. cit.*, p. 361.
16. "Krizis vlasti," *Den'*, #154 (September 3, 1917).
17. "Vo Vremennom Pravitel'stve," *Den'*, #163 (September 14, 1917), and "Krizis vlasti," *Rech'*, #223 (September 22, 1917).
18. "Plekhanov o programe mira," *Rabochaia gazeta*, #186 (October 14, 1917).
19. "Sovet respubliki: zasedanie 12 Okt.," *Edinstvo*, #163 (October 14, 1917).
20. P. Kh—v, "Vneshniaia politika i russkaia diplomatiia," *Rabochaia gazeta*, #187 (October 15, 1917).
21. "V sovete respubliki," *Ibid.*, #190 (October 19, 1917).
22. B. Avilov, "Prodovol'stvennoe delo," *Novaia zhizn'*, #145 (October 5, 1917).
23. N. Cherevanin, "Ekonomicheskaia pozitsiia revoliutsionnoi demokratii i gazeta *Den'*," *Rabochaia gazeta*, #172 (September 28, 1917).
24. Volobuev, *op. cit.*, pp. 383-404.
25. P. Maslov, *Kritika agrarnykh programm i proekt programmy* (Tiflis, 1917), pp. 7-14. F. Dub—kov, "Agrarnyia pis'ma," *Rabochaia gazeta*, #137 (August 19, 1917).
26. Current Soviet historians try to minimize the differences between the Kadets and the Soviet parties on the question of land tenure in order to strengthen their own argument that the peasantry could expect similar treatment from all non-Bolshevik groups. V. I. Kostrikin, *Zemel'nye komitety v 1917 godu* (Moscow, 1975), p. 98. Keep, *op. cit.*, discussed the theoretical structure of the land committee, pp. 163-167.

27. Alexis N. Antsiferov, *Russian Agriculture during the War* (New Haven, 1930), pp. 273-274, and Kravchuk, *op. cit.*, pp. 30-31. Keep, *op. cit.*, attributed the passage of this law to Chernov, p. 168.

28. Ia. Piletskii, "Zemel'nyi vopros u es—erov," *Novaia zhizn'*, #151 (October 12, 1917). The Menshevik land tenure program, usually called municipalization, was not based on political self-interest nor on a desire to see peasants in possession of all the arable land. It was designed primarily to assure the destruction of the old oriental order in Russia and pave the way for the development of capitalism in Russian agriculture. *Chetvertyi (ob"edinitel'nyi) s"ezd RSDRP, aprel' (aprel'-mai) 1906 goda: protokoly* (Moscow, 1959), pp. 55, 56, 111, 136, 137. G. V. Plekhanov, *Sochineniia*, D. Riazanov, ed., XV (Moscow, 1926), pp. 31-34, 67-70.

29. Eric R. Wolf, *Peasant Wars of the Twentieth Century* (New York, 1969), p. 91.

30. Raf. Grigor'ev, "Razval men'shinstva," *Novaia zhizn'*, #140 (September 29, 1917).

31. "Iz zhizni R.S.—D.R.P.," *Rabochaia gazeta*, #183 (October 11, 1917), and *Ibid.*, #184 (October 12, 1917), and *Ibid.*, #193 (October 22, 1917).

32. "Izbiratel'naia kampaniia men'shevikov oborontsev," *Den'*, #187 (October 12, 1917), and *Ibid.*, #188 (October 13, 1917), and *Ibid.*, #189 (October 14, 1917).

33. F. Dan, "Torzhestvo kruzhkovshchiny," *Rabochaia gazeta*, #185 (October 13, 1917).

34. Lev Deich, "Agoniia men'shevizma," *Edinstvo*, #155 (October 4, 1917).

35. Sorokin, *op. cit.*, p. 36. Sorokin's opinion of Dan's abilities may have been altogether too critical, but certainly Dan was unable to pull the party together.

36. Getzler, *op. cit.*, p. 162.

37. St. Ivanovich, "Pered novym udarom," *Den'*, #197 (October 24, 1917).

38. "K s"ezdu sovetov," *Rabochaia gazeta*, #173 (September 29, 1917).

39. Sukhanov, *op. cit.*, VI, p. 197.

40. V. Bazarov, "Bol'sheviki i problema vlasti," *Novaia zhizn'*, #138 (September 27, 1917).

41. Iv. Kubikov, "Na chto oni nadeiutsia?" *Rabochaia gazeta*, #183 (October 11, 1917).

42. "K s"ezdu sovetov," *Rabochaia gazeta*, #194 (October 24, 1917).

43. "Vremennyi Sovet Rossiiskoi Respubliki: rech' F. I. Dana," *Rech'*, #251 (October 25, 1917).

44. Stankevich, *op. cit.*, p. 259.

45. A. N. Potresov, "Bez podderzhik," *Den'*, #198 (October 25, 1917).

46. F. Dan, "K istorii poslednikh dnei Vremennogo Pravitel'stva," *Letopis' revoliutsii* (Berlin, 1923), pp. 167-175.

47. A detailed description of the preparations for Lenin's seizure of power is not germane to this discussion. Those who wish to investigate the problems facing Lenin might consult Robert V. Daniels, *Red October: the Bolshevik Revolution of 1917* (New York, 1967), S. Mel'gunov, *Kak bol'sheviki zakhvatili vlast': oktiabr'skii perevorot 1917 goda* (Paris, 1953), Mints, *Istoriia*, II, III (Moscow, 1968, 1973), or Alexander Rabinowitch, *The Bolsheviks Come to Power: the Revolution of 1917 in Petrograd* (New York, 1976).

48. N. Podvoisky, "Voennaia organizatsiia Ts. K.R.S.—D.R.P. (bol'shevikov) i voenno-revoliutsionnyi komitet 1917 g.," *Krasnaia letopis'*, #8 (1923), pp. 38-39.

49. "Voennyi zagovor," *Rabochaia gazeta,* #196 (October 26, 1917).

50. "Ekstrennoe zasedanie Tsentr. Isp. Kom. Sov. R.S. i Kr. Dep.: doklad F. I. Dana, *Izvestiia,* #207 (October 26, 1917).

51. "S"ezd sovetov," *Rabochaia gazeta,* #196 (October 26, 1917).

52. "Vtoroi vserossiiskii s"ezd sovetov," *Novaia zhizn',* #163 (October 26, 1917).

53. Haimson, *op. cit.,* pp. 43-51.

54. G. Aronson, *K istorii pravogo techeniia sredi men'shevikov* (New York, 1960), p. 23.

55. *Ibid.,* p. 25.

56. Mel'gunov, *op. cit.,* p. 373.

57. "Soveshchanie zemsk i gorodsk predstavitelei," *Rabochaia gazeta,* #210 (November 11, 1917).

58. "Ekstrennye vserossiiskii s"ezd R.S.—D.R.P. (ob"edin.)," *Novy luch,* #1-3 (December 1-3, 1917).

59. "Vykhod iz sostava Tsentr. Komiteta R.S.—D.R.P.," *Rabochaia gazeta,* #201 (November 2, 1917).

Conclusion

1. O. V, "Aziatskii sotsializm," *Vpered!* #160 (September 19, 1917).

2. Haimson, *op. cit.,* p. 361.

Bibliographical Note

For the good fortune of historians, the Mensheviks (tongue tied in the years after 1917), were filled with enthusiasm and confidence during the months that passed between February and October. As a result, the events they did not wish to discuss in their post-revolutionary memoirs were analyzed over and over again during the course of the revolution itself, so the available source material is quite extensive. *Rabochaia gazeta* holds the most important fund of information. It was the official daily newspaper of the Menshevik party and was published in Petrograd throughout 1917. It contains articles of opinion, notes from speeches and meetings and communications between Petrograd and other areas of the former empire. I do not believe that a more complete and reliable source exists for the history of Menshevism during the revolution. *Vpered!* was the official Menshevik daily newspaper in Moscow. The Moscow Mensheviks were outside the area of most intense political activity, but their observations are very important for the researcher. *Novaia zhizn*, a daily Petrograd newspaper supposedly edited by Maxim Gorky, was used repeatedly by the left-wing Mensheviks, particularly to attack the party leaders' policy of coalition, and *Den* (edited by Potresov in Petrograd) served the purposes of the Menshevik right. Along with *Rabochaia gazeta* these sources constitute the main body of material available for study.

Important statements of fact and opinion from the Menshevik point of view can also be found in *Izvestiia*, the daily organ of the Executive Committee of the Petrograd Soviet, in Plekhanov's *Edinstvo*, and in the considerable body of pamphlet material written by Menshevik authors during 1917. Most of the arguments and facts appearing in these pamphlets, however, also appeared in either *Rabochaia gazeta* or *Novaia zhizn*. Useful scraps of information can also be found in memoirs, but with the exception of Sukhanov and Tsereteli, these sources are not terribly helpful for reconstructing the action of 1917.

All these key sources are readily available to scholars writing outside the Soviet Union. The main collections are located at the Hoover Institute for War, Revolution and Peace in Palo Alto, California, and at the International Institute for Social History in Amsterdam, the Netherlands.

The major Soviet holding on the Mensheviks is fund #275 of the Central Party Archive—Institute for World Literature (TsPA—IML). It has not to my knowledge been examined by western scholars, but Soviet historians using its documents have revealed no information that is unavailable in the west.

Bibliography

Primary Sources

Aksel'rod, P. B. Bor'ba za mir i vosstanovlenie Internatsionala. Petrograd, 1917.

_____. Dve taktiki: doklad, prochitannye na s"ezde v Stokgol'me. St. Petersburg, 1907.

_____. Istoricheskoe polozhenie i vzaimnoe otnoshenie liberal'noi i sotsialisticheskoi demokratii v Rossii. Geneva, 1898.

_____. Pis'mo v redaktsiiu 'Rabochago Dela.' Geneva, 1899.

Broido, E (L'vova). Zhenskaia inspektsiia truda. Petrograd, 1917.

_____. Zhenshchina—rabotnitsa. Petrograd, 1917.

Cherevanin, N. Organizatsionnyi vopros: s predisloviem L. Martova. Geneva, 1904.

Cherevanin, N., Vl. Gorn, and V. Mech. Bor'ba obshchestvennykh sil v russkoi revoliutsii. Moscow, 1907.

Dan, F. I (Gurvich). 8 chasovoi rabochii den'. Petrograd, 1917.

_____. O voina i mire. Petrograd, 1917.

_____. Zadachi Uchreditel'nago Sobraniia. Petrograd, 1917.

Delo. Moscow, 1916—1917.

Delo naroda. Petrograd, 1917.

Den' (Novyi den'). Petrograd, 1917.

Diubua, A. Chto takoe Uchreditel'noe Sobranie. Petrograd, 1917.

Edinstvo. Petrograd, 1917.

Ezhov, V (S. O. Tsederbaum). Soldat za kem ty poidesh na vyborakh? Petrograd, 1917.

Figner, Vera. Zapechtelnnyi trud. Moscow, 1921.

Garvi, P (Chatskii). Kapital protiv truda. Petrograd, 1917.

_____. Professional'nye soiuzy. Petrograd, 1917.

Golos rabotnitsy. Petrograd, 1917.

Gorev, B (Gol'dman). Kto takie lenintsy i chego oni khotiat. Petrograd, 1917.

_____. Chego zhdet Rossiia ot Uchreditel'nago Sobraniia. Petrograd, 1917.

_____. Soslovie, klass, partiia. Petrograd, 1917.

Iskra. Leipzig, Munich, London, Geneva, Vienna, 1900—1905.

Iskra. Petrograd, 1917.

Ivanovich, S. O (Portugeis). Anarkhiia i anarkhisty. Petrograd, 1917.

_____. Neprikosnovennost' lichnosti. Petrograd, 1917.

_____. Svoboda sobranii. Petrograd, 1917.

Izvestiia petrogradskogo soveta rabochikh i soldatiskikh deputatov. Petrograd, 1917.

Izvestiia zagranichnago sekretariata organizatsionnago komiteta rossiskoi sotsialdemokraticheskoi rabochei partii. Geneva, 1915—1917.

Kheisin, M. Rabochaia kooperatsiia i sotsial-demokratiia. Petrograd, 1917.

Kubikov, I. Pervoe maia v Rossii. Petrograd, 1917.

Letuchii listok men'shevikov-internatsionalistov. Petrograd, 1917.

Levitskii, V (V. O. Tsederbaum). Bor'ba evropeiskikh rabochikh za svobodu koalitsii. Moscow, 1917.

_____. Kakaia armiia nuzhna svobodnoi Rossii? Petrograd, 1917.

Liber, M (Gol'dman). Zadachi rabochego klassa v russkoi revoliutsii. Moscow, 1917.

Martov, L (Iu. O. Tsederbaum). Proletariat i natsional'naia oborona. Petrograd, 1917.

_____. Prostota khuzhe vorovstva. Petrograd, 1917.

_____. Protiv voiny! sbornik statei (1914—1916). Moscow, 1917.

_____. Rabochii klass v Rossii i ego trebovaniia. Moscow, 1917.

_____. Sotsialisty-revoliutsionery i proletariat. Petrograd, 1917.

Martov, L, P. Maslov, and A. Potresov, eds. Obshchestvennoe dvizhenie v Rossii v nachale XX-go veka. 4 vols. St. Petersburg, 1909—1914.

Martynov, A (Pikker). Dve diktatury. Geneva, 1905.

_____. Istoricheskii ocherk nashikh poriadkov: do reformennye poriadki i ikh krushenie. Berlin, n.d.

Maslov, P. P. Agrarnyi vopros v Rossii: s istoricheskim obzorom krest'ianskogo dvizheniia. 2 vols. St. Petersburg, 1906.

_____. Agrarnyi vopros v Rossii s marksistskoi tochki zreniia. St. Petersburg, 1905.

_____. Chto delat' s zemlei. Moscow, 1917.

_____. Imperializm i voina. Moscow, 1917.

_____. Kritika agrarnykh programm i proekt programmy. Tiflis, 1917.

_____. Ob agrarnoi programme iksa. otvet na kritiku nashego proekta programmy N. Lenina. Geneva, 1903.

_____. Politicheskie partii i zemel'nyi vopros. Moscow, 1917.

Mirov, V. Postoiannaia armiia ili vooruzhenie vsego naroda? Petrograd, 1917.

Nashe slovo. Paris, 1915—1916.

Novaia zhizn'. Petrograd, 1917.

Panin, M. Kustarnichestvo i partiinaia organizatsiia. Geneva, 1904.

Partiinye izvestiia. Petrograd, 1917.

Petrashkevich, S. Pro zemliu i sotsializm. Petrograd, 1917.

Piletskii, Ia. Sotsial-demokratiia i krest'ianstvo. Petrograd, 1917.

Pravda. Petrograd, 1917.

Rabochaia gazeta (Luch, Zaria, Klich, Plamia, Fakel, Molniia, Molot, Novyi Luch). Petrograd, 1917.

Rabochaia mysl'. St. Petersburg, 1898—1901.

Rabochee delo. Geneva, 1899—1902.

Rech'. Petrograd, 1917.

Rozanov, Vlad. Demokraticheskaia respublika i vseobshchii mir. Petrograd, 1917.

_____. Imperializm. Petrograd, 1917.

_____. Organizatsiia verkhovnoi vlasti. Petrograd, 1917.

_____. Proiskhozhdenie voiny. Petrograd, 1917.

_____. Uchreditel'noe Sobranie. Petrograd, 1917.

_____. Voina 1914 goda i russkoe vozrozhdenie. Petrograd, 1917.

Tiumenev, A. Kak reshaiut sotsial-demokraty vopros o zemle. Petrograd, 1917.
Vestnik Vremennago Pravitel'stva. Petrograd, 1917.
Vlast' naroda. Petrograd, 1917.
Volgin, A. Analiz russkoi revoliutsii. Petrograd, 1917.
Volia naroda. Petrograd, 1917.
Vpered! Moscow, 1917.
Zaitsev, I. Vseobshchee izbiratel'noe pravo. Petrograd, 1917.

Memoirs and Document Collections

Abramovich, Raphael R. The Soviet Revolution 1917—1939. New York, 1962.
Aleksandrova, V. Perezhitoe (1917—1921 g.g.). New York, 1962.
Anan'in, E. A. Iz vospominanii revoliutsionera, 1905—1923 g.g. New York, 1961.
Aronson, G. Bol'shevistskaia revoliutsiia i men'sheviki. New York, 1960.
_____. K istorii pravogo techeniia sredi men'shevikov. New York, 1960.
_____. Martov i ego blizkie: sbornik. New York, 1959.
_____. Revoliutsionnaia iunost' vospominaniia, 1903—1917. New York, 1961.
Browder, Robert Paul, and Alexander F. Kerensky, eds. The Russian Provisional Government 1917: Documents. 3 vols. Stanford, 1961.
Buchanan, G (Sir). My Mission to Russia and Other Diplomatic Memories. 2 vols. London, 1923.
Chernov, V. Rozhdenie revoliutsionnoi Rossii (fevral'skaia revoliutsiia). New York, 1934.
Dan, F (Gurvich). "K istorii poslednikh dnei Vremennogo Pravitel'stva," Letopis' revoliutsii. Berlin, 1922.
_____. The Origins of Bolshevism. Joel Carmichael, trans. New York, 1964.
_____. Za god; sbornik statii. Petrograd, 1919.
Denikin, A. I. Ocherki russkoi smuti. 2 vols. London, 1922.
Dvinov, B. Moskovskii sovet rabochikh deputatov 1917—1922; vospominaniia. New York, 1961.
_____. Pervaia mirovaia voina i rossiiskaia sotsialdemokratiia. New York, 1962.
Ermansky, O. A (Kogan). Iz perezhitogo (1887—1921 gg.). Moscow, 1927.
Frankel, Jonathan, ed. and trans. Vladimir Akimov on the Dilemmas of Russian Marxism 1895—1903. Cambridge, 1969.
Garvi, P. A. Professional'nye soiuzy i Rossii: v pervye gody revoliutsii 1917—1921. New York, 1958.
_____. Revoliutsionnye siluety. New York, 1962.
Gaponenko, L. S, ed. Revoliutsionnoe dvizhenie v russkoi armii: 27 fevralia—24 oktiabria 1917 goda, sbornik dokumentov. Moscow, 1968.
Getsler, I. M, ed. Stat'i posviashchennye Iu. O. Martovu. New York, 1961.
Golder, Frank Alfred. Documents of Russian History. New York, 1927.
Gosudarstvennaia duma: stenograficheskie otchety. St. Petersburg, 1906—1917.
Ivanovich, S. O. Piat' let bol'shevizma: nachala i kontsy. Berlin, 1922.

Kerensky, A. "Iz vospominaniia," Sovremennyia zapiski. XXXVII (1929).

_____. Russia and History's Turning Point. New York, 1965.

_____. The Catastrophe. New York, 1927.

Lenin, V. I. Polnoe sobranie sochinenii. 5th ed. 55 vols. Moscow, 1967—1970.

Lunacharsky, Anatoly Vasilievich. Revolutionary Silouettes. Michael Glenny, trans. New York, 1967.

Martov, Iu. Obshchestvennye i umstvennye techeniia v Rossii 1870—1905 g.g. Moscow, 1924.

_____. Istoriia rossiiskoi sotsial-demokratii Moscow, 1923.

Martynov, A. S. O men'shevizme i bol'shevizme. Moscow, 1923.

Maslov, P. P. Itogi voiny i revoliutsii. Moscow, 1918.

_____. Krest'ianskie dvizheniia v Rossii do 1905 g. Moscow, 1924.

Miliukov, P. N. Istoriia vtoroi russkoi revoliutsii. Sofia, 1921.

_____. Vospominaniia. M. Karpovich, and B. El'kin, eds. New York, 1955.

Nikolaevskii, B. I. Men'sheviki v dni oktiabr'skogo perevorota. New York, 1962.

Padenie tsarskogo rezhima: stenograficheskie otchety doprosov i pokazanii dannykh v 1917 g. v. chrezvychainoi sledstvennoi komissii Vremennogo Pravitel'stva. P. E. Shchegolev, ed. 7 vols. Moscow, 1924—1927.

Paleologue, Maurice. An Ambassador's Memoirs. F. A. Holt, ed. 3 vols. New York, 1925.

Plekhanov, G. V. Sochineniia. D. Riazanov, ed. 2nd ed. 24 vols. Moscow, 1923—1927.

Pokrovsky, M. N, and Ia. A. Iakovlev, eds. 1917 god v dokumentakh i materialakh. 10 vols. Moscow, 1925—1939.

Potresov, A. N. Posmertnyi sbornik proizvedenii. B. Nikolaevsky, ed. Paris, 1937.

Potresov, A. N, et. al. Samozashchita: marksistsky sbornik. Petrograd, 1916.

Protokoly i stenograficheskie otchety s"ezdov i konferentsii kommunisticheskoi partii sovetskogo soiuza: vtoroi s"ezd R.S.D.R.P. iiul'-avgust 1903 goda—protokoly. Moscow, 1959.

_____. chetvertye (ob"edinitel'nyi) s"ezd R.S.D.R.P. aprel' (aprel'-mai) 1906 goda—protokoly. Moscow, 1959.

Raionnye sovety petrograda v 1917 godu (protokoly, rezoliutsii, postanovleniia obshchikh sobranii i zasedanii ispolnitel'nykh komitetov). S. N. Valk, Kh. Kh. Kamalov, V. I. Startsev, and A. L. Fraiman, eds. 3 vols. Moscow, 1964, 1965, 1966.

Resolutions and Decisions of the Communist Party of the Soviet Union; Vol. I: The Russian Social Democratic Labour Party from 1898 to October 1917. Ralph Carter Elwood, ed. Toronto, 1974.

Savinkov, B. K delu kornilova. Paris, 1919.

Schwarz, Soloman M. The Russian Revolution of 1905: The Workers' Movement and the Formation of Bolshevism and Menshevism. Gertrude Vakar, trans. Chicago, 1967.

Shliapnikov, A. "Iiul'skie dni v Petrograde," Proletarskaia revoliutsiia. IV and V (1926).

_____. "Iiun'skoe nastuplenie," Proletarskaia revoliutsiia. III (1926).

_____. Semnadtsatye god. 4 vols. Moscow, 1923.

Shvarts, S. Men'shevizm i bol'shevizm i ikh otnoshenii k massovomu rabochemu dvizheniiu. New York, n.d.

Sorokin, Pitirim A. Leaves from a Russian Diary and Thirty Years After. Boston, 1950.

Sotsialisticheskii vestnik: organ zagranichnoi delegatsii RSDRP. Berlin, Paris, New York, 1921—1965.

Stankevich, V. B. Vospominaniia 1914—1919. Berlin, 1920.

Sukhanov, N. N. Zapiski o revoliutsii. 7 vols. Berlin, 1922.

Trotsky, Leon. The History of the Russian Revolution. Max Eastman, trans. Ann Arbor, 1957.

Tsereteli, I. G. Vospominaniia o fevral'skoi revoliutsii. 2 vols. Paris, 1963.

_____. "Rossiiskoe krest'ianstvo i V. M. Chernov v 1917 godu," Novyi Zhurnal. XXIX (1925).

Tyrkova-Williams, A. From Liberty to Brest-Litovsk. London, 1919.

Vandervelde, Emile. Souvenirs d'un militant socialiste. Paris, 1939.

_____. Trois aspects de la revolution russe. Paris, 1918.

Velikaia oktiabr'skaia sotsialisticheskaia revoliutsiia; dokumenty i material: Revoliutsionnoe dvizhenie v Rossii posle sverzheniia samoderzhavia. Moscow, 1957.

_____. Revoliutsionnoe dvizhenie v Rossii v aprele 1917; aprel'skii krizis. Moscow, 1958.

_____. Revoliutsionnoe dvizhenie v Rossii v mae—iiune 1917; iiun'skaia demonstratsiia. Moscow, 1959.

_____. Revoliutsionnoe dvizhenie v Rossii v iiule 1917 g; iiul'skii krizis. Moscow, 1959.

_____. Revoliutsionnoe dvizhenie v Rossii v avguste 1917; razgrom kornilovskogo miatezha. Moscow, 1959.

_____. Revoliutsionnoe dvizhenie v Rossii v sentiabre 1917; obshchenatsional'nyi krizis. Moscow, 1961.

_____. Revoliutsionnoe dvizhenie v Rossii nakanune oktiabr'skogo vooruzhennogo vosstaniia. Moscow, 1962.

Volin, S. Deiatel'nost' men'shevikov i profsoiuzakh pri sov. vlasti. New York, 1962.

_____. Men'sheviki na Ukraine (1917—1921). New York, 1962.

Volsky, N. V. Encounters with Lenin. Paul Rosta and Brian Pearce, trans. London, 1968.

Vserossiiskaia konferentsiia men'shevistskikh i ob"edinennykh organizatsii RSDRP. Petrograd, 1917.

Woytinsky, W. S. Stormy Passage: a Personal History Through Two Russian Revolutions to Democracy and Freedom, 1905—1960. New York, 1961.

Zapiski sotsialdemokrata. Paris, 1931—1934.

Zaria. Berlin, 1922—1925.

Zeman, Z. A. B, ed. Germany and the Revolution in Russia, 1915—1918: Documents from the Archives of the German Foreign Ministry. London, 1958.

Zhordaniia, Noi. Moia zhizn'. Ina Zhordaniia, trans. (from the Georgian) Stanford, 1968.

Zinoviev, G. Sochineniia. Leningrad, 1925.

Secondary Works

Antsiferov, Alexis N, Alexander D. Bilimovich, Michael O. Batshev, and Dimi-
   try N. Ivantsov. Russian Agriculture during the War. New Haven, 1930.
Anweiler, Oskar. Die Rätebewegung in Russland, 1905—1921. Leiden, 1958.
_____. "The Political Ideology of the Leaders of the Petrograd Soviet in the
   Spring of 1917," Revolutionary Russia. Richard Pipes, ed. New York,
   1969.
Ascher, Abraham. Pavel Axelrod and the Development of Menshevism. Cam-
   bridge, 1972.
_____. "The Kornilov Affair," The Russian Review. XII (October 1953).
Augustine, Wilson R. "Russia's Railwaymen, July—Oct, 1917," Slavic Review,
   XXIV (1965).
Avrich, Paul. The Russian Anarchists. Princeton, 1967.
_____. "Russian Factory Committees in 1917," Jahrbücher für Geschichte
   Osteuropas. XI (1963).
Barber, John. Soviet Historians in Crisis, 1928—1932. New York, 1981.
Baron, Samuel H. The Father of Russian Marxism. Stanford, 1963.
_____. "Plekhanov's Russia: the Impact of the West on an 'Oriental' Society,"
   Journal of the History of Ideas. XIX (1958).
Bourguina, Anna. Russian Social Democracy, the Menshevik Movement: a Bib-
   liography. Stanford, 1968.
Chamberlin, William Henry. The Russian Revolution 1917—1921. 2 vols. New
   York, 1960.
Cole, G. D. H. The History of Socialist Thought: the Second International
   1889—1914. III, pt. 1. London, 1956.
Daniels, Robert V. Red October: the Bolshevik Revolution of 1917. New York,
   1967.
Deutscher, Isaac. The Prophet Armed: Trotsky, 1879—1921. New York, 1954.
Fainsod, Merle. International Socialism and the World War. Cambridge, 1935.
Feldman, S. "The Russian General Staff and the June 1917 Offensive," Soviet
   Studies. XIX (1968).
Ferro, Marc. La revolution de 1917: La chute du tsarisme et les origines d'Oc-
   tobre. Paris, 1967.
_____. "The Russian Soldier in 1917: Undisciplined, Patriotic, and Revolution-
   ary," Slavic Review. XXX (1971).
_____. "Les debuts du soviet de Petrograd 27/28 fevrier 1917," Revue histo-
   rique. CCXXIII (1960).
Getzler, Israel. Martov: a Political Biography of a Russian Social Democrat.
   London, 1967.
Haimson, Leopold H, ed. The Mensheviks from the Revolution of 1917 to the
   Second World War. Gertrude Vakar, trans. Chicago, 1974.
_____. The Russian Marxists and the Origins of Bolshevism. Cambridge, 1955.
Hamilton, Mary Agnes. Arthur Henderson. London, 1938.

Hasegawa, Tsuyoshi. "The Formation of the Militia in the February Revolution: an Aspect of the Origins of Dual Power," Slavic Review. XXXII (1973).

Meynell, Hildamaire. "The Stockholm Conference of 1917," International Review of Social History. V (1960).

Hilferding, Rudolf. Das Finanzkapital; eine Studie über jüngste Entwicklung des Kapitalismus. Berlin, 1955.

Hill, Christopher. Lenin and the Russian Revolution. London, 1947.

Hobson, J. A. Imperialism: a Study. London, 1948.

Katkov, George. Russia 1917: The February Revolution. New York, 1967.

———. Russia 1917: The Kornilov Affair. London, 1980.

Keep, J. L. H. The Rise of Social Democracy in Russia. Oxford, 1963.

———. The Russian Revolution, a Study in Mass Mobilization. New York, 1976.

Kennan, George F. Russia and the West under Lenin and Stalin. Boston, 1960.

Koebner, Richard, and Helmut Schmidt. Imperialism: the Story and Significance of a Political Word, 1840—1960. Cambridge, 1964.

Johnson, Humphrey. Vatican Diplomacy in the World War. Oxford, 1933.

Lane, David. The Roots of Russian Communism: a Social and Historical Study of Russian Social-Democracy, 1898—1907. Assen, 1969.

Mel'gunov, S. P. Kak bol'sheviki zakhvatili vlast': oktiabr'skii perevorot 1917 goda. Paris, 1953.

———. Martovskie dni, 1917 goda. Paris, 1961.

Menshevik Collection of Newspapers, Periodicals, Pamphlets and Books related to the Menshevik Movement. Stanford, 1967.

Michelson, A. M, P. N. Apostol, and M. W. Bernatzky. Russian Public Finance During the War. New Haven, 1928.

Miliukov, P. N. Istoriia vtoroi russkoi revoliutsii. 2 vols. Sofia, 1921.

Pidhainy, Oleh Semenovych. The Formation of the Ukrainian Republic. Toronto, 1966.

Postnikov, S. P. Bibliografiia russkoi revoliutsii i grazhdanskoi voiny (1917—1921). Iana Slavika, ed. Prague, 1938.

Rabinowitch, Alexander. Prelude to Revolution: the Petrograd Bolsheviks and the July 1917 Uprising. Indiana, 1968.

———. The Bolsheviks come to Power: the Revolution of 1917 in Petrograd. New York, 1976.

Radkey, Oliver H. The Agrarian Foes of Bolshevism. New York, 1958.

Roobol, W. H. Tsereteli — a Democrat in the Russian Revolution: a Political Biography. Philip Hyams and Lynne Richards, trans. The Hague, 1976.

Rosenberg, William G. Liberals in the Russian Revolution: the Constitutional Democratic Party, 1917—1921. Princeton, 1974.

Schiebel, Joseph L. Aziatchina: the Controversy Concerning the Nature of Russian Society and the Organization of the Bolshevik Party. Seattle, 1972.

Senn, Alfred Erich. The Russian Revolution in Switzerland 1914—1917. Madison, 1971.

Struve, P. B, K. I. Zaitsev, N. V. Dolinsky, and S. S. Demosthenov. Food Supply in Russia During the World War. New Haven, 1930.

Tokei, Ferenc. "Le mode de production asiatique dans l'oeuvre de K. Marx et F. Engels," La Pensee. CXIV (1964).

Treadgold, Donald W. Lenin and His Rivals: The Struggle for Russia's Future, 1898—1906. New York, 1955.

Trotsky, Leon. The History of the Russian Revolution. Max Eastman, trans. Ann Arbor, 1957.

Wade, Rex A. The Russian Search for Peace, February—October 1917. Stanford, 1969.

―――. "The Triumph of Siberian Zimmerwaldism: (March—May 1917). Canadian Slavic Studies. II (1967).

Warth, Robert D. The Allies and the Russian Revolution. Durham, 1954.

Wettig, Gerhard. "Die Rolle der russischen Armee in revolutionären Machtkampf 1917," Forschungen für osteuropäischen Geschichte. XII (1967).

White, James D. "The Kornilov Affair," Soviet Studies. XX (July 1968).

Wittfogel, Karl A. Oriental Despotism: a Comparative Study of Total Power. New Haven, 1955.

Wolf, Eric R. Peasant Wars of the Twentieth Century. New York, 1969.

Wolfe, Bertram D. "Backwardness and Industrialization in Russian History and Thought," Slavic Review. XXVI (1967).

Zagorsky, S. O. State Control of Industry in Russia During the War. New Haven, 1928.

Zaleski, Eugene. Mouvements ouvriers et socialistes: La Russie, I. Paris, 1956.

Zenkovsky, Serge A. Pan-Turkism and Islam in Russia. Cambridge, 1967.

Soviet Works

Andreev, A. M. Sovety rabochikh i soldatskikh deputatov nakanune oktiabria: mart—oktiabr' 1917 g. Moscow, 1967.

Astrakhan, Kh. M. Bol'sheviki i ikh politicheskie protivniki v 1917 godu. Leningrad, 1973.

Burdzhalov, E. N. Vtoraia russkaia revoliutsiia: vosstanie v Petrograde. Moscow, 1967.

―――. Vtoraia russkaia revoliutsiia: Moskva, front, periferiia. Moscow, 1971.

Drezen, A. K. ed. Burzhuaziia i pomeshchiki v 1917 godu. Moscow, 1932.

Dubrowski, S. Die Baurenbewegung in der Russischen Revolution 1917 g. Moscow, 1967.

Dumov, N. G. "Sovremennaia anglo-amerikanskaia istoriografiia o krakhe kadetskoi partii v 1917 g," Istoriia SSSR. IV (1969).

Freidlin, B. M. Ocherki istorii rabochego dvizheniia v Rossii v 1917 g. Moscow, 1967.

Gaponenko, L. S. Rabochii klass Rosii v 1917 godu. Moscow, 1970.

Garmiza, V. V. "Kak esery izmenili svoei agrarnoi programme," Voprosy Istorii. VII (1965).

Gulub, P. Partiia, armiia, i revoliutsiia otvoevanie partiei bol'shevikov armii na storonu revoliutsii mart 1917—fevral' 1918. Moscow, 1967.

Gusev, K. V, and Kh. A. Eritsian. Ot soglashatel'stva k kontrrevoliutsii (ocherki istorii politicheskogo bankrotstva i gibeli partii sotsialistov-revoliutsionerov). Moscow, 1968.

Gusev, K. V, and V. P. Naumov, eds. Velikii oktiabr' v rabotakh sovetskikh i za rubezhnykh istorikov. Moscow, 1971.

Ignat'ev, A. V. Russko-angliiskie otnosheniia nakanune oktiabr'skoi revoliutsii (fevral'—oktiabr' 1917 g.) Moscow, 1966.

————. Vneshniaia politika Vremennogo Pravitel'stva. Moscow, 1974.

Ioffe, A. E. Russko-frantsuzskie otnosheniia v 1917 g. fevral'—oktiabr'. Moscow, 1958.

Ioffe, G. Z. Fevral'skaia revoliutsiia 1917 goda v anglo-amerikanskoi burzhuaznoi istoriografii. Moscow, 1970.

Ivanov, N. Ia. Kornilovshchina i ee razgrom. Leningrad, 1965.

Kabanov, V. V. Oktiabr'skaia revoliutsiia i kooperatsiia (1917 g.—mart 1919 g.). Moscow, 1973.

Kanev, S. N. Oktiabr'skaia revoliutsiia i krakh anarkhizma. Moscow, 1974.

Kim, G. F, and V. H. Nikiforov. Obshchee i osobennoe v istoricheskom razvitii stran vostoka. Moscow, 1966.

Komin, V. V. Bankrotstvo burzhuaznykh i melkoburzhuaznykh partii Rossii v period podgotovki i pobedy velikoi oktiabr'skoi sotsialisticheskoi revoliutsii. Moscow, 1965.

Kostrikin, V. I. Zemel'nye komitety v 1917 godu. Moscow, 1975.

Kravchuk, N. A. Massovoe krest'ianskoe dvizhenie v Rossii nakanune oktiabria (mart—oktiabr' 1917 g. po materialam velikorusskikh gubernii evropeiskoi Rossii). Moscow, 1971.

Lebedev, V. V. Mezhdunarodnoe polozhenie Rossii nakanune oktiabr'skoi revoliutsii. Moscow, 1967.

Lozinskii, Z. Ekonomicheskaia politika Vremennogo Pravitel'stva. Leningrad, 1929.

Miller, V. I. Soldatskie komitety russkoi armii v 1917 g. (vozniknovenie i nachal'nyi period deiatel'nosti). Moscow, 1974.

Mints, I. I. Istoriia velikogo oktiabria. 3 vols. Moscow, 1967—1973.

————. Lenin i oktiabr'skoe vooruzhennoe vosstanie v Petrograde. Moscow, 1964.

Okorokov, A. Z. Oktiabr' i krakh russkoi burzhuaznoi pressy. Moscow, 1970.

Pershin, P. N. Agrarnaia revoliutsiia v Rossii: istoriko-ekonomicheskoe issledovanie. 2 vols. Moscow, 1966.

Pokrovskii, M. N, ed. Ocherki po istorii oktiabr'skoi revoliutsii. 2 vols. Moscow, 1927.

Pushkareva, I. M. Zheleznodorozhniki Rossii v burzhuazno-demokraticheskikh revoliutsiiakh. Moscow, 1975.

Ruban, N. V. Oktiabr'skaia revoliutsiia i krakh men'shevizma (mart 1917—1918 g.). Moscow, 1975.

Sobolev, G. L. Revoliutsionnoe soznanie rabochikh i soldat Petrograda v 1917 g. Leningrad, 1973.

Soboleva, P. I. Oktiabr'skaia revoliutsiia i krakh sotsial-soglashatelei. Moscow, 1968.

Startsev, V. I. Ocherki po istorii petrogradskoi krasnoi gvardii i rabochei militsii (mart 1917—aprel' 1918). Moscow, 1965.

Stepanov, Z. V. Rabochie petrograda v period podgotovki i provedeniia oktiabr'skogo vooruzhennogo vosstaniia (avgust—oktiabr' 1917 g.). Moscow, 1965.

Trapeznikov, S. P. Leninizm i agrarno-krest'ianskii vopros. 2 vols. Moscow, 1967.

Vasiukov, V. S. Vneshniaia politika Vremennogo Pravitel'stva. Moscow, 1966.

Vodolagin, V. M. Oktiabr'skoe vooruzhennoe vosstanie v sovetskoi istoricheskoi literature. Moscow, 1967.

Volobuev, P. V. Ekonomicheskaia politika Vremennogo Pravitel'stva. Moscow, 1962.

_____. Proletariat i burzhuazniia Rossii v 1917 godu. Moscow, 1964.

Zlokazov, G. I. Petrogradskii sovet rabochikh i soldatskikh deputatov v period mirnogo razvitiia revoliutsii (fevral'—iiun' 1917 g.). Moscow, 1969.

Znamenskii, Oleg Nikolaevich. Iiul'skie krizis 1917 goda. Moscow, 1964.

INDEX